STUDIES IN IMPERIALISM

General editor: Andrew S. Thompson
Founding editor: John M. MacKenzie

When the 'Studies in Imperialism' series was founded more than twenty-five years ago, emphasis was laid upon the conviction that 'imperialism as a cultural phenomenon had as significant an effect on the dominant as on the subordinate societies'. With well over a hundred titles now published, this remains the prime concern of the series. Cross-disciplinary work has indeed appeared covering the full spectrum of cultural phenomena, as well as examining aspects of gender and sex, frontiers and law, science and the environment, language and literature, migration and patriotic societies, and much else. Moreover, the series has always wished to present comparative work on European and American imperialism, and particularly welcomes the submission of books in these areas. The fascination with imperialism, in all its aspects, shows no sign of abating, and this series will continue to lead the way in encouraging the widest possible range of studies in the field. 'Studies in Imperialism' is fully organic in its development, always seeking to be at the cutting edge, responding to the latest interests of scholars and the needs of this ever-expanding area of scholarship.

The souls of white folk

Manchester University Press

SELECTED TITLES AVAILABLE IN THE SERIES

RACE AND EMPIRE
Eugenics in colonial Kenya
Chloe Campbell

MADNESS AND MARGINALITY
The lives of Kenya's White insane
Will Jackson

SCIENCE, RACE RELATIONS AND RESISTANCE
Britain, 1870–1914
Douglas A. Lorimer

ENDING BRITISH RULE IN AFRICA
Writers in a common cause
Carol Polsgrove

MUSEUMS AND EMPIRE
Natural history, human cultures and colonial identities
John M. MacKenzie

The souls of white folk

WHITE SETTLERS IN KENYA,
1900S–1920S

Brett L. Shadle

MANCHESTER
UNIVERSITY PRESS

Copyright © Brett L. Shadle 2015

The right of Brett L. Shadle to be identified as the author of this work has been asserted by him in accordance with the Copyright, Designs and Patents Act 1988.

Published by MANCHESTER UNIVERSITY PRESS
ALTRINCHAM STREET, MANCHESTER M1 7JA
www.manchesteruniversitypress.co.uk

British Library Cataloguing-in-Publication Data
A catalogue record for this book is available from the British Library

Library of Congress Cataloging-in-Publication Data applied for

ISBN   978 1 5261 0681 0 paperback

This edition first published 2017

The publisher has no responsibility for the persistence or accuracy of URLs for any external or third-party internet websites referred to in this book, and does not guarantee that any content on such websites is, or will remain, accurate or appropriate.

Typeset
by Servis Filmsetting Ltd, Stockport Cheshire
Printed in Great Britain
by Lightning Source

High in the tower, where I sit above the loud complaining of the human sea, I know many souls that toss and whirl and pass, but none there are that intrigue me more than the Souls of White Folk.

W. E. B. Du Bois, *Darkwater*

CONTENTS

List of figures—viii
Preface—ix
Abbreviations—xi
Swahili terms—xii

1	Introduction: The souls of white folk	1
2	Race, civilization, and paternalism	26
3	Prestige, whiteness, and the state	58
4	Chivalry, immorality, and intimacy	85
5	The law and the lash	116
6	Conclusion	145

Select bibliography—161
Index—178

LIST OF FIGURES

1.1 'Race committee, July 4 1900'. Courtesy of Winterton Collection of East African Photographs, Melville J. Herskovits Library of African Studies, Northwestern University 20

2.1 'B.E.A. colonist to idle native: "You're expected to bear your share in the development of the Country and we hope to make you into a thrifty and industrious member of the community"', from *East African Standard* (21 June 1919), p. 16 29

4.1 Russell Bowker, from T. J. O'Shea (compiler and ed.), *Farming and Planting in British East Africa* (Nairobi: Newland, Tarlton, 1917), facing p. vii 93

5.1 'Officers and committee of the Colonists' Association of British East Africa', from Somerset Playne (compiler), F. Holderness Gale (ed.), *East Africa (British): Its History, People, Commerce, Industries, and Resources* (London: Foreign and Colonial Compiling and Publishing, 1909), p. 166 131

PREFACE

I often ask my students to guess what scholars read first when they pick up an academic book. I tell them it is not the introduction, not the conclusion, not the bibliography. It is the preface, to see what conference the author attends, to discover who is friends with whom, to track the intellectual lineage of the author, all of which then becomes gossip at the next professional meeting. We are a strange collection of human beings.

This book was not one I intended to write. I had begun writing a historical examination of sexual violence in Kenya, with one chapter on settler ideas about the fear of black-on-white rape. But the chapter kept growing, and became a book. And then other chapters in the book overshadowed 'black peril', which was reduced to one theme among many. Thus in the years this book has been gestating and mutating, I have received assistance from many people, in ways that they might not recognize.

Perhaps to his chagrin, I start with Jon Glassman. I first took on Kenya's settlers long ago in a research paper when I was his advisee at Northwestern University. Jim Brennan, another advisee, was also writing on the settlers. We threatened to create a Delamere Chair in Settler History, and install Jon as its first holder. He was not amused.

Meals and drinks, conversations and emails, with many people have informed my thinking (and often, more importantly, made time in various cities more pleasant): David Anderson, Ann Asugah, Melissa Baker, Jim Brennan, Matt Carotenuto, David Cline, Havana Gari, Matt Heaton, Parakh Hoon, Stacey Hynd, Rachel Jean-Baptiste, Theresa Kircher, John Lonsdale, Kate Luongo, Keguro Macharia, Michael Murungi, Wambui Mwangi, Paul Ocobock, Joel Onyancha, Myles Osborne, P. S. Polanah, Helen Schneider, Martin Shanguhyia, Heather Switzer, Liz Thornberry, Richard Waller, Calvin White, Jr, and Michael V. Williams. Dutch and Ginger Featherston have helped herd my children during my trips overseas. Special thanks to the members of Concerned Kenyan Writers, from whom I have learned much.

Parts of the book have been presented previously, often in embarrassingly premature form. My thanks to organizers, co-panellists, and commenters at African Studies Association conferences in 2007, 2008, 2011; the European Conference on African Studies (2009); the Canadian Association of African Studies (2010); Critical Whiteness Studies Symposium at the University of Iowa (2010); Images of

PREFACE

Whiteness – Exploring Critical Issues at Oxford (2011); Whiteness Beyond the West at Virginia Tech (2011); ASPECT Working Paper Series at Virginia Tech (2013); and talks at the University of Arkansas and Roanoke College. A few who deserve special thanks on this count include Ira Bashkow, Jesse Boucher, Komal Dhillon, Will Jackson, Katy Powell, Tom Spear, Dan Thorp, and Chris Youé. Thanks also to Dane Kennedy, Janet McIntosh, Allison Shutt, and the anonymous readers for Manchester University Press who commented on chapters of the book.

The staff at the Kenya National Archive have made the reading room a second home for many years now. Deepest thanks to the mzee, omukofu, the old man, the one who knows where everything is, and one of the most helpful and genuinely kind persons I have ever worked with, Richard Ambani.

Students in courses on whiteness, African history, and settler colonialism at Virginia Tech have helped me refine my thinking, and are due a collective thanks. Graduate students in the course 'Whiteness beyond the West' were instrumental in organizing the conference of the same name. At the institutional level, I have benefited from the financial support of the College of Liberal Arts and Human Sciences and the Department of History at Virginia Tech. Mark Barrow, Francois Debrix, and Sue Ott Rowlands have all been supportive over the years. Linda Fountaine, Jan Francis, and Kathy McIntyre are the ones who make everything actually happen. My undying gratitude to the Interlibrary Loan department, who must have tired of me long ago. Everyone at Manchester University Press has been extraordinarily helpful and responsive throughout.

Most of all, I must thank Marie, Elliot, and Alden. They keep me grounded. When Marie helps a child to walk, my vanity at having come up with a nice sentence is undone. Coaching (if poorly) Elliot's and Alden's soccer teams helped me forget day-long struggles to write a coherent paragraph. This non-academic world reminds me that if authoring a book is a person's greatest accomplishment in life, it's unlikely to have been a full life. To them I dedicate this book, with love and gratitude.

ABBREVIATIONS

AS	*African Standard*
CO	Colonial Office
DAR	District Annual Report
DC	District Commissioner
EA	*East Africa*
EAS	*East African Standard*
EAUA	*East Africa and Uganda Argus*
EAUM	*East Africa and Uganda Mail*
EAWL	East African Women's League
KNA	Kenya National Archive
KO	*Kenya Observer*
LegCo	Legislative Council
NA	British National Archive
RH	Rhodes House
SS	Secretary of State for the Colonies
TEA	*Times of East Africa*

SWAHILI TERMS

Askari	African policeman or soldier
Kiboko	hippopotamus; whip made of dried hippopotamus hide
Mtoto (pl: watoto)	child (usu. *toto* when used by settlers)
Mshenzi (pl: washenzi)	savage, uncivilized person (usu. *shenzi* when used by settlers)
Mzungu (pl: wazungu)	white person
Panga	machete
Serikali	government

CHAPTER ONE

Introduction: The souls of white folk

The sun rose at quarter to seven on 14 March 1907. Ewan Reginald Logan prepared for another unexceptional working day. At thirty-eight years old, he found himself Town Magistrate of Nairobi, a sad collection of tin shacks and dirt roads far from his England home. Each day, he heard a dreary litany of assault and theft cases, mostly involving Africans. He suffered abuse in the press from white settlers who (with 'all deference') were 'woefully disappointed' with his supposed leniency on African offenders.[1] A thankless job, and about to get worse. For as he entered his office just after ten o'clock, he beheld a gang of white men barreling down Government Road toward his court. Then murmurs, then shouts, in British and Anglo South African voices. Logan sent out his Goan clerk to investigate, but the crowd ignored him. And so E. R. Logan, Town Magistrate of Nairobi, capital of British East Africa, stepped out of his front door.

This is what he saw. Some forty or fifty white men, shoulder to shoulder, filled the courtyard. In the centre stood three well-known settlers, Ewart Grogan, Russell Bowker, and Captain Thord Gray. On the ground lay three young African men. Grogan fondled a *kiboko*, a hippopotamus-hide whip. This did not bode well. Logan tried to intervene, he insisted that, whatever the complaint, the law must be followed. Scoffing, Grogan replied that he was going to thrash the men. Why? 'Because I want to.' They had been impertinent to two white women. A defeated Logan returned to his office and sent for the police. He heard the crack of the whip. Had he been so inclined, Logan could have counted the number of times the kiboko sliced the air. Seventy-five. Twenty-five times by Grogan. Twenty-five times by Bowker. Twenty-five times by Gray. Twenty-five on each black back.

THE SOULS OF WHITE FOLK

The image of the settler

Since the late nineteenth century, Kenya has held a special place in the hearts of Britons, Americans, and others in the West. The geography of Kenya is exceptional, to be sure. The animals, too, are rightly renowned for their size and their variety, for their killing and their being killed. But aside from glossy photo spreads, it is the histories of Kenya's white settlers – Grogan included – that continue to populate bookshelves.[2] Brave men and women seeking adventure or escaping strait-laced Edwardian England, falling in love with the flora and fauna (always under an 'African sun'),[3] becoming emotionally close to their exasperating but deeply loyal 'noble savage' domestic servants. They pioneered untamed (and supposedly unoccupied) lands and created a new country. They were lords and ladies who loved Africa, worked in the sun and drank on the veranda, swapped lovers, and created something from nothing. Settlers appear to have lived life to the fullest in an gorgeous, exotic land. Far indeed from the drab succession of days suffered through by contemporary suburbanites. These are the stories that continue to be told about what was, and is, seen as 'the *fun* colony'.[4]

Settlers' ideas about themselves, about Africans, about the government are repeated uncritically in popular works. In this stream of books, settlers are exceptional, all in good ways: 'They played hard and worked hard, never excusing or regretting ... They all possessed a common bond: independence, tenacity, ambition, and fearlessness.'[5] Settlers understood Africa better than any outsider, *yea*, they even became indigenous: Beryl Markham was 'almost more African than European in her thinking and attitudes'.[6] Colonization brought the rule of law, though with some difficulty: 'The European notion of impartial justice is incomprehensible in Africa where revenge is all'.[7] Settlers were the doting paternalists of their adoring, appreciative workers: 'The farm wife was called *Mama* ... by the Africans, who turned to her to help solve their problems'.[8] Administrators did nothing to assist their more well-informed and well-intentioned fellow whites: 'official policy was to defer to native rights in all areas of conflict' with settlers.[9] Maasai, Somali, and other pastoralists deserve admiration: 'fierce, handsome, and shrewd East African trading and cattle-raising people'.[10] Those who adopted European ways of life, the Christian Africans, are comical: 'the parody of the white man'.[11]

Such fawning works – and there are many – too often ignore the seamier side of European settlement in Kenya. Another image of the white settler came from the pen of J. M. Kariuki, a leader in the anti-colonial struggle and a champion of the worker and the peasant.

INTRODUCTION

'As a tribe', he wrote in 1963, 'the Europeans had certain characteristics which were, perhaps, not pleasant'. Perhaps, an understatement. Whites were

> Quick to anger, inhospitable, aloof, boorish, and insensitive, they often behaved as if God had created Kenya and us for their use. They accepted the dignity of man as long as his skin was white ... Many Europeans refused to talk to educated Africans in any language but their deplorably bad Swahili; old men were addressed as boys and monkeys; Africans were barred from hotels and clubs; Africans with land near European farms were not allowed to plant coffee; there was a wholesale disregard for human dignity and little respect for anyone with a black skin.[12]

Historians of Kenya have tended more toward J. M.'s views.

What are we to make of such widely divergent images of Kenya's white settlers? How do we square the romantic, benevolent settler with the brutal, exploitative settler? In part, it is a matter of what we wish to see. Some consider Karen Blixen's *Out of Africa* a classic love story. It is also the story of a smug woman who sees herself as a mother to 'her [adult African] children'. Settler memoirs, taken uncritically, can sweep one up in the adventure: brave men and women bringing progress to the wilds, bringing gifts of peace, justice, and modern medicine to Africans. Read more sceptically, and alongside court transcripts, government files, and African-authored sources, we find the racism, the violence, the infantilization of Africans.

How can we write a history that is revealing of settler lives, of the white men and women who claimed Kenya as their home? We should take seriously settlers' assertions (if not the reality) of their civilizing mission and their benevolent paternalism. We should listen to their complaints of colonial officials meddling in (what settlers claimed to be) mutually beneficial relations with Africans. Settlers, after all, believed this. But we must also dig more deeply. We must inquire into the origins of these attitudes, and their implications for settlers and Africans.[13]

Through a reading of settler memoirs, letters, and diaries, government reports and court transcripts, and locally owned, pro-settler newspapers, we can see the issues which settlers daily reflected on and debated. We can witness the creation of a settler self-image. We hear their foundational ideas about the settler project. We can find the emotional core of white settlement in their (real and imagined) relations with Africans, state officials, and one another.

The souls of white folk

Within the souls of white settlers, I argue, we find a series of interlacing ideas. White settlement was based on the equation of civilization with (a difficult to define) whiteness; was emotionally enriched through notions of paternalism and trusteeship; appeared constantly under threat from Africans, colonial administrators, the judiciary, and fellow settlers; and was shored up daily through rituals of prestige, deference, humiliation, and violence. These ideas help explain 'black peril', the recurrent settler fear of African men raping white women. Such rape posed an existential threat, in that it targeted each part of the settler soul: paternalism paid back with ingratitude, white prestige and the inviolate white body brushed aside, violence by rather than against the dominated, white women and their impotent white male defenders humiliated. These are the issues I explore in this book.

Settlers, like administrators, were supremely confident that civilization, race, and fitness to rule could not be pulled apart. Whites in general, and Britons in particular, had achieved the highest level of civilization ever the Earth had witnessed. Not hampered by cultural relativism, settlers had no qualms about insisting that the civilized world must enlighten the darker corners of the globe. As bearers of civilization, whites had not just a right but a duty to rule the uncivilized, to guide them toward a better existence. Settlers admitted that two thousand years had passed before the spark of Roman and Christian innovations had fully bloomed into the civilization they carried with them to Kenya. Africans would advance more quickly under white tutelage, but it would still take them hundreds of years to catch up.

The civilizing mission contributed to settlers' being emotionally enriched through ideas of paternalism and trusteeship. In their newspapers, books, and letters, many settlers (from famed Karen Blixen and Beryl Markham to near-impoverished farmers) demonstrated a deep belief in their burdens toward Africans. In often gory detail, they related the time they spent in their very intimate doctoring of their African servants and squatters. They described episodes of protecting their servants from arrest. They waxed lyrical about their African workers-cum-serfs, their domestic servants-cum-retainers. Far from cynical rhetoric, the white man's burden took a very personal, emotional meaning for many white settlers. In their own eyes, settlers were parents, guardians, and lords over their African children, wards, and serfs. This paternalism would become one of the defining features of settler thinking: it was both a *duty* to civilize Africans and emotionally and psychologically *pleasurable* to do so.

Paternalism might create bonds between whites and a few Africans.

INTRODUCTION

What, settlers wondered, about the millions of anonymous Africans amongst whom they lived? How could all those Africans be controlled? The Maxim gun could end but not prevent an uprising. Settlers instead invested enormous faith and energy in what they called prestige, a kind of protective barrier surrounding them.[14] Settlers argued (or fervently hoped) that Africans naturally held whites to be superior, almost godlike. This, whites believed, permitted them to travel, work, and live in almost total security despite their being fantastically outnumbered by Africans. So long as settlers had prestige, Africans could not conceive of rebellion. So long as the white race had prestige, every individual white was safe. The sign of prestige: deference. Africans must tip their hats, step off a path to let a white person pass, say 'bwana' or 'memsahib'. Lack of deference in the most minor way suggested that prestige was fraying. Accordingly, settlers constantly, obsessively, monitored Africans for any sign of 'insolence'.

The burden Africans were told to bear – deferring to every member of the white race – placed a burden on whites as well. As the sociologist Erving Goffman points out, to retain prestige requires a certain public 'demeanour'. An elite must always act as an elite should. To do otherwise would encourage the dominated to question the need for deference. Why, the inferior would wonder, should I defer to a drunkard, a libertine, a fool, a cheat? In Kenya, prestige was connected to race, such that any white person's *individual* failure to maintain prestige threatened the prestige of *all* white people. Keeping up appearances was thus a matter of public concern. Whites demanded that each among them lived and behaved in certain ways, lest they all lose prestige. Most thought this meant abiding by bourgeois norms. Settlers who fell into penury, became vagrants, turned to crime, or 'went native' failed miserably to possess the demeanour necessary to inspire prestige. For their part, white working men demanded economic protection from their white employers so that they could keep up white prestige. White prisoners expected segregated cells for the same reason.

What complicated matters further is that 'white' was not – is not – self-evident.[15] Race is not a biological category, but one we humans have invented. What race means, and how many races there are, and how individuals are categorized are all matters for ongoing debate. Settlers described Kenya as a 'white man's country', a land that whites – not Africans or Indians – could dominate. Depending on whom one asked, however, 'white' could have different meanings. For in the thinking of many English-speakers around the world in the early twentieth century, there were multiple white races: Anglo-Saxon, English, Irish, Dutch, Afrikaner, and so on. Settlers believed that whites were superior to non-whites, and that some white races were superior to other white races.

For most settlers, the English, or British, or Anglo-Saxon race could claim the highest civilization, a particular genius of rule, a robust adventurous spirit. But what of the other, somewhat inferior, white races? Kenya's British settlers – including here Anglo South Africans, Americans, Canadians, New Zealanders, and Australians – welcomed western Europeans. They could help in the civilizing project. But whites from other parts of Europe, well, their whiteness was suspect. The *Kenya Observer* queried the European and African Trades Organization in 1923 for taking such a 'wide and unintended and sinister an interpretation' of 'European' – for the EATO was alleged to be importing Italian artisans.[16] Similarly, during his travels in western Kenya Lord Hindlip was brought 'news that a "Mzungu" (white man) was living up in that region ... This foreigner may have been a Goanese or a low-class white man or Greek ...' A white man *or* a Greek: for Hindlip, these were not quite the same thing.

Unfortunately enough for Hindlip, Greeks were, in Kenya, white. From the British perspective, the differences between themselves and Italians or Greeks were patently obvious. Africans (so settlers believed) were not so discerning. To them, one light-skinned person was barely distinguishable from another.[17] Hence Hindlip could not be sure if in using *mzungu* his African informants were referring to a poor white, a Greek, or a Goan – even though Hindlip likely considered none of the three groups *fully* white. (For a poor white did not live as a white man should.) British lord, American tycoon, Danish royalty? Russian peasant, Italian labourer, itinerant Greek trader? All were equally white in African eyes. Just as the demeanour of 'poor whites' reflected back on, and lowered the prestige of, all whites, so too did the demeanour of 'whites' – those who, from a British perspective, were not white, or not quite white.[18]

Settlers were not the only whites to demand prestige – government officials did too, but in ways that settlers found troubling. Settlers rarely tired of grousing about the colonial government. Officials were 'negrophile'. They threw roadblocks in front of all settlers attempts to gain land and attract labour. They looked down on the common settler. In his 1931 introductory guide for visitors to Kenya, H. O. Weller explained that 'To get and keep on friendly terms with his hosts [a visitor] should naturally avoid local politics when staying with Government officials, and help slang the Government – especially the P[ublic] W[orks] D[epartment] and the Agricultural Department – when with settlers'.[19]

Rarely did settlers acknowledge that their own presence in Kenya owed everything to the colonial government. The vast settler lands were alienated by or with the collusion of Nairobi. Labour was regularly sent out of the 'native reserves' by British district officers and government-salaried African chiefs. Settlers had an influence on the government all out of proportion to their numbers.[20] Based on shared racial identities and, for the better settlers, shared social backgrounds, colonial officials felt an affinity towards their fellow whites.

Yet there is a level of truth in settler complaints. Settlers and colonial officials had different goals. Government officials, while concerned about racial prestige, were fully engrossed in building up the prestige of *serikali*, government. Whereas settlers insisted that prestige must attach to white skin, colonial officials argued it attached to those representing the Crown. Thus when John Rennie – a private citizen – assaulted an African policeman – a public servant – he was arrested by a white official. Settlers believed the criminal charge was an outrageous assault on white prestige.

Settlers defined civilization in large part through gender norms; indeed, whites marked African savagery through gender. Settlers misinterpreted bridewealth as the purchase and sale of women. They claimed that African men demurred from physical labour in favour of treating their wives as 'beasts of burden'. Until African men learned to treat their womenfolk properly, settlers insisted, they could never be considered civilized. This is not to say that whites themselves strictly adhered to the middle-class gender norms then common in their homelands. White women played active roles in their farms and in the public sphere, and gained the vote before their sisters in Britain. Some flouted convention in their dress, and in their smoking and drinking. Yet in the end, white men and women celebrated women's domesticity, and men's defence of their womenfolk's honour and bodies, and thus their superiority over Africans.

Across the empire, Europeans obsessed over the dangers of sex across the colour line. Scholars have argued that this was due to fears over miscegenation and a loss of racial purity.[21] In Kenya, settlers paid attention to sexual matters, but primarily for reasons of prestige. Newspaper editors, women's groups, and male and female letter-writers proclaimed the need for sexual discretion *among* whites. If whites could not adhere to their own sexual morality how, pray tell, could Africans be convinced of white superiority? More worrying was inter-racial sex. Concerns over mixed-race children were largely absent from settler discourse until the 1940s. Instead, inter-racial sex was dangerous because it could suggest emotional intimacy and, thus, an inversion of the racial order. White men who had sex with African women sometimes came in for condemnation for what it meant to white prestige. How, the complaint went, could a civilized man lower himself to share a bed with an 'unwashed savage', and what would Africans think? Prevailing ideas about male sexuality, however, meant that such acts could be dismissed as simply animal functions, devoid of emotional connection.

For white women, the thinking went, sex was not a biological necessity but an expression of tenderness and love. Sex between a settler woman and an African man was inherently an act of emotional as well as physical intimacy. It suggested a level of equality.[22] This was bad enough, but it got worse. Whites believed African men lacked civilized emotions of love and romance, that they dominated and exploited their womenfolk. To have sex with a white woman (the African man would supposedly conclude) lowered her to the debased status of an African woman. When a white woman fell in love with an African man or displayed her flesh in front of a domestic servant, her prestige vanished. Worse still, by whites' logic once a single white woman had fallen, the prestige of all white woman was endangered. Once a white woman showed herself to be uncivilized, to be as mortal – and as immoral – as the colonized, the prestige of all white women was shown to be a sham. No white woman would be safe.

As settlers tried to navigate through all these ideas of whiteness, prestige, gender, and sex, they also found themselves caught between two traditions of rule, two traditions of dominating Africans. The first was the personal relationship between ruler and ruled, as reflected in settlers' ideas about paternalism and prestige. In the tradition of so many paternalists, settlers resorted to violence to chastise their child-like charges. While the physical pain of corporal punishment fades, the psychological effect is more long-lasting. It is the performance itself that carries meaning, for corporal punishment humiliates the sufferer. A beating – with fist, boot, or whip – reinforces a hierarchy.[23] Just as a parent spanks a child, or a teacher a student, settlers believed corporal punishment on an 'insolent' African was essential to creating or re-establishing lines of power. The whipped African became a child punished by his white 'parent'. The whipped African was no longer an adult man. (Settlers spoke freely of their physical chastisement of African men, but very rarely of any violence toward women.)

At the same time, settlers were also wedded to the idea of a modern, liberal democratic state with an impartial legal system. Yet they wished the state to be impartial only when dealing with intra-white concerns. For inter-racial disputes, they believed that the state machinery must favour whites. Many colonial officials and judges disagreed. Colonial officials considered it their duty to protect 'their' Africans from rapacious settlers. Judicial officials, mostly imported from Britain, believed in applying the law equally, regardless of race or station in life. Settlers

INTRODUCTION

railed against a judicial system that allowed Africans to charge settlers with assault, for it undermined their personal control over Africans. Settlers condemned magistrates who weighed equally the words of an African and a white person, for it suggested racial equality. Africans would see not the genius of English law (settlers claimed) but only that a white magistrate had sided with a black man against a white man. It was humiliating to whites and undermined white prestige.

Without prestige: black peril. The hysteria among whites over black-on-white rape. Scholars have advanced many explanations for these periodic explosions of fear across the European colonized world.[24] Perhaps white men stoked fear of rape to reassert control over their womenfolk. Perhaps it was to unify white communities split by social or economic conflict. Yet we need not think of black peril as simply a tool used for certain ends. What if, instead, we consider black peril an honest (if baseless) *fear*?[25] Rather than wondering why certain people may have invented perils at particular times, we should ask why the fear of the *rape of white women* so consumed white people.

In short, the African rapist sullied each corner of the settler soul. He lowered the erstwhile parental white woman to the level of the degraded African woman. Instead of deferring to white prestige, the African humiliated the white woman as well as her menfolk who had failed to protect her. The violence that whites used to punish and humiliate Africans was turned against them. All of the tools – emotional, psychological, and corporeal – that settlers relied upon appeared impotent. Moreover, settlers believed that Africans knew all of this. According to this thinking, if an African could rape a white woman and escape with his life, he must feel invincible. This, in turn, emboldened *all* Africans, and made *all* white women targets: the rape of a single white woman put *all* white woman at risk. Similarly, settlers believed, if the African masses knew that an African had raped a white woman and lived, that white prestige was a chimera, they would feel empowered to rob, beat, murder, and rape whites at will. All that made up the settler soul was threatened, assaulted, extinguished.

While always distracted by financial and land matters, it was these concerns – civilization, whiteness, paternalism, prestige, law, and the lash – that shaped settlers' lives. These factors determined which actions settlers must take and which they must avoid; with whom they could have certain emotional and physical relationships; under what circumstances they must mock, or care for, or thrash an African. They determined how settlers would react to the threat of 'black peril'.

This story begins around 1902, when the colonial government beckoned white people to make their homes in East Africa. It culminates in 1928, with the first execution of an African for raping a white woman.

This book is a kind of snapshot of the settler soul over that quarter century. Over those years white settlement took root, and the settler soul flourished. Particular aspects of it mutated slightly during those two and a half decades. Leading settlers of the 1920s, their eyes on the holy grail of self-government, had little patience for Grogan's brazen vigilantism. The postwar battle with Indians over political supremacy brought out more explicit talk of the white man's burden to civilize Africans. But white violence against Africans did not fade away in the 1920s, and paternalistic attitudes did not emerge ex nihilo in 1923. In reading the diaries, letters, newspaper columns, and court cases, one is struck by the continuities over the years. Select at random a letter to the editor, and one is hard pressed to determine if it was published in a 1903 edition of the *African Standard*, a 1917 edition of the *Critic*, or a 1928 edition of the *East African Standard*. The language, the obsessions, the emotions expressed in 1903 were repeated every year through 1928. If I have failed to discover significant alterations in the settler soul over these years, it is not for lack of trying.

Fears and contentments

Thus were the souls of white folk in Kenya. Certainly, there were exceptions. Some rejected any interest in civilizing Africans or acting the trustee.[26] A handful did not believe Africans to be childlike. A few held fast to the notion that the law must treat all persons, regardless of race, equally. But the cacophony of other voices drowned out these more conscientious men and women. New immigrants learned to adopt the attitudes of their fellow settlers, or they learned to keep their own counsel.[27]

The fears, the unease, that plagued the settler soul did not always consume them. The benefits of being white in colonial Kenya were immense. As trustees, as *pater* and *mater*, as members of the ruling race, settlers achieved a status much higher than they might have had elsewhere. This is what made settlement in Kenya so attractive. The historian M. P. K. Sorrenson once remarked that 'In East Africa all white men were aristocrats, though some were more aristocratic than others'. Perhaps it could also be phrased: not all white men were aristocrats on Mombasa-bound ships, but they all became aristocrats once their feet touched Kenyan soil.[28] For the farmers, Berman points out, 'settlement became not simply or even primarily a means of profit, but rather an attempt to create a way of life rooted in non-capitalist, indeed, pre-capitalist values'.[29] By the twentieth century, such a life could be created only in a racialized society like Kenya. Lord Delamere, Grogan, Berkely and Galbraith Cole, on down to vagrants and criminals, settlers received – or, at least, demanded – the 'wages of whiteness'.[30]

INTRODUCTION

Settlers also believed Kenya to be their home. They created spaces which would be permanent and white. They built brick or stone homes, and planted flower gardens to mark off their space from the bush. The Muthaiga Club reproduced the elite clubs of Britain, although it allowed much more rowdiness. Settlers constructed churches and established branches of organizations celebrating their Scottish heritage or their public schools. Kenya could make whites feel confident and secure and *important*. Abraham Block (born in Lithuania but raised in South Africa) came to East Africa in 1903 to seek a brighter future. Late in life he was asked why he had not moved to Britain once he had made his fortune in Kenya. He seemed incredulous at the question. 'Why should I retire to England?' he retorted. 'In this country I am somebody; in England I would only be a number on a door.'[31] A life so sweet, surely it was divine to be a white person in Kenya.

None the less, even in private spaces, even in the segregated clubs and white homes, there the Africans would be found. The cooks, the domestic servants, the rickshaw 'boys' waiting outside, the workers lining up for their pay. Even the sundowner: a whisky at dusk that became the most striking image of the settler life. A well-earned relaxation after hard labour in the scorching sun, gazing out over an Eden more beautiful for not being London or Manchester or Johannesburg. The sundowner also marked the beginning of night, the time the settlers did not control. The darkness was owned by lions and Africans prowling Nairobi streets, by hyenas and Africans laughing somewhere in the bush. Even in the spaces they most tightly controlled, settlers could feel, viscerally, the African presence.

Having spent many years now plumbing settler souls, I admit that I have found little about them that was redeeming – and this is not just to judge them by the standards of a new millennium, for one hundred years ago their critics were legion. But an inventory of white settlers' sins would be of rather little use.[32] I have no desire simply to condemn settlers, just as I have no patience for those who celebrate them. We do need to understand settlers, in their totality, their hopes and frustrations, their tenderness and violence, their loves and hatreds.

What of the objects of their tenderness and violence, of their love and hatred? Where are the Africans in this story? Some readers may be frustrated by the foregrounding of settlers in this book, with Africans seemingly relegated to the shadows. The new wave of research on whiteness is in fact sometimes criticized for repeating the old mistake of obsessing over whites, of allowing whites to 'suck out all the air' from the academic room.[33] Africans are not absent, of course, but I cannot claim that they are the primary actors in this story. They were sometimes 'insolent' or 'cheeky' – which we might easily understand as attempts to assert their dignity or to strike back at their oppressive colonial masters. They sometimes refused to express gratitude, which might well reflect their unwillingness to be the helpless savage for the settlers' paternalistic romance.

But to include Africans' intentions, their goals, their understandings of settlers and of colonialism, would be to write a very different book. These are important topics, and scholars have already explored many aspects of them. My understanding of colonialism, white settlement, and whiteness has been shaped by a variety of scholarly works about Africans, by the novels of the Kenyan author Ngũgĩ wa Thiong'o, by Africans' words that come through in the archive, and by African American writers of the early to mid-twentieth century who suffered with a similar white soul.[34] But here, the settler perspective, the settler soul, must be understood, and on its own terms. For this project, then, it does not matter so much *why* Africans were 'insolent', or indeed even *if* they were insolent in any particular case. What is important here is that settlers *believed* Africans to be insolent, and to explore why that mattered. African voices are not absent, but neither are they central.

The history of white settlement

Few whites could be found in East Africa prior to 1903. Missionaries had been active along the coast for some years, but rarely went very far inland. Britain staked claim to Kenya almost as an afterthought. The Imperial British East Africa Company had established forts along the old caravan route between Mombasa and the lake region, but it cared only for the Kingdom of Buganda. When the company folded, the Foreign Office stepped in for fear of losing to the Germans influence over Buganda and the headwaters of the Nile. The East African Protectorate was declared over the area in 1895, although no one thought first to inform the Africans.[35] (By the time it was renamed the Colony and Protectorate of Kenya in 1920, Africans were all too aware of their status as subjects of the Crown.)

The new imperial commissioner remained more interested in Uganda than the geography that had to be traversed to reach the lake. Soon after the protectorate was born, the Foreign Office successfully claimed British taxpayer funds to establish a railway, the more quickly to skim through the dangerous wastelands. Costs ran ever higher as the iron snake crept almost imperceptibly away from the coast. Government officials found themselves protecting the railway and its workers from lions and Africans alike. 'Pacification' became more important, and more bloody, to be followed quickly by the imposition of taxes and other signs of British sovereignty.

INTRODUCTION

With each cost over-run on the railway, with each costly sally into the wilds to machine-gun down spear-wielding youth, with each tax collection composed of eggs and ostrich feathers, the colonial government faced a crisis. East Africa must pay for itself, and soon. There appeared to be two paths. Kenya might follow the West African colonies, in which African peasants produced valuable cash crops for export. Africans in this locale, according to the government, were not sufficiently advanced in agriculture and commerce to make this a realistic option. White settlement might be the better choice.

As early as 1897, the Commissioner of the Protectorate Arthur Harding broached the idea of white settlement. In unpromising numbers, a few set up shops or tried their hands at farming, mostly around Fort Smith, or traipsed about in regions well out of British influence. Five years later, the number had inched up, with perhaps thirty in Nairobi, a new railway town. More could be found in Mombasa engaged in various types of commerce. It was on 5 January 1902 that one might – certainly only in retrospect – see the dawning of a new era. For it was on that date that the new commissioner, Sir Charles Eliot, informed the Foreign Office that 'the East Africa highlands are for the most part a white man's country'. He had already met with nineteen white settlers in Nairobi, promising 'to promote and encourage the settlement of Europeans'.[36] Though white settlement would take some time to get under way in any significant numbers, and still many factors could easily have derailed the whole programme, Eliot's decision helped set the course of Kenya's tortured history.

According to Eliot, a few other administrators, and the vocal European population already there, Kenya demanded white settlers. Stolid British farmers and ranchers could make the (supposedly) unexploited, fantastically fertile soil produce a bounty such as the world had not yet seen. The country seemed almost impossibly well suited to white settlement. The cool, wet, central highlands set atop the equator cried out for farmers. The vast Rift Valley impatiently awaited fields of wheat and herds of cattle. The plains seemed a veritable zoo, but one which permitted visitors to cut down the animals. Not all was rosy, of course. It would be some years before fears of debilitating actinic solar rays dissipated and whites quietly removed protective spine pads from their jackets.[37] Malaria and blackwater fever, not to mention lions, buffalo, and hippos, pushed their share of whites into their graves. But for hardy (or desperate) souls, East Africa had much to offer.

Still, attracting Britons to an unproved land along the equator was a tough sell. By April 1903, Eliot had little reason to feel satisfied with his promotion of British settlement. Only a hundred whites had established themselves around Nairobi (which in 1906 would replace

Mombasa as the administrative headquarters of the protectorate). Not all of them had arrived from Great Britain, but had come by way of South Africa. This land, just emerging from a terrible war, appeared a more promising reservoir from which to populate the white man's country. Eliot dispatched a representative in August 1903 to talk up Kenya, while two South Africans undertook their own promotional scheme. The results helped ensure that large swaths of East Africa would, legally if not morally, pass into white hands. While in 1903, 117 whites made applications for land grants, the next year 599 immigrants made three hundred applications.[38] Most early settlers sought land just outside Nairobi or in the Rift Valley. Afrikaner immigrants headed toward Uasin Gishu. Over the next several years settlers claimed land in Ukambani and Laikipia. By May, 1910, four thousand square miles had been alienated, although half had been distributed in large concessions, often to land speculators, and were left undeveloped and unoccupied.[39] The war limited the growth of white settlement, but peace helped spur it. The Soldier Settlement Scheme brought several hundred veterans and their families to East Africa. The government illegally claimed African lands in Trans-Nzoia and Laikipia for many of them, and turned over land around Kericho to the short-lived British East Africa Disabled Officers' Colony.

The settlement of veterans marked the closing of the land frontier – aside from the alienation of land when gold was discovered in Kakamega, no further lands would be opened for white settlers.[40] By 1925, twelve thousand square miles of land had been alienated to them. Extensive tracts remained unused. Until the end of the decade much of it was cultivated by African 'squatters' who worked their own plots in exchange for several months of labouring each year for the white landowner.[41] The 'Reserves' – gazetted in 1926, in which whites could not purchase land – contained fifty thousand square miles.

Even with the ending of land alienation, the number of white settlers continued to grow – farms were subdivided, and salaried workers in the towns increased. But whites always remained a tiny minority in the colony. It is difficult to know with precision how many settlers there were in Kenya at any given point. In 1906, there were 1813 Europeans, which included missionaries and government officials. By 1916 the number had grown to 5438, and reached 12,529 a decade later. There were always more Indians than whites: in 1926, they numbered 26,749, twice the European population. The African population according to colonial censuses can also be taken only as broad estimates, but it was always vastly greater than either of the immigrant groups – perhaps two and a half to three million. The number of white settlers – in relative and absolute terms – is surprisingly small given their outsized influence on Kenyan history, and the furore they caused in the Colonial Office and humanitarian circles in Britain.[42]

Settler politics

From very early on, fault lines among the settler population were readily apparent. Winston Churchill witnessed this during a visit to East Africa in 1907:

> Every white man in Nairobi is a politician; and most of them are leaders of parties. One would scarcely believe it possible, that a centre so new should be able to develop so many divergent and conflicting interests, or that a community so small should be able to give to each such vigorous and even vehement expression. There are already in miniature all the elements of keen political and racial discord, all the materials for hot and acrimonious debate. The white man *versus* the black; the Indian *versus* both; the settler as against the planter; the town contrasted with the country; the official class against the unofficial; the coast and the highlands; the railways administration and the Protectorate generally; the King's African Rifles and the East Africa Protectorate Police; all these different points of view, naturally arising, honestly adopted, tenaciously held, and not yet reconciled into any harmonious general conception, confront the visitor in perplexing disarray.[43]

Organizing had indeed arrived early. The Colonist Association was formed as early as 1902 in Nairobi. Hard on its heels came the Planters' and Farmers' Association in 1903, at first purely of commercial concern but soon enough consumed by politics. It incorporated the old Colonist Association in 1905, and took its name. Lord Delamere was able to hold leadership only briefly, when a more radical bunch – mostly South Africans – took over under Ewart Grogan. (Delamere regained power after Grogan's trial for the 1907 flogging.) Meanwhile, the Pastoralist Association championed the small farmers, although its leader, Robert Chamberlain, had himself applied for 32,000 acres.[44] By 1910, the antagonism between Delamere and Chamberlain had relaxed enough to allow for the creation of a larger organization, the Convention of Associations.

The Convention, locally known as the settlers' parliament, was intended to give settlers a strong voice through which to impose itself on the government. Each of the long list of settler groups could send representatives to the annual meeting in Nairobi. But the Convention only partly unified settlers, still split by their various local concerns – and angry words were often exchanged at the Convention's annual meetings.[45] Large landowners heavily invested in cattle, wheat, timber, and the like, shared few of the economic concerns of smaller farmers trying to scrape by on maize or a few coffee bushes.

Town and country marked another division – indeed, Duder argues that this was the most important political and economic split amongst the settlers. Those on the farms often made it to Nairobi once or twice a year, if that. They came for the races, the bars, the clubs, the fashions – the highlife that town-dwellers enjoyed all year round. Other, smaller towns – Nakuru, Eldoret, Kisumu – were little more than manure-flecked outposts with a sprinkling of shops, banks, bars, and post offices. Merchants had their own interests, of which locusts and labour supplies were not uppermost. Policies meant to protect wheat farmers meant higher bread prices for Nairobi residents. Safari outfitters like the famed Newland and Tarlton made their fortunes entirely from visitors who spent a few months spilling the blood of creatures big and small.

Perhaps the most commented-on division amongst the settlers was class. The image of the Kenya settlers is certainly not the Nairobi artisan, the Rift Valley farm manager, the Afrikaner subsistence farmer, the Thika family asking the bank manager Mr Playfair for yet another loan. It is, instead, the barons, the earls, the lords and ladies, the generals and colonels and majors. It is the men and women who could support lavish parties and constant safaris with fortunes made elsewhere, or who had gobbled up vast estates and earned fantastic wealth through land speculation. The well-off men and women are also said to have dominated the scene politically. They could better socialize with and influence government officials who largely shared their middle- and upper-class background and public school education. Delamere and Hindlip could take their complaints directly to the House of Lords, and many others had important political connections in London.

If we look solely at high politics, then the Delameres and the Grogans and the officers who came after the First World War may indeed have dominated the scene. Norman Leys, a former medical officer in Kenya who turned himself into a bitter critic of white settlement, certainly believed this to be true. In his exposé, titled simply *Kenya*, Leys focused on the exploitative laws and land expropriation which he laid at the feet of the 'big men'. 'But the working farmer, the clerk, the skilled tradesman, the people who live wholly or mainly by their earnings, do not appear [in his book]. If they have evaded their responsibility for events, they have at least avoided the disgrace of the events to be narrated in the next chapter' – cases of excessive brutality against Africans.[46] (As we will see, the 'small men' were in fact hardly innocent on that count.)

The influence of the elites on high society is just as notable. More than one observer has pointed to elites as the formative element in settler society.[47] Their large, well-appointed homes, their entertaining, their clubs – such became the standard in Kenya to which all settlers aspired.

INTRODUCTION

Indeed, many settlers tried to reinvent themselves in Kenya, boosting themselves up the class hierarchy. Their attempts were sometimes too obvious, especially for Harold Robertson, a champion of the working man and editor of the *Critic*. Under the heading 'Kenya Social Events', he noted that 'Last week Mrs Doublebarrelled-name gave a magnificent dance at her beautifully appointed bungalow (furniture on the instalment plan ... piano, on instalment)', remarked on the 'Engagement of "Mr Highup-In-The-Air"', owner of a 'splendid coffee plantation (mortgaged to the hilt and run on a colossal overdraft)', and offered 'Congratulations to Mr and Mrs Title-Angler on the birth of a son'.[48]

Yet the attempts of some settlers to equal the lives of their social betters should not obscure the fact that many of them failed. In one of his 'Nutshell Novels', Robertson told the story of one John Smithers, a pimply faced London warehouse clerk who came to Kenya, added '-Smythe' to his name, and 'lives on chits and stories about blue blood ancestors'. In the end, however, this social climber lost his job and was left wandering the streets, friendless, and tossed aside by those who had lured him with offers of good employment.[49] Elites may have set the standard to which settlers could aspire, but they did not set the standard by which most settlers actually lived.

The story of white settlement cannot be the story of just the politicians, the more visible men and women, the titled. White settlement was truly made by many hands. It did not take Lord Delamere to teach Abraham Block that in East Africa his white skin, his racial prestige, made him 'somebody'. The crowd cheered on Grogan as he flogged the rickshaw 'boy' – he had no need to convince them that it was the proper thing to do. John Simpson was not under the spell of Lord Cranworth when he dismissed his wife's query: would they ever make money of their farm? 'To make money did not seem to be his ultimate concern', she recalled. 'It was as though he were a pioneer for the joy of it, for its own blessed sake.'[50] In reconstructing the souls of white folk, we must attend to *all* those white folk.

Moreover, the non-elites were not always so quiet. The working men had their champions, such as Robertson who stood on the side of 'the poor and humble townsmen'.[51] A proposal to slap a steep duty on wheat imports would certainly help local producers, but not consumers, he pointed out: 'That is to say, no one section of the community must be pampered at the expense of another'.[52] Under the nom de plume Rab the Rhymer, his arrows found their mark:

> Oh! I'd love to be a farmer!
> Not the kind who ploughs the land
> And sweats from morn till dewey eve

With rough and horny hand;
But one who plays at politics
And grinds his axe all the day –
It really *is* a topping game
And somehow seems to pay!
Oh! I'd love to be a farmer!
Yes! There's really such a charm
In being *called* a farmer though
One doesn't *need* to farm![53]

Lower down the scale still were the Afrikaners, most of whom lived a hard scrabble life of subsistence farming, hunting for the pot and for skins, training and driving oxen, and serving as farm managers for the more wealthy. Barely visible in most accounts are the flotsam and jetsam who constantly washed from shore to shore of the empire. Criminals, shady adventurers, unskilled men seeking any work to keep body and soul together, unattached women of questionable backgrounds – these people too found their ways to Kenya. Economically and politically they had little in common with a baron or general – in London or in Nairobi. Yet as whites in East Africa, they all shared certain beliefs, certain attitudes.

Regionally, too, there were differences. Residents of Mombasa were thought to be of a more even keel than their dramatic, hot-tempered, upcountry fellows.[54] While upcountry white footballers refused to play an African team from Uganda, Rennie Stevenson of the Mombasa Soccer Team did 'not see anything to be worried about' in meeting them on the pitch.[55] James Patton in 1923 pointed out that whites in Mombasa 'do less carping' than their Nairobi brethren, and counselled 'respect for modern and commonsense' against the blustering of Grogan.[56] A. Morrison of Mombasa, when running for Legislative Council in 1924, proposed to work with Arab members to fight for interests of the coast, rather than join with other settlers in the Reform Party.[57]

Delamere and Smithers-Smythe, Cranworth on his vast estate and Mary Morgan locked up for vagrancy, the footballers from upcountry and the coast – they did have some things in common. They were of one soul. Even when settlers disagreed, they did so in a common language. They believed in the supremacy of the white race, of the equation of civilization and whiteness, the importance of white prestige, the power of humiliation, the necessity of the lash, the rightness of a racialized legal system, and the monstrosity of black peril. When a crisis emerged, like black peril, all settlers could be expected to come together, because – regardless of class, nationality, or means of earning a living – they were white. Peter de Polnay remarked that in 1930, when aboard a ship steaming to Mombasa, he unexpectedly found new social conventions: 'The passengers talked to me as you speak to a member of your club. Their chumminess at first astonished me, not realising that in a sense I was already in East Africa, where white men stick together, and consider each other friends merely because of their colour.'[58]

In acknowledgement to Du Bois

Many readers may be familiar with W. E. B. Du Bois's magisterial 1903 reflection on the state of African America, and America itself, *The Souls of Black Folk*. Less well known is the essay from which the present book takes its name, 'The Souls of White Folk', from Du Bois's 1920 *Darkwater: Voices from within the Veil*. Early in his long career as an academic and political thinker, Du Bois had realized what many other 'race leaders' had missed. Freedom could not be won through the politics of respectability, by demonstrating that black people could be as civilized as whites. Booker T. Washington argued that hard-working African Americans would eventually convince white Americans to accept them into the body politic. Preachers and reformers chastised the lazy and dirty and immoral of their race, lest it give white Americans justification for Jim Crow. Du Bois understood that the failures of black people did not cause racism, and improving black people would not solve racism. The roots of the problem lay in the souls of white folk. In his *Souls of Black Folk*, Du Bois warned his readers that 'the *problem* of the Twentieth Century is the *problem* of the *color-line*'. It was only by laying bare the souls of white folk, however, that he could explain the origins of that colour line.

In Du Bois's preliminary examination of the souls of white folk, we see the souls of Kenya's white settlers. Du Bois pointed to whites' recently adopted 'assumption that of all the hues of God whiteness alone is inherently and obviously better than brownness or tan'. From there follows the civilizing mission and paternalism (a 'burning desire to spread the gift abroad, the obligation of nobility to the ignoble' which brings 'much mental peace and moral satisfaction'), then the sensitivity to insolence (whites bristle 'when [the non-white's] attitude toward charity is sullen anger rather than humble jollity; when he insists on his human right to swagger and swear and waste'), then to fear ('the spell is suddenly broken and the philanthropist is ready to believe that Negroes are impudent, that the South is right, and that Japan wants to fight America'). From there to rage and violence: 'After this the descent to Hell is easy'.

These were the ideas, the emotions, that animated the souls of white folk, in the United States as much as in Kenya. The title of the present book is a recognition that, as in so many areas of the study of race, much is owed to the pioneering work of Du Bois.[59]

There is also something to be gained when the title brings to mind *The Souls of Black Folk*. If he had written nothing else – if he had not produced journalism, history, sociology, and fiction in such prodigious amounts, if he had written nothing more than the first chapter of *Souls of Black Folk*, Du Bois's name would still be remembered. For in 'Of Our Spiritual Strivings', he lays out, excruciatingly, what it was to be black in America – and the inability to be simply *American*. African Americans live as if behind a veil. Of the world, and yet not of it. Existing in 'a world which yields him no true self-consciousness, but only lets him see himself through the revelation of the other [white] world'. The black American walks through life with a 'sense of always looking at one's self through the eyes of others, of measuring one's soul by the tape of the world that looks on in amused contempt and pity'.

It may seem profane to apply these ideas to Kenya's white settlers. It may be. But there is profit from such an exercise. White settlers too lived behind a veil, albeit one of their own making. They too constantly observed themselves through others' eyes, but it was the eyes of the dominated. Their fear was that Africans would measure the white soul – using the tape the settlers had made – and find that soul lacking.

1.1 'Race committee, July 4 1900'

INTRODUCTION

Settlers feared Africans would gaze at them with 'amused contempt and pity'. Settlers always chose their words and performed their actions with the briefest but crucial pause for self-censorship: how will the Africans perceive us? Du Bois writes of the tragedy of the dominated. Settlers' lives were in some ways tragic as well, but the tragedy was one they themselves had authored.

Notes

1 'Wanted: severer sentences', *TEA* (11 Aug. 1906), p. 4. For a short biography of Logan, see Somerset Playne (compiler) and F. Holderness Gale (ed), *East Africa (British): Its History, People, Commerce, Industries, and Resources* (London: Foreign and Colonial Compiling and Publishing, 1909), p. 45.
2 The most recent on Grogan include Edward Paice, *Lost Lion of Empire: The Life of 'Cape to Cairo' Grogan* (London: HarperCollins, 2001); Julian Smith, *Crossing the Heart of Africa: An Odyssey of Love and Adventure* (New York: Harper, 2010).
3 See Binyavanga Wainaina, 'How to write about Africa', *Granta* 92 (2005), located at www.granta.com/Archive/92/How-to-Write-about-Africa/Page-1 (accessed 24 Feb. 2014).
4 The phrase is Will Jackson's, summarizing the image. Will Jackson, 'Dangers to the colony: loose women and the "poor white" problem in Kenya', *Journal of Colonialism and Colonial History* 14 (2013). Or, as Boyles puts it, less clearly distancing himself from the sentiment, Kenya was 'a peach of a colony'. Denis Boyles, *African Lives: White Lies, Tropical Truth, and Rumblings of Rumor – from Chinese Gordon to Beryl Markham, and Beyond* (New York: Weidenfeld and Nicolson, 1988), p. 4.
5 Ulf Aschan, *The Man whom Women Loved: The Life of Bror Blixen* (New York: St Martin's, 1987), p. 34.
6 Mary S. Lovell, *Straight on Till Morning: The Biography of Beryl Markham* (New York: St. Martin's, 1987), p. 17.
7 Errol Trzebinski, *The Lives of Beryl Markham: Out of Africa's Hidden Free Spirit and Denys Finch Hatton's Last Great Love* (New York: Norton, 1993), p. 40.
8 Errol Trzebinski, *The Kenya Pioneers* (New York: Norton, 1986), p. 151.
9 Boyles, *African Lives*, p. 25.
10 Judith Thurman, *Isak Dinesen: The Life of a Storyteller* (New York: St Martin's, 1982), p. 114.
11 Thurman, *Isak Dinesen*, p. 57.
12 However, there were, J. M. reassured his readers, 'many individual exceptions' to the rule. J. M. Kariuki, *'Mau Mau' Detainee* (Baltimore: Penguin, 1963), pp. 41, 49.
13 I am deeply grateful for the pioneering work of other historians who have explored some of these issues. Of special relevance in Kenya: Michael Gordon Redley, 'The Politics of a Predicament: The White Community in Kenya, 1918–32' (Ph.D. diss., University of Cambridge, 1976); C. J. D. Duder, 'The Soldier Settlement Scheme of 1919 in Kenya' (Ph.D. diss., Aberdeen University, 1978); Dane Kennedy, *Islands of White: Settler Society and Culture in Kenya and Southern Rhodesia, 1890–1939* (Durham, NC: Duke University Press, 1987); C. J. D. Duder, 'Love and the lions: the image of white settlement in Kenya in popular fiction, 1919–39', *African Affairs* 90 (1991): 427–38; C. J. D. Duder, 'An army of one's own: the politics of the Kenya Defence Force', *Canadian Journal of African Studies* 25 (1991): 207–25; C. J. D. Duder and Chris Youé, 'Paice's place: race and politics in Nanyuki District, Kenya, in the 1920s', *African Affairs* 93 (1994): 253–78; Carolyn Martin Shaw, *Colonial Inscriptions: Race, Sex, and Class in Kenya* (Minneapolis: University of Minnesota Press, 1995), ch. 7; Chloe Campbell, *Race and Empire: Eugenics in*

Colonial Kenya (Manchester: Manchester University Press, 2007); John Lonsdale, 'Kenya: home county and African frontier', in Robert A. Bickers (ed.), *Settlers and Expatriates: Britons Over the Seas* (Oxford: Oxford University Press, 2010); Will Jackson, *Madness and Marginality: The Lives of Kenya's White Insane* (Manchester: Manchester University Press, 2013). For works from farther afield, see Carol Summers, *From Civilization to Segregation: Social Ideas and Social Control in Southern Rhodesia, 1890–1934* (Athens: Ohio University Press, 1994); Grace Elizabeth Hale, *Making Whiteness: The Culture of Segregation in the South, 1890–1940* (New York: Pantheon, 1998); Joel Williamson, *The Crucible of Race: Black/White Relations in the American South since Emancipation* (New York: Oxford University Press, 1984).

14 My thinking on this point has been influenced by James C. Scott, *Domination and the Arts of Resistance: Hidden Transcripts* (New Haven: Yale University Press, 1990); Allison K. Shutt, '"I told him I was Lennox Njokweni": honor and racial etiquette in Southern Rhodesia', *Journal of African History* 51 (2010): 323–41; Shutt, 'The settlers' cattle complex: the etiquette of culling cattle in colonial Zimbabwe, 1938', *Journal of African History* 43 (2002): 263–86; Ann Laura Stoler, *Carnal Knowledge and Imperial Power: Race and the Intimate in Colonial Rule* (Berkeley: University of California Press, 2010); Jennifer Ritterhouse, *Growing up Jim Crow: How Black and White Southern Children Learned Race* (Chapel Hill: University of North Carolina Press, 2006); George Orwell, *Shooting an Elephant, and Other Essays* (New York: Harcourt, Brace, 1950); Alan Paton, *Too Late the Phalarope* (New York: Scribner, 1953); Doris Lessing, *The Grass Is Singing* (London: M. Joseph, 1950). See also Summer, *From Civilization to Segregation*, p. 62.

15 The following draws on the burgeoning field of 'whiteness studies'. For critical works in the history and study of whiteness, see David Roediger, *The Wages of Whiteness: Race and the Making of the American Working Class* (New York: Verso, 1991); Richard Dyer, *White* (London and New York: Routledge, 1997); Matthew Frye Jacobson, *Whiteness of a Different Color: European Immigrants and the Alchemy of Race* (Cambridge, MA: Harvard University Press, 1999); John Hartigan, Jr, *Odd Tribes: Toward a Cultural Analysis of White People* (Durham: Duke University Press, 2005); Bruce Baum, *The Rise and Fall of the Caucasian Race: A Political History of Racial Identity* (New York and London: New York University Press, 2006); Matt Wray, *Not Quite White: White Trash and the Boundaries of Whiteness* (Durham, NC: Duke University Press, 2006); Steve Garner, *Whiteness: An Introduction* (London and New York: Routledge, 2007); Nell Irvin Painter, *The History of White People* (New York: Norton, 2010). I suggest that we must pay much closer attention to locales outside Europe and the US, to places where 'whites' were in the minority and were thus forced to reckon more directly with definitions of whiteness. For suggestive works on 'whiteness beyond the west', see Melissa Steyn, *'Whiteness Just Isn't What It Used to Be': White Identity in a Changing South Africa* (Albany: State University of New York, 2001); Ira Bashkow, *The Meaning of Whitemen: Race and Modernity in the Orokaiva Cultural World* (Chicago: University of Chicago Press, 2006); Judy Rohrer, *Haoles in Hawai'i* (Honolulu: University of Hawai'i Press, 2010); David McDermott Hughes, *Whiteness in Zimbabwe: Race, Landscape, and the Problem of Belonging* (New York: Palgrave Macmillan, 2010); Richard Schroeder, *Africa after Apartheid: South Africa, Race, and Nation in Tanzania* (Bloomington: Indiana University Press, 2012); Jackson, *Madness and Marginality*; Janet McIntosh, 'Unsettled: Denial and Belonging among White Kenyans' (ms, 2014).

16 'On Dangerous Ground', *KO* (15 Oct. 1923), p. 3.
17 It appears that, among whites, only the Afrikaners were specially identified by Africans; they were known as *kaburu*, from goat – a reference to the long beards Afrikaners favoured, reminiscent of goats' hairy chins.
18 A phrase borrowed from Wray, *Not Quite White*.
19 Henry O. Weller, *Kenya Without Prejudice* (Nairobi: East Africa, 1931), p. 57.

INTRODUCTION

20 The literature on the intermeshing of government and settler is vast. For a sampling, see Bruce Berman, *Control and Crisis in Colonial Kenya: The Dialectic of Domination* (London: James Currey, 1990); Bruce Berman and John Lonsdale, *Unhappy Valley: Conflict in Kenya and Africa* (Athens: Ohio University Press, 1992); Anthony Clayton and Donald Savage, *Government and Labour in Kenya, 1895–1963* (London: Cass, 1975); Robert M. Maxon, *Struggle for Kenya: The Loss and Reassertion of Imperial Initiative, 1912–1923* (Hackensack, NJ: Fairleigh Dickinson University Press, 1993); Norman Leys, *Kenya* (London: Cass, 1973 [1924]); W. McGregor Ross, *Kenya from Within: A Short Political History* (London: Frank Cass, 1968 [1927]). Settlers' complaints of government inattention can be found in virtually every book they wrote, in every issue of every paper they published.

21 Among the most influential recent texts on this point is Stoler, *Carnal Knowledge and Imperial Power*.

22 In Fanon's words, the colonized man concludes that 'By loving me she proves that I am worthy of white love. I am loved like a white man. I am a white man.' Frantz Fanon, *Black Skin, White Masks* (New York: Grove Press, 2008), p. 63.

23 Myra C. Glenn, *Campaigns against Corporal Punishment: Prisoners, Sailors, Women, and Children in Antebellum America* (Albany: SUNY Press, 1984); Susan Dwyer Amussen, 'Punishment, discipline, and power: the social meanings of violence in early modern England', *Journal of British Studies* 34 (1995): 1–34; Henrice Altink, '"An outrage to all decency": abolitionist reactions to flogging Jamaican slave women, 1780–1834', *Slavery and Abolition* 23 (2002): 107–22; Abby M. Schrader, *Languages of the Lash: Corporal Punishment and Identity in Imperial Russia* (Dekalb: Northern Illinois University Press, 2002).

24 Mrinalini Sinha, *Colonial Masculinity: The 'Manly Englishman' and the 'Effeminate Bengali' in the Late Nineteenth Century* (Manchester: Manchester University Press, 1995), p. 47; Norman Etherington, 'Natal's black rape scare of the 1870s', *Journal of Southern African Studies* 15 (1988): 36–53; Jacquelyn Dowd Hall, 'The mind that burns in each body: women, rape and racial violence', in Ann Snitow, Christine Stansell, and Sharon Thompson (eds), *Powers of Desire: The Politics of Sexuality* (New York: Monthly Review Press, 1983); Carmel Harris, 'The "terror of the law" as applied to black rapists in colonial Queensland', *Hecate* 8 (1982): 22–4; John Pape, 'Black and white: the "perils of sex" in colonial Zimbabwe', *Journal of Southern African Studies* 16 (1990): 699–720; Jeremy Martens, 'Settler homes, manhood, and "houseboys": an analysis of Natal's rape scare of 1886', *Journal of Southern African Studies* 28 (2002): 379–400; David M. Anderson, 'Sexual threat and settler society: "black perils" in Kenya, c. 1907–1930', *Journal of Imperial and Commonwealth History* 38 (2010): 47–74; Kennedy, *Islands of White*; Charles Van Onselen, *Studies in the Social and Economic History of the Witwatersrand, 1886–1914* (Harlow: Longman, 1982).

25 A point made long ago by W. J. Cash, *The Mind of the South* (New York: Vintage, 1941), p. 118.

26 Tommy O'Shea, when running for the LegCo, admitted that he 'came as a white settler, and I do not pretend that my interest in the native is other than that of the average white settler'. 'Plateau South elections', *EAS* (9 Feb. 1924), p. 8A.

27 As Duder and Youé put it, 'Racial solidarity was a veneer, but subscription to it was indispensable to the maintenance of white supremacy. Private views were subsumed by the prevailing ideology.' 'Paice's place', p. 270.

28 M.P.K. Sorrenson, *Origins of European Settlement in Kenya* (Oxford: Oxford University Press, 1968), p. 228. Margery Perham found herself coming under this spell in 1930. Margery Perham, *East African Journey: Kenya and Tanganyika, 1929–30* (London: Faber and Faber, 1976), p. 190.

29 Berman, *Control and Crisis*, p. 134. Similarly, Duder argues that officers involved in the Soldier Settlement Scheme 'were members of an elite before coming to Kenya and their main reason for participation in the scheme was to preserve that status from the threat of post-war inflation'. Duder, 'Soldier Settlement Scheme', p. iv.

30 A phrase coined by Du Bois, popularized by Roedigger.
31 Quoted in Trzebinski, *Kenya Pioneers*, p. 104. McGregor Ross was, as per his custom, uncharitable as to the ends of such attitudes: 'The type of life lived, and pursuit followed, in new lands such as Kenya, led to a strange evaporation of humility and the easy substitution of self-sufficiency and arrogance in its place'. *Kenya from Within*, p. 125.
32 McGregor Ross admitted that his critique of settlers was sardonic in many passages, 'But was ever [a] writer provided with such a field for satire? Has there anywhere flourished, in our generation, a group of British people as aptly symbolized, as is the small political group in Kenya, by a turkey-cock – everlastingly gobbling, strident, aggressive, ugly to look at?' *Kenya from Within*, p. 454.
33 This phrase I borrow from Keguro Macharia.
34 Ngũgĩ wa Thiong'o, *Weep Not, Child* (London: Heinemann, 1964); *A Grain of Wheat* (London: Heinemann, 1967); *Petals of Blood* (London: Heinemann, 1977); W. E. B. Du Bois, *Souls of Black Folk* (Chicago: McClurg, 1903); James Weldon Johnson, *Along this Way: The Autobiography of James Weldon Johnson* (New York: Viking, 1933); Johnson, *The Autobiography of an Ex-Colored Man* (Boston: French, 1912); Richard Wright, *Black Boy: A Record of Childhood and Youth* (New York: Harper 1945); Wright, *Native Son* (New York: Harper, 1940); Ralph Ellison, *Invisible Man* (New York: Random House, 1952).
35 The boundaries of the East African Protectorate in 1895 differ from those of independent Kenya. The Uganda Protectorate extended into the Rift Valley until 1902, while in the northeast a large piece of land was turned over to Italian Somaliland in 1925.
36 Quoted in Sorrenson, *Origins of European Settlement*, p. 36.
37 Kennedy, *Islands of White*, ch. 6.
38 Charles Eliot, 'The progress and problems of the East Africa Protectorate', *Proceedings of the Royal Colonial Institute* 37 (1905–6): 81–100, numbers from 86, 94.
39 Sorrenson, *Origins of European Settlement*, pp. 103–7, 123–6.
40 On the Kakamega gold rush, see Priscilla Shiralo, *A Failed Eldorado: Colonial Capitalism, Rural Industrialization, African Land Rights in Kenya, and the Kakamega Gold Rush, 1930–1952* (Lanham, MD: University Press of America, 2008).
41 Tabitha Kanogo, *Squatters and the Roots of Mau Mau* (Athens: University of Ohio Press, 1987).
42 Duder notes that critics in Britain were sometimes surprised to find out how few settlers there were, compared to how much trouble they caused.
43 Winston Churchill, *My African Journey* (London: Holland, 1908), pp. 14–15.
44 Sorrenson, *Origins of European Settlement*, pp. 93–4.
45 See, for example, 'The convention', *Leader* (5 Aug. 1911), n.p.
46 Leys, *Kenya*, p. 172.
47 See, for example, Duder, 'Soldier Settlement Scheme', pp. 124, 762.
48 'Kenya social events', *Critic* (23 Sept. 1922), p. 13.
49 'Nutshell novels: John Smithers-Smythe', *Critic* (7 Oct. 1923), p. 23. For actual examples of inventing 'double-barrelled' names, see Duder, 'Soldier Settlement Scheme', pp. 770–1.
50 Alyse Simpson, *Red Dust of Kenya* (New York: Crowell, 1952), p. 57.
51 'Things we want to know', *Critic* (3 June 1922), p. 15. See also Duder, 'Soldier Settlement Scheme'.
52 'Hands off the people's food', *Critic* (13 May 1922). See also 'An open letter', *Critic* (12 Aug. 1922), pp. 16–17.
53 Rab, 'I'd love to be a farmer', *Critic* (3 June 1922), p. 11.
54 McGregor Ross, *Kenya from Within*, p. 125; Duder, 'Soldier Settlement Scheme', p. 664.
55 'Apostles of fear', *East African Chronicle* (28 Aug. 1920), pp. 5–6.
56 James Paton, letter to ed., *EAS* (1 Oct. 1923), p. 5.

INTRODUCTION

57 'The coming elections', *EAS* (22 March 1924), p. 27. He failed in his attempt, losing 45 votes to 60 for P. H. Clarke. 'The elections', *EAS* (4 Apr. 1924), p. 30.
58 Peter de Polnay, *My Road* (London: Allen, 1978), p. 77.
59 As Roediger notes, much of what seems to be new in recent work on whiteness was articulated long ago by African-American writers. David Roediger, *Black on White: Black Writers on What It Means to Be White* (New York: Random House, 1998).

CHAPTER TWO

Race, civilization, and paternalism

In a curious way, white settlers in early colonial Kenya could be seen as the inheritors of nineteenth-century abolitionism. Africans in Kenya required liberation. The chains to be shed were not iron but mental and cultural. Kenyans must be lifted from the degradation not of slavery but of savagery. Like Britons of the previous century, settlers would also do good by doing well: harnessing African labour and developing the land created prosperous whites even as it civilized Africans. Thus the *Times of East Africa* in 1905 called on the incoming commissioner, James Hayes-Sadler, to devote himself to the interests of settlers. 'We do not mean that the interests of the natives of the Protectorate are to be neglected', it reassured Hayes-Sadler. 'On the contrary, it is our firm conviction that those interests will be best served by promoting the welfare of the white population.'[1]

The comparison between settlers and anti-slavery advocates becomes perverse, however, when the influence of racial thinking is taken into account. As the nineteenth century wore on, scientists constructed ever-more elaborate rankings of people by race, and by their race's level of development. Settlers had little doubt that they, as whites, were more civilized than Africans, and that this would remain the case for generations or centuries to come. Under white tutelage, Africans would, slowly, reach the level of Europeans. In the meantime, equality did no one any good. Africans were children, or pupils, and settlers their parents or teachers. The abolitionist icon showed an African slave on bended knee, asking 'Am I not a man and a brother?' Settlers would have appreciated the image of a black man on his knees, but the caption must be 'Am I not your child?'

Race, obviously, was the dividing line in colonial Kenya. Whites brought civilization to Africa. Africans must defer to whites as higher beings. Whites ruled, Africans were the ruled. These were truisms to which every settler held. Ewart Grogan summed it up in 1906: 'No distinction other than colour is politically possible since every grade of intelligence or wealth ... exist in our midst without reference to colour. There can be no intelligence or wealth test here. Let us be honest and call a spade a spade. Our boundary line is colour.'[2] Honest, perhaps, but not without complications. For settlers justified settlement through the language of civilization, but some Africans claimed to have become civilized. They became Christians, learned English, dressed in western-style clothing. These individuals posed a problem for settlers. A 'civilized' African might claim equality with whites, and would find allies in settlers' pesky critics back in Britain. In order to turn back these striving Africans, settlers turned to humiliation. These so-called 'semi-civilized' Africans were, settlers scoffed, rogues, thieves, layabouts, promiscuous. The 'raw' African was to be preferred to the 'mission boy' whose head had been filled with nonsense about racial equality. Through laughter and insult, settlers instructed Africans as to what, precisely, the dividing line in Kenya must be: race, not civilization.

Settlers felt much more comfortable with those Africans who did not express pretentions toward civilization, but who (appeared) to accept white trusteeship. For settlers found great emotional and psychological satisfaction from their roles as trustees. They often thought of themselves as parents of their African charges, or feudal lords and ladies with retinues of loyal retainers. They thought themselves selfless in their care of Africans. Africans' lack of gratitude only reinforced settlers' belief in blacks' childishness. Settlers often spoke of their love for Africans. It was instead a love for their new status as trustees, as parents, as commanders of servants. Kenya was, indeed, a happy place for whites.

Race and civilization

Europeans' self-appointed duty to spread civilization across the world had become nearly unquestionable (in Europe) by the late nineteenth century. Colonialism would bring rational government, law and order, and economic development. Missionaries concerned themselves with the moral and cultural sides of African life, for to be a Christian meant to follow European civilization. Settlers in Kenya too believed in the civilizing mission. But in small doses. Teaching Africans about democracy and equality they considered to be dangerous. Instead, settlers argued that the long, slow process of civilizing Africans must begin by teaching them the value of hard work. To be effective, this would have to be done under white supervision, under white tutelage.

Civilization and evolution

In settler thinking, civilizing Africans was no small thing, and could not be accomplished quickly. Although western Europeans, and Britons in particular, enjoyed a racial genius for rule (the thinking went), this had admittedly not always been the case. Two thousand years ago, the British Isles were home to Druids and various savage, warfare-loving tribes. The Romans provided the spark for progress. Only with the Roman invasions did the British enter into a centuries-long climb up the social-evolutionary ladder.[3] Africans in the early twentieth century could be compared to Britons' pre-Roman ancestors, an idea shared by settlers, administrators, missionaries, and anthropologists alike.[4] Although a few settlers held fast to a belief in innate, unalterable African inferiority,[5] most expressed confidence in whites' ability to lift them from savagery to civilization.

Catching up to the modern world would be a long struggle. Great minds debated the means of uplifting backwards races. Followers of Lamarck and Bagehot believed that characteristics acquired over an individual's lifetime could be passed down to the next generation – use-inheritance. Exceptional individuals could create positive habits, passing on to subsequent generations a higher level of life.[6] Individual success propelled evolution. By 1900, scientists had dismissed these ideas, but settlers paid them no mind. Ideas of use-inheritance remained influential in settlers' thinking on social and cultural evolution. Whites would patiently teach an African many tenets of civilization. Only a few of those lessons would truly strike home. Still fewer lessons would be passed to the next generation. But when whites began to tutor that next generation, they would have something – something small, to be sure, but something – on which to build.

Thus while whites could accelerate Africans' climb up the ladder of social evolution, Africans could not immediately be lifted to the top rung. An early Thika settler, Sandy Herd, recalled that 'It was generally agreed that time and time only was the answer without any short cut'.[7] Virtually all whites believed it would be many generations before Africans could approximate the civilization whites already enjoyed. The *East African Standard* rejected the 'wholly fantastic theorizing' that other races could jump forward in a generation what had taken whites 'very many centuries of evolution'.

> It is assumed too readily that what has been a long, weary and dangerous climb for the most virile and persistent races of the earth, is but an easy leap for others more lethargic. No race is, in fact, so readily adaptable that in a few years it can unlearn the traditions of its thousands of years of history, and replace them with the outlook, ideas and aspirations taken from the latest revolutionary textbook of a wholly foreign race.

RACE, CIVILIZATION, AND PATERNALISM

> The advance of races other than white to the ranks of rulers on the lines of the white domination of to-day ... must proceed by the same patient process as has emerged in the ability of the white races to rule.[8]

Karen Blixen was perhaps the most optimistic, calculating a ratio of three years for Africans to make advances that had taken Europeans a hundred years; Africans might catch up in as little as sixty years.[9] For most whites, however, Africans' evolution was a matter of centuries, not decades.[10]

Trusteeship

While virtually all non-African observers agreed that Africans required assistance along the path toward civilization, not all trusted settlers as their guides. Bureaucrats in the Colonial Office, the humanitarian lobby in Britain, and, in Kenya, district officers and missionaries all claimed the mantle of 'trusteeship'. In their own ways, each group adhered to the belief that it had a solemn duty to help and protect

2.1 'B.E.A. colonist to idle native: "You're expected to bear your share in the development of the Country and we hope to make you into a thrifty and industrious member of the community"'

Africans. They often differed as to what kind of assistance Africans needed. (Few thought to ask Africans.) Settlers loudly proclaimed that while they all – as Britons, as imperialists, as whites, or as bearers of Christian European civilization – shared the duty of trusteeship, settlers were the best placed to actually put trusteeship to work.[11] This was an argument settlers never ceased to make, for their claims to trusteeship were never fully accepted.

Administrators had their own ideas of trusteeship. The early district officers in Kenya were, to put it mildly, of mixed background.[12] But by the 1910s, London more carefully selected the men who would fill the ranks of cadets and district commissioners. These officers, most educated in public schools, Oxford or Cambridge, and from the middle or upper classes, developed a 'paternalistic authoritarianism' over Africans. They drew only partially on ideas of a modern, bureaucratic state for their inspiration. At the local level district officers held to an 'ideology of domination "aristocratic" in its cultural roots and mythology, with an emphasis on honor, duty, and noblesse oblige'.[13] They would preserve law and order, protect the weak from the powerful, and limit the disruptions outside influences might have on the 'organic communities' under their command. By a judicious mix of their standing as a disinterested third party and a sentimental attachment to 'their people', administrators believed they could benefit all Africans under their rule.

This 'paternalistic authoritarianism' did not mesh well with settlers' claims to trusteeship. In 1905, following a petulant Colonists' Association memorandum to the Secretary of State, the senior administrator C. W. Hobley wrote that 'The officials of the administration are not antagonistic to the settler community'. Conflict did arise, he admitted, owing to different ideas of trusteeship. 'All [administrators] ask', Hobley continued, 'is that the settlers will co-operate with them in a liberal spirit and assist them in furthering the progress of the country by just treatment of the natives and in other ways.'[14] Co-operation meant adhering to administrators' ideas of trusteeship. Few settlers would take this bargain.

The question of trusteeship became most prominent in 1923.[15] For several years European and Indian settlers had politicked over control of Kenya. Settlers defended themselves through the language of trusteeship. To grant Indians political power would be to sentence Africans to yet further centuries of savagery. Indians, settlers' accusations went, were dishonest, exploitative, unsanitary, and morally depraved. Did one ask an adulterer, idolator, or thief to teach children the Ten Commandments? Moreover, settlers argued that Great Britain had made a pact with Africans. The Convention of Associations resolved in February 1923:

That, whereas our Administrators have entered into treaties, agreements and negotiations with native and African peoples in the belief that they were asking them to entrust their future to the protection of an Imperial Race, which would guide their development by the liberal traditions of Western Civilisation, this Convention considers that the adoption of a policy which will gradually but inevitably transfer those responsibilities to an Asiatic Race, steeped through many centuries in the traditions of Eastern despotism, would be a flagrant breach of faith.[16]

(One wonders how many landless Gikuyu and widowed Nandi would have agreed with this interpretation of conquest.) The motion passed, at which point the attendees stood and lustily sang the national anthem.[17]

Despite their flag-draped double-barrelled racism, settlers would be disappointed. In July the Colonial Office released a White Paper titled 'Indians in Kenya', more commonly referred to as the Devonshire Declaration (so named after the then-Secretary of State). The crucial passage:

> Primarily, Kenya is an African territory, and ... the interests of the African natives must be paramount, and that if, and when, those interests and the interests of the immigrant races should conflict, the former should prevail.

The state would retain the position of trustee, although settlers would never be excluded from their role as agents in Africans' development. As the East African Commission of 1924–25 explained, 'It is in very truth a white man's burden, and all Europeans in Africa must share in the work'.[18] Settlers continued to assert their role as guides and teachers of Africans. Africans chafed under all this, evidenced by 'insolence', breakaway Christian churches, and western-style political movements.

It would be easy to dismiss settler talk of trusteeship and the white man's burden as lies and propaganda. Settlers needed labour, hence they claimed that Africans could be civilized only by working for whites. Settlers feared Indian enfranchisement, hence they demonized Asians as having a retarding effect on Africans' progress. Yet we ought not to imagine settler discourse as nothing more than empty rhetoric. Like administrators, London officials, and missionaries, settlers shared a worldview steeped in ideas of race, civilization, and evolution. Whites were more advanced than Africans, and must assist in the latter's advancement. Settlers may well have used these ideas for particular economic and political ends. They could do so only because trusteeship had purchase among themselves and their fellow whites.

Humiliation and the 'civilized' African

Whites proclaimed it their duty to civilize Africans, but a civilized African could be troublesome. He might demand his rights. To prevent such an awkward situation, settlers reminded Africans that becoming civilized was a centuries-long process. No one alive in 1910 or 1920, settlers insisted, would live to see a civilized Kenyan African. Those Africans who had pretensions to civilization? Settlers humiliated them.[19] Humiliation is a symbolic transaction of power. To be humiliated is to be forced into a position of subordination. To be laughed at or bullied displays one's inferiority – lack of intelligence, or social grace, or physical strength – in relation to the aggressor. It demonstrates that one is at the bottom of the community, or even beyond its boundaries. Unless the humiliated are able to respond, verbally or physically, their lower status is confirmed.[20] Settlers well understood the power of humiliation. They told the African man in western-style clothing that he had fallen lower in morality than his unclothed brother. They condemned mission-educated Africans as thieves. Settlers instead praised Africans who accepted their place on the racial/civilizational hierarchy.

Civilization, morality, and clothing

The long road to civilization could be fraught with danger, whites believed. Settlers with vast herds certainly raged against lawless cattle thieves from the Reserves, but it was not the unschooled, isolated savages who most rankled whites. Those who committed – or were thought to commit – burglaries were those who had come into contact with western ways.[21] Africans in 'pristine savagery', the *Standard* claimed in 1906, were 'infinitely more moral' than those who had picked up bits of civilization.[22] Civilization also brought urbanization and prostitution.[23] Prior to colonization, according to settler-turned-novelist Nora Strange, prostitution in its 'dictionary meaning of the word was unknown'. Selling sex was one of the 'ugly aspects' of the introduction of civilization.[24] Police officer Robert Foran spoke for many when he despairingly admitted that the 'advance of civilisation had also brought in its train many evils', including 'large numbers of native prostitutes' in the new colonial towns.[25] Prostitution soon bore its bastard scourge, venereal disease, hitherto (settlers claimed) unknown in East Africa.[26]

Ragged trousers on a white man lowered his social standing. Pressed trousers on Africans lowered their morals. This, at least, was the story settlers loved to tell. It was virtually uncontested that western-style clothing erased Africans' sexual morality. Nora Strange's district officer in her novel *Courtship in Kenya* authoritatively stated 'that every additional garment an Embu woman puts on represents another good-bye to her morals'.[27] One of the tribal stereotypes circulating in early colonial Kenya was in fact complementary, in its own way. It was said that the Luo, who at this time covered relatively little of their bodies, were in fact the 'most moral of the East African tribes',[28] perhaps in all of Africa.[29]

This is not to say that Europeans necessarily revelled in the sight of Africans walking city streets unclothed. But covering the body did not require western-style finery. For they were equally convinced that western clothing had ill effects on Africans' attitudes. The moment an African man donned a hat, jacket, trousers and shirt – or any combination thereof – he became haughty to other blacks.[30] Ethel Younghusband, wife of a King's African Rifles officer, believed that 'the less the native is clothed the nicer he is, and the more modest and well behaved'. 'Directly a native begins putting on garments of civilisation', she warned, 'he gets wrong ideas with them, and smells infinitely more unpleasant'.[31] Settlers humiliated Africans who wore western clothing, comparing them to monkeys or giraffes.[32] A well-placed blanket always had better effect than a cast-off (or stolen) dress or pair of trousers.

Christianity and education

Settlers most distrusted Christian Africans, especially that class known as 'mission boys'. Missionaries such as Archdeacon W. E. Owen who preached equality between the races (even while exercising a racist paternalism over his followers) were condemned.[33] Harold Robertson insisted that the 'entirely illogical efforts being made to force Christianity (or rather dogmas and ceremonies based on Christian teachings) upon the native mind by means of get-there-quick methods will assuredly bring disaster in their train'.[34] Just as they laughed at Africans in trousers, settlers smirked at the Old Testament names some converts selected.[35]

Christianity could not speed up social evolution. Hilda Peirson dismissed the idea of using mission-trained African women to care for white children. 'No doubt', she wrote in 1924, 'they very quickly learn to sew, knit, cook, scrub and clean, and even to read and write, but how long does it take to eradicate the effects of the surroundings in which they have lived for generations?'[36] Most converts did little good, and caused much harm. 'Is it not true', queried D. Sparrow of Uasin Gishu, 'that many educated Natives – so-called – Christians are unreliable, they steal, lie, are troublesome, trouble-brewers, create dissatisfaction among the raw boys who, as a rule, are more trustworthy, honest and better labourers and servants'.[37] Thus many whites preferred to hire a 'heathen ... because he is not puffed up with nonsensical ideas and does not adopt the manner towards Europeans that is so objectionable in the averaged [sic] mission trained boy'.[38]

For many years liberal education would be inappropriate. Educated Africans, it was said, believed themselves too good for real, physical labour. H. Ryle Shaw of Ruiru considered that 'A smattering of reading and writing generally gives savages insufferable conceit and disdain of manual work, and is simply useful to them (of course, I am speaking of the mass) for forging passes, testimonials, orders on stores and dates on labour tickets'.[39] Sometimes educated Africans presumed themselves to be 'as on an equality with the white man'.[40] They became a 'class of useless native parasites in European garb'.[41] They 'develop[ed] exaggerated ideas'.[42]

The dangers of too-quick civilizing did not mean that whites should walk away and leave Africans to their barbaric ways. 'The simplicity of savage life', 'Critolaoa' of Nairobi reminded whites, 'is not all beer and skittles'.[43] Instead of useless, dangerous liberal education, Africans must be civilized through learning the value of labour, of regular, physical toil.[44] There were benefits to religion and western education, but 'To obtain the best fruits of [their] advantages a substratum of useful service and contact with real European life has first to be laid'.[45] Substituting liberal education for training in agricultural science and crafts was in fact an 'injustice' to Africans.[46]

The noble savage

There was little love lost between settlers and the Africans who adopted western civilization. Instead, settlers glorified those peoples who actively refused western ways. Most important were the pastoralists, particularly the Somali and Maasai. In the early years of settlement few settlers had kind words for them.[47] Settlers boasted that they brought peace to communities who had lived under constant fear of Maasai raids. But like Native Americans in the US, once Maasai had been pushed off into a reserve they posed little threat to whites. Their independence, pride, courage, and rejection of modern ways could now be celebrated.[48]

Settlers – perhaps upper-class English settlers especially – saw in the pastoralists a type of person long lost 'back home'. V. M. Carnegie praised her Somali servant Omar: 'In manner Omar resembled the best type of old family retainer, perfectly frank but never familiar, and with the native good breeding that I sometimes think is the birthright of Eastern races'.[49] Other settlers saw in pastoralists all that they desired in themselves: a strict code of honour, a supreme self-confidence, a firm belief in the superiority of one's culture, a bravery unshaken in the face of scabbard-wielding foes or snarling lions. The American hunter Edgar Bronson echoed many settlers when he dubbed the Maasai the 'gentlemen *par excellence* of the British East Africa plateau'. J. Bland-Sutton praised them as 'dignified', while W. S. Rainsford believed them 'Very intelligent, with a certain dash of independence, that other natives lack'.[50] Delamere, Galbraith Cole, and Lord Colvile all counted themselves as 'friends of the Maasai', Delamere to the extent that he (allegedly) refused to punish them for stealing his cattle.[51]

The 'westernized' Africans had only a veneer of civilization; scratch the surface and the savage remained. But underneath they were no longer the good savage. Not the moral, naked Luo. Not the noble, proud Maasai. Pseudo-civilized Africans had jettisoned all the worthy restraints of tribal morality, yet had not internalized – indeed, were evolutionarily unprepared to internalize – a higher morality. The Africans whom settlers most admired were those who would not interrupt the equation of whiteness with civilization. Other Africans must be reminded of their place.

A 'boy' with a hat

The case of L. M. Tebajanga is an especially poignant example of the kinds of humiliation suffered by Africans 'acting European'. Tebajanga, a Ugandan, was literate in English and likely a Christian.[52] One day in early March 1922, Tebajanga was walking down a Nairobi street, wearing 'a beautiful military helmet', his hands full with packages to be brought to his employer. He came upon three white men, none of whom, he noted, wore uniforms or any sign of rank (that is, none represented government). One of the men crossed the road and stood before Tebajanga, ordering him to remove his helmet. 'This was not done', Tebajanga wrote in a letter to the *East African Standard*, 'as I wanted to know the reason why'. The white man again insisted, and threatened to smash the hat and 'brain' the black man. Tebajanga still refused, and he and the three white men all stood in silence, eyes locked. Tebajanga finally walked on, at which point his hat was pushed off his head. He asked why; 'Sorry to say that no answer was given [other] than "Because you are a black man – boy, I mean."' The white men then continued on their way.

Tebajanga found the incident to be deeply humiliating, and in his letter to the editor he struggled to make whites understand this:

> Do you know what he made me feel like when he talked like that? It is not I who can explain the bitter feelings which hurt my heart more than I can tell you, but only one thing I may say: I suddenly felt a tug which sent my heart into my brains. What I want you to make me understand is: How

and why should I lift my hat to every white man who is neither titled, my master, nor my friend? Are not all the creatures of one Creator?[53]

In his letter, Tebajanga drew on one of the best counters to humiliation, or the best way to draw allies: empathy. He asked white readers to understand what the white men 'made me feel', to describe how it sent 'my heart into my brains'. He hoped that if whites truly understood his humiliation, if they could empathize with him, such acts would cease. He explicitly connected the incident with his *emotions*, ones which he expected his readers to share.

Unfortunately for Tebajanga, settlers knew full well his humiliation, for that was their intention. For humiliation to really hit its mark, the humiliator should *understand* his opponent, to understand what would most hurt him. To humiliate Tebajanga, the white men and the editor had to understand his self-image, his belief in an equality based on civilization. Thus they knocked off his western-style hat, they called him boy. The responses to Tebajanga's letter were as insulting as the incident he described. For Tebajanga's query – 'How and why should I lift my hat to every white man who is neither titled, my master, nor my friend?' – the editor became the teacher of a slow pupil. Think harder, he told Tebajanga, for 'the patience and intelligence that compiled this letter can surely persist a little longer till they discover the answer – or else turn themselves to more productive problems'.[54] Tebajanga would not be permitted into the ranks of the civilized.

The joy of paternalism

Whites emigrated to Kenya for many reasons: to hunt exotic animals, to experience the thrill of civilizing virgin land and savage peoples, to escape social conventions or enervating modern life, to make their fortunes. Yet leaving their families and homes for a faraway land must have been bittersweet. In Kenya, however, settlers found emotional comfort in the strangest of places. Settlers told stories about themselves in which they parented childlike Africans, in which they sacrificed for their African dependants. They gloried in being waited upon by retinues of African servants. They created an emotional life based on a strict racial hierarchy. No matter what Africans did – if they were thankful, or if they were ungrateful – they reinforced settlers' self-image.

Firm and just parents

The language of social evolution was very much tied up with ideas of human maturation. The civilized child matured through stages – emotional, self-centred, and obsessed with the present, to rational, control of the ego, and able to plan for the future. Civilized races or nations were thought to have undergone a similar process. Once they had been savage, but had matured to civilized people; as a race, they had matured from childhood to adulthood. When Kenya's Governor Grigg addressed a London audience in 1927, they all understood when he spoke of Britain's own 'rise from our barbarous childhood'.[55]

The imagery of maturation and evolution was constant in settler discourse. Like a child, Kenya itself was striving towards adulthood – from dependence on the mother country towards independence, or a relationship of equality tempered by an offspring's deference to and love for the parent. Kenya was a 'young colony', a 'juvenile', in its 'infancy'.[56] Like a child, Kenya would move through stages toward adulthood and independence.[57] One of the most important steps came in 1912, when grants-in-aid from London ceased. The child no longer relied on the financial support of the parent. 'We have emerged', boasted the *Leader*, 'from the days of childhood, and are preparing, by the discontinuance of the Grant-in-Aid, to keep our own accounts, and to live, as a community, without recourse to chits ... The youngest colony has been mothered fairly well and is answering admirably to the teachings of the Motherland.'[58] A mere five months later, the *Leader* squirmed under the motherland's control: Kenya was in the 'predicament of a youth who has begun to earn his own living, who, whilst being praised for being economical in his habits ..., the parental control is not relaxed a jot, and his opinions respecting his future are not allowed to weigh in the kindly but over-cautious counsels of his elders'.[59] By 1924, the *Standard* could boast that the white community 'has passed its infancy and is advancing into the virile, glowing youth with the promise of mature, and dignified manhood of Empire service and influence'.[60]

Settlers used maturation as a metaphor for Kenya's growth, but were much more literal in its application to Africans. The African race was a childlike race.[61] Moreover, Africans' stunted social evolution *as a race* could be witnessed in the developmental delay of *each* African. African (and other non-European) children were thought to grow emotionally and mentally at the same pace as European children, or even a bit more quickly.[62] The difference: at some point prior to full maturity, African growth stopped. From the late 1800s through the first decades of the twentieth, such thinking was common sense among European scholars and scientists.[63] Attitudes in Kenya were the same. 'On an average', Mrs M. C. Monckton informed readers of the *Standard* in 1922, 'the mentality of the native is like that of a little child and moreover a child who never grows up'.[64] Less charitably, Eve Bache believed that the African had 'the mentality of a child – usually of a backward child'.[65]

Like the colony in which they lived, Africans remained children so long as they needed to depend upon whites for guidance and training. The idea of 'self-determination' so popular after the First World War was good for neither British children nor African adults. Thomas Raynes pointed to Haiti as an example of what would happen when independence was granted too soon. Linking evolution, paternalism, and independence, Raynes warned that disaster would result

> unless [the Kenyan African] is kept with unwearied patience continually under influence, until his brain begins to evolve, for it is by the process of evolution alone, which is or ought to be spontaneous that real progress can take place, and I fear that an enormous time must elapse before any hope can be entertained of dear brother Jerogi [i.e., Njoroge, a common Gikuyu name] standing alone and progressing of his own volition.[66]

'Onlooker' explained how Gikuyu must 'be carefully fathered until the difficult period of adolescence is passed, and the time of maturity is reached when they may stand the tests of adversity on a footing equal to that enjoyed by other men'.[67]

Ideas of Africans as childlike infected settlers' personal interactions with Africans. The most obvious sign was the ubiquitous use of 'boy' to refer to every African male, regardless of his age. This was a custom new arrivals (at least from Britain, perhaps not South Africa and the United States) had to learn. When writing for British audiences, settlers often set off 'boy' in quotes to remind readers that the term had little to do with age.[68] Reflecting on her childhood in early colonial Kenya, Elspeth Huxley recalled that 'The term "boy", then in universal use, has come to seem derogatory and insulting, as of course in English terms it is; these were men, not boys'. Yet she dismissed any notion that settlers intended it to be degrading ('At the time, no one thought anything of it, it was just the custom') or that Africans necessarily took it as degrading ('French waiters do not object to being called garçons, so far as I know').[69]

Huxley overstates the obliviousness of her fellow settlers, and overlooks the impact of 'boy'. Until they had a stronger grasp of the nuances of the term's meaning in English, African servants may well have thought little of being referred to as 'boy'. This was not so for men like Tebajanga, and most Africans by at least the 1940s and 1950s resented the word.[70] But from their first arrival in East Africa, using 'boy' for adult Africans held great symbolic power for white settlers. It placed African men in perpetual childhood. No matter his age or station in life, so long as he was a 'boy' a man was not a man.[71] He could not be the equal of a white person. If Africans were children, whites must be their parents.

African women, however, remained women. According to white ideas about African societies, bolstered by the claims of more than a few African men, African women had essentially no rights. They were perpetual jural minors. They were the property of their fathers until marriage, at which point they became the property of their husbands. A simplistic view of African gender and generational relations, certainly, but settlers were not known for their ethnographical skills. It also made sense in social evolutionary terms, for were not British women still in the process of claiming legal rights so long denied them? Obviously, if civilized women had only recently become responsible adults under the law, then African women must remain for some years legal minors. There was no need to refer to adult African females as 'girls', for there was no question – not for generations, perhaps – of African women claiming equality with Europeans. African women did not need reminding of their dependence on their menfolk and, through them, whites.

Kindness and ingratitude

Whites believed that Africans, like European children, lacked certain emotions or ways of thinking. They were cruel, they could not empathize with other sentient beings. Africans' (alleged) cruelty to animals was legendary among whites. They tortured animals for sport. They secretly impaled settler cattle in hopes that the employer would distribute its meat. They bloodied and blinded oxen with their whips. Whites would have to inculcate – usually via corporal punishment – in Africans a sense of empathy toward dumb beasts, just as in Britain children were taught – usually through novels with anthropomorphic animal narrators – to treat animals with kindness.[72]

Africans' lack of kindness, settlers insisted, showed also in their treatment of fellow human beings. It was conventional wisdom that, as T. Howitt put it, 'Kindness was an unknown quantity to natives in their present state of civilization'.[73] African men's treatment of women was 'callous'.[74] The example that most disturbed whites was the Gikuyu treatment of their dying relatives, who were sometimes left in the forest to die rather than bring ritual uncleanliness to their homes. The cruelty of this was, to whites, obvious and grotesque. Whites asked their readers to imagine (using that civilized sense of empathy) being deserted in the forest to die alone, cold, uncomforted, unloved. Imagine the terror of hearing hyenas drawing near even before one took one's last breath. And who was most likely to be deserted in the woods but the elderly, parents and grandparents, those to whom a person should feel deep and enduring gratitude? Indeed, for Europeans the relationship between parent and child best exemplified giving and sacrifice – the gift of life, the investment of time, resources, and emotional energy – and thus the need for gratitude. Africans, the story went, felt no such gratitude.[75] Kindness and gratitude were not inborn, like anger or fear, but had to be taught. Settlers, as parents, had this duty.

Because Africans had not yet mastered these civilized emotions, the argument went, settlers had to modulate their treatment of Africans. Because Africans did not yet believe kindness a virtue, whites must not indulge Africans. On Empire Day 1928, Col. Swinton-Home lectured European children 'on what they owed to the Native, and to treat him with firmness and justice, but not to spoil him'.[76] For, as the *Standard* had pointed out a decade and a half before, the African 'mistakes kindness for weakness'. This could easily turn dangerous.[77] *The Advertiser* reported on a settler who had welcomed some Africans into his tent during a downpour. The result? 'They rewarded his kindness by half killing and robbing him.'[78] Instead, as again Howitt explained, 'what was wanted was that [Africans] should be treated with firmness and justice'.[79] This was not simply what settlers desired, but what (according to settlers) *Africans* desired. Settlers tried to convince themselves (and many likely succeeded) that Africans appreciated, even sought out, the firm, just, paternalistic rule of whites.[80]

Yet very often settlers did feel compelled to act with kindness toward Africans, most especially Africans closest to them – their longtime farm workers and domestic servants. This was most evident, and settlers never allowed anyone to forget it, in their provision of medical care to Africans.[81] Virtually every settler reminiscence discusses, often in gory detail, how they tended to the medical needs of Africans on their farms and in their homes. Some set aside time each day for a 'sick parade', addressing anything from simple aches to serious burns on children who had fallen into a kitchen fireplace.[82] Settlers distributed aspirin, brandy, digestive aids, applied plasters, and pulled teeth. In emergency cases, they sewed together flesh torn asunder by pangas or transported the critically injured to the nearest mission or government hospital.

At these rough clinics settlers experienced the most intimate connection they would ever have with Africans. (Excepting, of course, sexual intercourse, which was all about the needs and desires of the European, not at all about those of the African.) Only a very few settlers had any background in nursing. The majority of settlers would never have poked and prodded another human being so extensively. They may have cared for children or the elderly, but for anything beyond a minor ailment a doctor would have been called. Before coming to Kenya, Elspeth Huxley's mother had never found herself soaked in the blood of a man whose blown-apart limb she tried to save.[83] Alyse

Simpson's husband had never before reached his hand in another man's mouth to remove a rotten tooth, until he fell into the position of dentist for his labourers.

This touching of bodies had, at least for settlers, a special emotional impact. Certainly for some the provision of medical care was a calculated move to keep their labour force healthy and working. Yet few settlers spoke of their clinics in this way, while they freely admitted that providing other perks, such as rudimentary schools, was done purely to attract labour. Sometimes their patients came from neighbouring farms or the reserves, meaning settlers had no direct economic interest in their health. Instead, settlers felt compelled out of kindness, out of a desire to alleviate suffering, to tend to the medical needs of their dependants – the Africans directly reliant on them, or all Africans to whom whites stood as trustees.[84]

Handing out pills and holding flesh, bathing in blood and putting a hand in a gaping mouth, settlers found themselves touching another human being as they never had before. Who else, settlers wondered, would take such time and effort to care for another human? Doctors, of course, but settlers rarely charged their patients. Only parents, or those who stood in the position of a parent, would willingly come into such intimate physical contact with another human, and do so without expectation of reward.

The question of reward did, none the less, bother settlers. Settlers gave much to Africans, or so settlers insisted. From medical care to cast-off clothing, to civilization itself, settlers congratulated themselves for selflessly providing Africans with a better life and a brighter future.[85] And yet – lamentations – they received nothing in return. Their gifts were met not with gratitude but with silence, or even hostility. (Hence the settler who offered the gift of shelter from the rain was not thanked but assaulted.) Many settlers saw in Africans, as in their own young children, a lack of gratitude. 'A Colonist' believed Africans could feel gratitude only 'in animal fashion that he distinguishes between friend and foe'.[86] Elspeth Huxley claimed – quite wrongly – that 'No words for thanking people existed in the Kikuyu's language'.[87]

After spending a full chapter of her book on the medical care she provided her African workers, Eve Bache assured her readers that 'They are not particularly grateful for our ministrations'.[88] She sighed at her workers' fickleness:

> [The white] is conscious of having in his employ dozens of raw savages with whom he is on the best of terms; who rely on him to settle their quarrels and heal their diseases; who often inform him that he is their father and call his wife touchingly *ma-ma*! He knows they will let him

down and have no real affection for him – they have very little for their own families – but he can't help it, such being the composition of the white man, becoming attached to them and taking a sincere interest in their welfare.[89]

Helpless, Bache and others continued to devote themselves to 'their' Africans.

Despite all that the settlers did for Africans, there was no emotional reciprocation – Africans felt no gratitude, no 'affection', for those who helped them. Why then did settlers continue to carry on with (what they claimed to be) such thankless tasks? In part, it helped cement whites' paternal standing over Africans. Philosophers debate the morality of committing an act that, at the time, the subject does not consent to, but will in the future appreciate and express gratitude for. The only example of such paternalism that seems to have universal approval is that of parents over children. Children do not appreciate the sacrifices of their parents until later in life, when they both feel and express – through words or actions – their gratitude. It could be expected then that Africans would one day, upon achieving racial maturity, give thanks to settlers. In the meantime, settlers must do what they, *in loco parentis*, knew to be in the best interests of their African charges.

Even setting aside the paternal contract, by charging that Africans lacked gratitude settlers could claim to have established a permanent racial hierarchy. At least in the European tradition, a gift freely given creates a relationship, but not necessarily an equal one. A hierarchy is created, at least until the gift (be it material or abstract) is repaid (in word or in kind). Perhaps not even then. As the sociologist Georg Simmel wrote in 1908, 'Once we have received something good from another person, once he has preceded us with his action, we no longer can make up for it completely, no matter how much our own return gift or service may objectively or legally surpass his own. The reason is that his gift, because it was first, has a voluntary character which no return gift can have.'[90] By insisting that Africans lacked gratitude to whites, settlers emphasized that they did in fact deserve gratitude, that they had freely given gifts to Africans, and thus that a hierarchy between white and black had been created which could never be altered.[91]

Some few settlers did believe Africans capable of gratitude, although perhaps not verbally. If not a word of thanks, what could Africans offer in return? What could an African give that could remotely approach the value of the gifts bestowed by Europeans? Certainly no material goods. Instead, whites sought services, and precisely the type that expressed hierarchy. The most shockingly obvious, perhaps, was the only type of intimate medical care Africans performed on whites: the removal of jiggers. Jiggers are small insects whose favoured place to lay eggs is under humans' toenails. Once discovered, the eggs must be removed with extreme care, for should the sac containing the eggs burst, the toe quickly becomes infested. Whites believed Africans to be expert in the removal of jigger eggs and pressed them into this duty. That is, Africans literally served at the feet of whites.

Servants and status

While, as a class, whites held trusteeship over all Africans, as individuals they also personally stood *in loco parentis* to at least a few Africans. Virtually every white person in Kenya had servants. One of the first duties upon arrival was to take on a 'boy' or two. Settlers 'loaned out' their servants to new arrivals, or passed them along to friends upon leaving Kenya.[92] Depending on the size and wealth of the household, a settler would require a cook (with a 'toto' as his assistant), one or more 'houseboys', a gardener, a syce for the horses, an ayah for the children, perhaps a personal attendant. Mrs F. Alcock fended off jealous comments from women in Britain by explaining how, without modern conveniences, having at least four servants was an absolute necessity.[93] Alyse Simpson knew 'full well that no White woman could possibly do her own cooking in the tropics'.[94]

And settlers enjoyed having servants. Colonel Arbuthnot, a settler from 1921 to 1923, recommended Kenya to other elites, for 'the servant may be trying, but many are quite good, and at any rate you don't have to cook your own meals and wash up! and there is no other colony where you have a white man's climate and black labour'.[95] Tempting, indeed. His days slipping away, Galbraith Cole returned to Kenya from convalescence in Britain for he 'longed for his own land, his sheep, and his servants, especially the Somali Jama Farah, who had been with him for many years and nursed him with great devotion'.[96] Karen Blixen, baroness only upon marriage, had felt the sting of being servantless when, as a young woman, she attended balls with her noble second cousins.[97] She made up for this in spades once she settled in Kenya: 'I think one can put up with any sort of hardship if one has plenty of servants'.[98]

Settlers quickly took to a reliance on their servants. J. G. Squiers recalled the absurdity of a settler, 'not given to doing things for himself ... used to being waited on hand and foot', now out in the bush during the First World War and expected to cook for himself.[99] Settler reliance on servants could be too extreme, some critics thought. 'Sir Hasirim' pointed out the difficulty of teaching Africans the innate value of labour when whites themselves revelled in being waited on by multitudes of servants. What lesson was learned by the servant who is made to fetch, fill, and light a pipe, even place it into his master's mouth?[100] Few took this to heart. No matter if a white man had never issued an order to another person in his life, in Kenya he could bark commands and have his every whim satisfied.

For settlers of a more elite background, plentiful servants and paternalism held extra value. Kenya was, and often still is, stereotyped as the land of lord and ladies, with peers thick on the ground. In twentieth-century Britain, few of this class could still retain the status and ease of life common only a few generations before. While they may have had servants 'back home', in Kenya they could recapture a more idyllic past. They would revert to an earlier, quieter, feudal way of life.[101] One could have extensive landholdings and hunt wild beasts (rhino rather than elk, lion instead of bear). One could have dozens, scores of simple peasant folk settled upon one's land. They would bow, they would work one's fields, they would look upon one as their *lord*. 'It was a feudal vision', as Huxley later recalled about the dreams many settlers had of Africa during her youth.[102] The vision could never accord with reality, but it did shape settlers' self-image.

Paternalism required the defence of one's dependents. As feudal lords, the family of Elspeth Huxley (née Grant) took it upon themselves to protect their serfs. In *Flame Trees of Thika*, Huxely describes how their Afrikaner neighbour, Mr Roos, thought their worker Sammy insolent. When Sammy ignored the white man's order, Roos kicked him. Jos Grant prevented Sammy from retaliating, and then refused Roos's order to flog Sammy for his 'insolence'. This was not because Grant rejected violence toward Africans. Rather, 'the Dutchman's arrogance annoyed him'.[103] For was it not arrogant for an outsider to demand a lord flog his servant? Similarly, Delamere, Blixen and others refused to allow police on to their estates. They refused to allow some alternative authority to enter their realms.[104]

Emotion and paternalism

Settlers had much invested emotionally in trusteeship and paternalism. When a settler proclaimed (as did Alyse Simpson) that she 'had a great liking for these natives, and I think they liked us, too', their words ought not be easily dismissed.[105] Settlers often believed themselves to have developed close personal relationships with their servants. Huxley recalls that, soon after Sammy's arrival at their home, she 'became friends' with him. His behaviour suggests more the loyal retainer than a friend: 'To the Kikuyu he was stern and often arrogant, but to us he was always polite and dignified.'[106] Sammy, as 'half a Masai', differed from the other Gikuyu labourers. He was proud, but 'this pride was so instinctive and so unselfconscious, that it imposed upon others the obligation to respect it'. Huxley's parents 'spoke to Sammy as they would speak to a fellow European'. This did not imply familiarity. Should he use a 'hectoring tone' Tilly would be angered. Sammy understood the nature of their relationship: 'Sammy gave them his complete loyalty.'[107]

Elspeth Huxley was not alone in seeing friendship where a relationship of clear hierarchy existed.[108] In her ghost-written autobiography of growing up on a Kenyan farm, Beryl Markham brags of her friendships with Africans, and her particular closeness with Ruta. As much as Markham (and her admirers) insisted that she and Ruta were friends, the relationship was clearly not one between equals. Sonny Bumpus, who knew the pair, noted that 'They seemed to be on terms of friendship rather than that of master and servant, although he always referred to Beryl as madam, and memsahib'. Another settler recalled that between the two 'She was the memsahib kidogo [little madam] and very imperious'.[109] In the same way, Juanita Carberry recalled having 'formed strong bonds of friendship with many of our houseboys'. After some time away at school in South Africa, she returned as a teenager.

> There was now, to my chagrin, a certain respectful distance between the African *totos* [*watoto*, children] and me. Before I went away they used to call me *nyawera*, or 'worker' because, unlike most colonial females, I was always busy, cleaning tack ... Now I had become, to my regret, *memsahib kidogo*, or little mistress, to distinguish me from June who was *memsahib mkubwa*, or big mistress.[110]

One wonders if the watoto had always been aware of the distance between them and the white child who would soon be their mistress.

Karen Blixen: paternalist par excellence

Perhaps more than most white settlers, Karen Blixen (1885–1962) promoted herself as a feudal lady, selflessly protecting her retinue of dedicated Africans.[111] In *Out of Africa*, an often-fictionalized account of her failures as a coffee planter between 1914 and 1931,[112] Blixen helped shape westerners' views of settler–African relations. *Out of Africa* is a complicated book. Blixen telescoped her experiences, barely acknowledged the man to whom she was married for a decade, and elided any mention of the syphilis that so often debilitated her. But her letters home from Kenya reveal that the book hits close to the mark on one key issue. With heartfelt conviction, she imagined herself a godlike mother figure to her workers and their families.

Karen Blixen sometimes became 'furious' with the Gikuyu and other 'natives', but in the end (her belief in) their acceptance, their need, of her paternalistic care won her over. 'There is something touching about them', she wrote to her mother in 1922, 'and about the amazing faith they have in me and in my ability to see them through all the circumstances of life, which disarms one's anger'.[113] 'I can't really define what it is that makes the natives so likable', Blixen wrote again a few months later, for 'in reality they have more bad qualities than good ones and they are all stupid and unreliable. I think it is the remarkable, – and brazen, – trust they have in one, which ends up by working like a "spell."'[114] She called Kamante her son, he and other servants called her 'mama'.[115]

Blixen fancied herself, and often Africans, superior to the middle-class English settlers amongst whom she lived. Not only were they boors, but they mistreated Africans. They demanded burdensome 'hut taxes' to drive Africans into the labour force; they treated Africans as less than human; they felt no compunction at drawing out the *kiboko* and giving Africans 'twenty five of the best'. 'Where the natives are concerned', she reported to a friend in Denmark, 'the English are remarkably narrow-minded; it never occurs to them to regard them as human beings'. Blixen smugly asserted her 'pro-native' leanings and (quietly) revelled in her belief that the English settlers thought her 'eccentric' in her dedication to African rights and well-being.[116]

Her superiority to English commoners comforted her, as did the similar paternalism of the upper-class English – Finch Hatton, Delamere, the brothers Cole, Governor and Lady Grigg – with whom she socialized. She congratulated herself that she felt class distinctions much more than racial ones.[117] Hence the special place in her heart for Farah and his Somali countrymen, for the Maasai, for the aristocratic Chief Kinyanjui.[118] Indeed, Karen Blixen exemplified the settler glorification of pastoralists. She assured her readers that Maasai had never been, nor could they be made, slaves. If imprisoned, they died within months. 'This stark inability to keep alive under the yoke', Blixen wrote, 'has given the Masai, alone amongst all the Native tribes, rank with the immigrant aristocracy'.[119] Her lyrical appreciation of Maasai warrior borders on the erotic.[120] Maasai and Somali alike had strict moral codes, would thank one for a good turn, and bitterly hold grudges for slights. Kamba, Gikuyu, Luo: they had no such cultural values.[121] Somali, epitomized by her retainer Farah, stood uppermost in her esteem. They 'have a bearing like Spanish grandees'.[122]

As much as Blixen's ego was enlarged through comparison with the uncultured English settlers, her character differed from theirs more in degree than in kind. She too believed Africans to be childlike. She too appointed herself *in loco parentis*. Childless herself, the adult Africans around her became her children.[123] She too believed the lash an essential tool for encouraging Africans to evolve.[124] Africans might in some ways – in their honour, their loyalty, their bravery – be superior to middle-class settlers in Kenya. But there was no getting around the fact of Africans' ultimate savagery.[125]

Blixen shared the common notion that Africans ought to be protected from the evils of western education and civilization. She too had little use for educated, Christian, 'westernized', Africans, and believed that Africans 'cannot learn as *much* as we can'.[126] In 1914 she refused to assist her beloved Farah in his quest for schooling, for she thought 'that [education] leads to [Africans] becoming unhappy and useless'.[127] Nine years later she had warmed, slightly, to the idea of educating Africans. 'I would so much like to run a school on the farm some day', she wrote her mother, 'although I don't really know whether it would not be better to let the natives keep their primitive life-style'. In the end, she concluded that 'In some form or other civilization will take possession of them', and so it was best to control that process, and guide it to proper channels.[128] There was, after all, 'so much in civilization which is dangerous'.[129] But within three years she had begun to despair of even such a limited beginning to the civilizing mission. 'I do not think', she wrote in 1926, 'that the natives here are sufficiently mature for this sort of education yet, – it is as if they have to jump over a stage that we in our long, slow development from barbarians to civilized people have had to go through; I sometimes get the feeling that through a kind of impatience we deliberately allow them to come into the world prematurely'.[130] For one who condemned her fellow settlers' worldview, Blixen sounded very much like them.

Conclusion

Africans chafed under many aspects of white trusteeship and paternalism. Obviously, they felt hostility toward alienation of their lands for 'advanced' farming by settlers, they despised being forced from their homes to work for whites, and the imposition of new political authorities pleased no one (except the chiefs and headmen who filled these new roles). As western-style political movements arose in the 1920s, it became equally clear that Africans did not see the need for whites to define African interests.[131]

Yet it is not beyond belief that Africans encouraged certain aspects of settler paternalism. Many Africans were well acquainted with patron–client relationships, with invented kinship. An unattached or impoverished individual might enter into an uneven but mutually beneficial relationship with a more powerful or more secure individual or clan. Many Gikuyu who settled on white farms in the Rift Valley understood themselves to be *ahoi* – clients.[132] Africans who sought protection with missionaries saw them as patrons.[133] Just as settlers might protect their clients against arrest or assault by other whites, Africans might ignore the commands of any European aside from their patrons. Thus rather than answering Roos's command, Sammy – attached to the Grant family – simply turned and walked away.[134] Thus a Somali man remonstrated with a Nairobi shop owner who had threatened him with violence: Boraleh asked 'why he wanted to beat a boy who was not his servant'.[135] Similarly, many settlers reported having been called 'father' or 'mother' by their African employees.[136] When her husband was found to have stolen some maize, one woman expressed surprise when he was prosecuted: 'Why, memsahib, ever since we first came here he has stolen your maize! Why not? You and *Bwana* are our mother and father'.[137]

Africans' thoughts on white trusteeship and paternalism meant little for settlers. It was of little consequence whether or not Africans reciprocated settlers' emotional stirrings. If an African called his memsahib mama, it demonstrated that the relationship was true and proper. If an African failed to express gratitude, it demonstrated that he had not reached emotional maturity. Settlers' self-image was secure in either case. Settlers worried most about those Africans who seemed to claim equality on settlers' own ground – civilization. Taking seriously the threat posed by men like Tebajanga could best be done by not taking those men seriously at all.

Notes

1. 'Our new commissioner', *TEA* (2 Dec. 1905), p. 4.
2. Letter to ed., *TEA* (5 May 1906), p. 3.
3. See, for example, 'The native', *KO* (2 Oct. 1923), p. 3; M. C. Monckton, letter to ed., *EAS* (17 June 1922), p. 5; 'The native problem', *EAS* (22 June 1922), pp. 2, 7; Elspeth Huxley, *Flame Trees of Thika* (New York: Morrow, 1959), p. 114.
4. On government employees, see Richard St. Barbe Baker, *Men of the Trees: In the Mahogany Forests of Kenya and Nigeria* (New York: L. MacVeagh, 1931), p. 127, and Bruce Berman, *Control and Crisis in Colonial Kenya: The Dialectic of Domination* (London: James Currey, 1990), pp. 108, 113. On anthropologists, see W. S. Routledge and Katherine Routledge, *With a Prehistoric People: The Akikuyu of British East Africa* (London: Frank Cass, 1968 [1910]), p. xvii.
5. Perhaps the most outstanding proponent was Dr R. W. Burkitt, considered by even fellow settlers to be extreme in some aspects of his biblically infused thinking. R. W. Burkitt, letter to ed., *EAS* (29 Aug. 1922), p. 5; J. R. Gregory, *Under the Sun: A Memoir of Dr. R. W. Burkitt of Kenya* (Nairobi: self-published, 1952), p. 36. 'X.Y.Z.' from Kitale believed that the sutures in Africans' craniums solidified more quickly than in whites', preventing their brains from reaching full size. Letter to ed., *EAS* (21 Oct. 1924), p. 5.
6. Mike Hawkins, *Social Darwinism in European and American Thought, 1860–1945: Nature as Model and Nature as Threat* (Cambridge: Cambridge University Press, 1997), p. 68.

7 KNA: MSS 105/1, Papers of Sandy Herd, 'Early Days in Nyeri', p. 3. See also, for example, Sidney Fichat in Correspondence relating to affairs in the East African Protectorate, Cd 4122 1908, quoted in M. P. K. Sorrenson, *Origins of European Settlement in Kenya* (Oxford: Oxford University Press, 1968), p. 239.
8 'The right to rule', *EAS* (30 Aug. 1922), p. 4. A year later, the editors of the *Standard* again warned against those who would mislead Africans, telling them that they 'can jump into the full panoply of citizenship in a day; having no need to go through [the] same travail as other races in their evolutionary advancement'. 'European trusteeship', *EAS* (1 Oct. 1923), p. 6.
9 Isak Dinesen, *Out of Africa* (New York: Random House, 1985 [1938]), p. 305.
10 For similar thinking elsewhere in the white world, see Carol Summers, *From Civilization to Segregation: Social Ideas and Social Control in Southern Rhodesia, 1890–1934* (Athens: Ohio University Press, 1994), p. 98; Susan Pedersen, 'Settler colonialism at the bar of the League of Nations', in Caroline Elkins and Susan Pedersen (eds), *Settler Colonialism in the Twentieth Century: Projects, Practices, Legacies* (New York: Routledge, 2005); Edward P. Wolfers, *Race Relations and Colonial Rule in Papua New Guinea* (Sydney: Australia and New Zealand Book Company, 1975), p. 26 n. 7; Margaret D. Jacobs, *White Mother to a Dark Race: Settler Colonialism, Maternalism, and the Removal of Indigenous Children in the American West and Australia, 1880–1940* (Lincoln: University of Nebraska Press, 2009); Leon Litwack, *Trouble in Mind: Black Southerners in the Age of Jim Crow* (New York: Knopf, 1998), p. 92.
11 'Native trusteeship', *EAS* (12 Apr. 1924), p. 5; 'The new faith', *EAS* (18 Nov. 1924), p. 4.
12 This paragraph draws heavily on Berman, *Control and Crisis*, ch. 3. See also John F. Murphy, 'Legitimation and paternalism: the colonial state in Kenya', *African Studies Review* 29 (1986): 55–65.
13 Berman, *Control and Crisis*, p. 104.
14 C. W. Hobley, 20 Oct. 1905, in G. H. Mungeam, *Kenya: Select Historical Documents, 1884–1923* (Nairobi: East African Publishing House, 1978), pp. 464–5.
15 S. H. C. Hawtrey of Thika admitted that there had been little discussion of trusteeship before the Indian crisis, 'But the feeling of personal interest, and personal trusteeship, has been evident for a very much longer time'. Letter to ed., *EAS* (10 Dec. 1924), p. 8.
16 'Convention of Associations', *EAS* (23 Feb. 1923), p. 6.
17 'Convention of Associations' session', *EAS* (27 Feb. 1923), p. 7.
18 Quoted in Robert Gregory, *India and East Africa: A History of Race Relations within the British Empire, 1890–1939* (Oxford: Clarendon Press, 1971), p. 287. See also E. S. Atieno-Odhiambo, 'The colonial government, the settlers, and the "trust" principle in Kenya', *Transafrican Journal of History* 2 (1972): 94–113.
19 Gopal Guru notes that 'Colonial rule in different parts of the world has subjected local people to both crude and subtle forms of humiliation'. This was no accident. Gopal Guru, 'Introduction: theorizing humiliation', in Gopal Guru (ed.), *Humiliation: Claims and Context* (New Dehli: Oxford University Press, 2009).
20 For more on humiliation and its relation to power and social structures, see Maury Silver, Rosaria Conte, Maria Miceli, and Isabella Poggi, 'Humiliation: feeling, social control and the construction of identity', *Journal for the Theory of Social Behaviour* 16 (1986): 269–83; Zhitian Luo, 'National humiliation and national assertion: the Chinese response to the Twenty-One Demands', *Modern Asian Studies* 27 (1993): 297–319; William Ian Miller, *Humiliation: And Other Essays on Honor, Social Discomfort, and Violence* (Ithaca: Cornell University Press, 1993); Evelin Linden, 'Humiliation and human rights: mapping a minefield', *Human Rights Review* 2 (2000): 46–63; Avishai Margali, *The Decent Society*, trans. Naomi Goldblum (Cambridge, MA: Harvard University Press, 1998); Paul Cohen, 'Remembering and forgetting national humiliation in twentieth-century China', *Twentieth-Century China* 27 (2002): 1–39; David Keen, *Conflict and Collusion in Sierra Leone* (Oxford: James Currey, 2005), esp. ch. 4; Victoria Fontan, 'Polarization

between occupier and occupied in post-Saddam Iraq: colonial humiliation and the formation of political violence', *Terrorism and Political Violence* 18 (2006): 217–38; *Social Alternatives*, Special Issue on Humiliation, 25 (2006).

21 Roger Noel Money, *Ginia: My Kenya Coffee Shamba, 1918–1939* (Perth: privately published, 2000), p. 126. See also 'A rumour', *Advertiser* (26 June 1908), p. 3.
22 'The reply', *EAS* (21 July 1906), p. 6. See also Sorabji M. Darookhanawala, 'Africa in Darkness' (1905), in Cynthia Salvadori with Judy Aldrick (eds), *Two Indian Travelers: East Africa, 1902–1905* (Mombasa: Friends of Fort Jesus, 1997), pp. 160–1. For similar thinking elsewhere in the white world, see Christine Dobbin, 'The Ilbert Bill: a study of Anglo-Indian opinion in India', *Historical Studies – Australia and New Zealand* 12 (1965): 87–104, 95; Raymond Evans, Kay Saunders, and Kathryn Cronin, *Exclusion, Exploitation, and Extermination: Race Relations in Colonial Queensland* (Sydney: Australia and New Zealand Book Company, 1975), chs 5–6; Claudia Knapman, *White Women in Fiji, 1835–1930: The Ruin of Empire?* (Sydney and London: Allen and Unwin, 1986), p. 121; Karen Tranberg Hansen, *Distant Companions: Servants and Employers in Zambia, 1900–1985* (Ithaca and London: Cornell University Press, 1989), pp. 38–9; Chilla Bulbeck, *Australian Women in Papua New Guinea: Colonial Passages, 1920–1960* (Cambridge: Cambridge University Press, 1992), p. 219; Summers, *From Civilization to Segregation*, pp. 73 n. 111, 98–103, 137–40; Patricia O'Brien, 'Remaking Australia's colonial culture?: white Australia and its Papuan frontier, 1901–1940', *Australian Historical Studies* 40 (2009): 96–112.
23 The founding of towns like Nairobi, the *Standard* editorialized in 1924, 'is an unfortunate necessity of Western life which, applied to African conditions, is pregnant with much evil'. 'The woman's part', *EAS* (7 June 1924), p. 13.
24 Nora Strange, *Kenya To-Day* (London: Stanley Paul, 1934), p. 102.
25 W. Robert Foran, *A Cuckoo in Kenya: The Reminiscences of a Pioneer Police Officer in British East Africa* (London: Hutchinson, 1936), p. 218. See also Lady Evelyn Cobbold, *Kenya: The Land of Illusion* (London: John Murray, 1935), p. 89.
26 Foran, *A Cuckoo in Kenya*, p. 218.
27 Nora Strange, *Courtship in Kenya* (London: Stanely Paul, 1932), p. 106. See also Lord Charles Allsopp Hindlip, *Sport and Travel: Abyssinia and British East Africa* (London: Unwin, 1906), p. 269; A. G. Anderson, *Our Newest Colony Being an Account of British East Africa and Its Possibilities as a New Land for Settlement* (Nairobi: East African Standard, 1910), p. 52; Lord Cranworth, *A Colony in the Making; or Sport and Profit in British East Africa* (London: Macmillan, 1912), p. 26; Alexander Davis, *Microcosm of Empire (British East Africa): A Political, Racial, and Economic Study* (Nairobi: Caxton, 1917), p. 57; Cobbold, *Kenya*, p. 158; C. H. Stigand, *The Land of Zinj: Being an Account of British East Africa, Its Ancient History and Present Inhabitants* (New York: Barnes and Noble, 1966 [1913]), pp. 292, 297; Julian Huxley, *Africa View* (New York: Greenwood, 1968 [1931]), p. 350.
28 R. Gorell Barnes, *Babes in the African Wood* (London: Longmans, Green, 1911), p. 219. 'U.T.U.', 'The tractable tribe', *EAS* (12 May 1921), p. 2. As early as 1885, Joseph Thompson argued that the Luo were 'the most moral tribes of this region', while the 'decently dressed Masai' wallowed in 'vice of the most open kind'. Joseph Thompson, *Through Masai Land with Joseph Thompson* (Evanston, IL: Northwestern University Press, 1962), p. 287. S. M. Darookhanawala, a Parsi from Zanzibar, similarly praised the Luo: despite being naked, he said, they possessed great integrity and morality. 'Africa in Darkness', pp. 132–5.
29 Florence Riddell, *Kenya Mist* (New York: Henry Hold, 1924), p. 209.
30 'Native welfare', *EAS* (20 June 1923), p. 4.
31 Ethel Younghusband, *Glimpses of East Africa and Zanzibar* (London: John Long, 1910), p. 84. The Acting DC of Central Kavirondo commented on mission-educated youth 'whose education is rather towards pride of self than pride of achievement', such that 'it may be difficult for such persons to obtain a wife without enduring the discomforts of manual labour [to raise bridewealth] and the doffing of gaudy

hats, ties and socks'. KNA: PC/NZA 3/28/4/1, Ag DC Central Kavirondo to Senior Commissioner, Nyanza, 4 Dec. 1926. For similar reactions elsewhere, see Evans, Saunders, and Cronin, *Exclusion, Exploitation, and Extermination*, pp. 89–90; Wolfers, *Race Relations and Colonial Rule*, pp. 46–7; John Butcher, *The British in Malaya, 1880–1941: The Social History of a European Community in Colonial South-East Asia* (New York: Oxford University Press, 1979), p. 98; Hansen, *Distant Companions*, pp. 42–3; Grace Elizabeth Hale, *Making Whiteness: The Culture of Segregation in the South, 1890–1940* (New York: Pantheon, 1998), pp. 156–9; Litwack, *Trouble in Mind*, pp. 28, 149–61; Julia Martinez and Claire Lowrie, 'Colonial constructions of masculinity: transforming Aboriginal Australian men into "houseboys"', *Gender and History* 21 (2009): 305–23, esp. pp. 311–2. Even a sympathetic observer like Hortense Powdermaker found, on her arrival in Rabaul, that the 'police boys with white caps perched on top of their bushy hair seemed slightly ridiculous'. *Stranger and Friend: The Way of an Anthropologist* (New York: W. W. Norton, 1966), p. 57.

32 'Life in Kenya', *EAS* (3 Feb. 1923), p. 8; 'An injustice to Africans', *EAUM* (24 Oct. 1903), p. 4; M. S. Hunt, *Through English Eyes: Sunny Days and Ways in Kenya Colony and Assam* (Derby: Central Educational, 1932), pp. 16–17; Younghusband, *Glimpses of East Africa and Zanzibar*, p. 74.

33 On Owen, see Cynthia Hoehler-Fatton, *Women of Fire and Spirit: History, Faith, and Gender in Roho Religion in Western Kenya* (New York: Oxford University Press, 1996); Brett Shadle, *'Girl Cases' Marriage and Colonialism in Gusiiland, Kenya, 1890–1970* (Portsmouth, NH: Heinemann, 2006), pp. 62–3; Opolot Okia, *Communal Labor in Colonial Kenya: The Legitimization of Coercion* (New York: Palgrave Macmillan, 2012).

34 'The black heathen and the white', *Critic* (24 June 1922), pp. 9, 29. See also Francis F., letter to ed., *EAS* (19 July 1919), p. 22. The Bible itself could have baneful influence when read by the half-educated, written as it was by 'Orientals'. 'The angel in the house', *EAS* (1 Apr. 1914), p. 6.

35 A. H. Spencer Palmer, letter to ed., *EAS* (6 Sept. 1924), p. 34.

36 Hilda Pierson, letter to ed., *EAS* (20 Sept. 1924), p. 8.

37 D. Sparrow, letter to ed., *EAS* (8 May 1922), p. 3. See also H. A. C. Wilson, *A British Borderland: Service and Sport in Equatoria* (London: J. Murray, 1913), p. 306; Laborare est Orare, letter to ed., *EAS* (1 Mar. 1919), p. 10; Huxley, *Flame Trees of Thika*, pp. 114, 117–18; D. A. Malcolm-Smith, letter to ed., *EAS* (7 June 1924), p. 12. Admittedly, not all 'mission boys' were bad, but it seemed that the good ones became preachers rather than entering the colonial labour market. 'Native training', *EAS* (18 Aug. 1923), p. 4; 'Christian', letter to ed., *EAS* (22 Mar. 1919), p. 4.

38 'Mission boys', *EAS* (5 July 1919), p. 17. Compare this to the incessantly ridiculed class of the 'babus' of India. Primarily attached to Bengalis, but extended to any educated Indian, the 'babu' appellation came to imply effeminacy, stilted and ungrammatical English, and reliance on white-collar employment rather than more physically exerting labour. Mrinalini Sinha, *Colonial Masculinity: The 'Manly Englishman' and the 'Effeminate Bengali' in the Late Nineteenth Century* (Manchester: Manchester University Press, 1995). Whites in Kenya fully exploited the 'babu' stereotype as well in their battles against Indians.

39 H. Ryle Shaw, letter to ed., *EAS* (30 Mar. 1918), p. 25. See also the comments of Miss Maclean in 'Labour from a woman's viewpoint', *EAS* (18 Nov. 1924), p. 4.

40 'Experientia Docet', letter to ed., *Leader* (8 May 1909), p. 6.

41 'Notes and comment', *Leader* (8 May 1909), p. 6.

42 'Timely warning', *EAS* (30 Oct. 1920), p. 22.

43 'Critolaoa', letter to ed., *Leader* (25 Feb. 1911), p. 11. The letter was a comment on a Nairobi YMCA debate on the resolution, 'That the barbarian is happier than civilized man', which was defeated, five votes for, ten against. 'What is happiness?', *Leader* (18 Feb. 1911), p. 6.

44 See, for example, 'Principles of education', *EAS* (15 Mar. 1924), p. 15; editorial comment to G. A. Grieve, letter to ed., *EAS* (22 Mar. 1924), p. 24A. The parallels

with the 'industrial education' of Booker T. Washington should be clear, and was indeed clear at the time. On his massive, bloody hunting expedition across Kenya in 1909, Teddy Roosevelt congratulated the American mission at Kijabe for focusing on 'industrial training' rather than churning out 'imitation white men'. 'Mr Roosevelt at Kijabe', *Leader* (14 Aug. 1909), p. 6.

45 'The prospects of British East Africa', *Leader* (8 Aug. 1908), p. 4.
46 'An injustice to Africans', *EAUM* (24 Oct. 1903), p. 4. The emphasis on industrial education and the positive influence of settlers was nearly unanimous among settlers. The visit of the Phelps-Stokes Commission in 1924 bolstered this thinking. 'Corner stones of education', *EAS* (1 Mar. 1924), p. 5; 'First impressions', *EAS* (8 Mar. 1924), p. 7; 'The election in West Kenya', *EAS* (15 Mar. 1924), p. 35; 'Envoys in the Rift Valley', *EAS* (29 Mar. 1924), p. 32; 'Sir Northrup McMillan at Nakuru', *EAS* (12 Apr. 1924), p. 35. If missionaries desired to teach African women, it should be things appropriate to proper women. As it stood, they produced 'women who can sing an English hymn, write a senseless letter, read senseless books, but not sew on a button, mend a baby's frock, let alone make one'. 'Evils of civilization', *EAS* (18 June 1910), p. 13.
47 'Masai raid on a farm', *TEA* (2 June 1906), p. 5; W. Russell-Bowker, letter to ed., *TEA* (27 Oct. 1906), p. 7; 'Lancastrian', letter to ed., *EAS* (20 June 1908), pp. 9–10; J. W. Gregory, *The Great Rift Valley: Being a Narrative of a Journey to Mount Kenya and Lake Baringo* (London: Frank Cass, 1968 [1896]), p. 86; Lord Hindlip, *British East Africa*, pp. 15–16. Sir Charles Eliot wrote in 1904 that Maasaidom was a 'beastly, bloody system' that should die off.
48 See also Carolyn Martin Shaw, *Colonial Inscriptions: Race, Sex, and Class in Kenya* (Minneapolis: University of Minnesota Press, 1995), pp. 190–1.
49 V. M. Carnegie, *A Kenyan Farm Diary* (Edinburgh: William Blackwood, 1930), p. 25. See also Cranworth, *Colony in the Making*, p. 25. More generally on westerners' fascination with Maasai, see Dorothy Hodgson, *Once Intrepid Warriors: Gender, Ethnicity, and the Cultural Politics of Maasai Development* (Bloomington: Indiana University Press, 2001).
50 Edgar Beecher Bronson, *In Closed Territory* (Chicago: McClurg, 1910), p. 62; J. Bland-Sutton, *Man and Beast in Eastern Ethiopia: From Observations Made in British East Africa, Uganda, and the Sudan* (London: Macmillan, 1911), p. 102; W. S. Rainsford, *The Land of the Lion* (New York: Doubleday, Page, 1909), p. 135. See also Younghusband, *Glimpses of East Africa and Zanzibar*, pp. 75–6; Gregory, *Under the Sun*, p. 52. Elspeth Huxley variously praised Maasai, Somali, and Galla: *The Mottled Lizard* (New York: Penguin, 1962), pp. 97–8 (on Galla); *Out in the Midday Sun* (New York: Penguin, 1988), p. 161 (on Maasai) and p. 162 (on Somali); *Flame Trees of Thika*, pp. 101, 105–6 (on Somali) and p. 210 (on Maasai).
51 Elspeth Huxley, *White Man's Country: Lord Delamere and the Making of Kenya* (New York: Praeger, 1935); *Out in the Midday Sun*, pp. 75, 105. Administrators were known to catch 'Maasai-itis', seeking to protect the proud pastoralists from encroaching civilization. C. W. Hobley, *Kenya from Chartered Company to Crown Colony* (London: Frank Cass, 1970 [1929]), p. 60.
52 He may have been the co-author of a later book, *The Life and Work of Canon Apolo Kivebulaya*. He is mentioned briefly in R. A. Snoxall, 'Ganda literature', *African Studies* 1 (1942): 55–76, at p. 59. Snoxall does not give a date for the publication, but considers Tebajanga among the 'younger modern' writers. I have not been able to find any further information about Tebajanga.
53 'How and why should I take off my helmet?', L. M. Tebajanga, letter to ed., *EAS* (6 Mar. 1922), p. 6.
54 Comment by editor following Tebajanga's letter. See also 'M. A. D. Hatter', letter to ed., *EAS* (10 Mar., 1922), p. 5.
55 Edward Grigg, 'British policy in Kenya', *Journal of the Royal African Society* 26 (1927): 193–208, quote from 201.
56 For examples: young: 'The native', *EAS* (25 Nov. 1916), p. 11; *East African Protectorate Economic Commission, Final Report* (Nairobi: Swift Press, 1919);

Davis, *Microcosm of Empire*, p. 6; Lord Francis Scott, 'The A.B.C. of Kenya', *The National Review* 81 (1923): 937–44, at p. 937; 'Forthcoming elections', *EAS* (1 Mar. 1924), p. 12; Brig.-General C. P. Fendall, 'Kenya problems', *English Review* (1925): 158–62, at p. 158; Col. A. G. Arbuthnot, 'Life and prospects in Kenya Colony', *Journal of the Royal Artillery* 53 (1926): 137–51; juvenile: 'Foreword', *Kenya Graphic* 2 (1923); infancy: V. M. Newland, 'The romance of settlement', *Kenya Graphic* 1 (1922), p. 69. See also Huxley's comment that in the early 1930s 'Nairobi was at an awkward age', between a frontier town and a true capital city. *Out in the Midday Sun*, p. 45.

57 In a 1924 speech, the member of LegCo for Nyanza, Conway Harvey, 'explained in detail the numerous stages of evolution from "pooh-bahdom" to "responsible Government"'. 'Kenya's problems under review', *EAS* (10 May 1924) p. 26A.
58 'A proud day', *Leader* (11 May 1912), p. 10.
59 'Adjustment', *Leader* (19 Oct. 1912), p. 10. Uasin Gishu – not incidentally, dominated by Afrikaners – still had some catching up to do: it was 'only in its infancy'. It would mature, but in its own time: 'It is better to nurture and raise a healthy youngster than strive too early for weedy manhood. Like babies, most young countries have to run the gamut of their infant troubles. We have no reason to expect that this country will escape the usual trials of its kind.' 'Uasin Gishu', *Leader* (13 July 1912), p. 10. A decade later, Governor Coryndon explained how there had been a desire to make the colony 'self-supporting at as early an age as possible' to encourage 'self-reliance and independence both in official and settler for much the same reason as youngsters are thrown into the world to earn their own living'. Robert T. Coryndon, 'Problems of eastern Africa', *Journal of the Royal African Society* 21 (1922): 177–86, quote from p. 185.
60 'Towards permanence', *EAS* (15 Dec. 1924), p. 4.
61 On Africans as children or a 'child race', see, for example, 'Forced labour', *Leader* (20 Feb. 1909), p. 7; 'Coddling the native', *EAS* (8 Mar. 1913), p. 22; 'The native: and how best to deal with him', *EAS* (31 May 1913), pp. 24–5; 'Women's world – by Molly', *EAS* (3 June 1916), p. 15; 'Our custodian', *EAS* (17 Jan. 1923), p. 1; 'Appointment of a new governor for Kenya', *EA* (4 June 1924), p. 768; E. May Crawford, *By the Equator's Snowy Peak: A Record of Medical Missionary Work and Travel in British East Africa* (London: Church Missionary Society, 1913), p. 140; Evelyn Brodhurst-Hill, *So This Is Kenya!* (London: Blackie, 1936), pp. 36, 191, 202; H. K. Binks, *African Rainbow* (London: Sidgwick and Jackson, 1959), p. 97.
62 Karen Blixen, letters to Ingeborg Dinesen, 16 Jan. 1917, and 10 Sep. 1922, in Isak Dinesen, Frans Lasson (ed.), Anne Born (trans.), *Letters from Africa, 1914–1931* (Chicago: University of Chicago Press, 1981), pp. 46, 132.
63 Stephen Jay Gould, *The Mismeasure of Man* (New York: Norton, 1996), pp. 114–20; Greta Jones, *Social Darwinism and English Thought* (Brighton: Harvester Press, 1980), p. 150.
64 M. C. Monckton, letter to ed., *EAS* (17 June 1922), p. 5. See also Rachel Stuart Watt, *In the Heart of Savagedom: Reminiscences of Life and Adventure during a Quarter of a Century of Pioneering and Missionary Labours in the Wilds of East Equatorial Africa* (London: Pickering and Inglis, 1920), p. 237; Routledge and Routledge, *With a Prehistoric People*, pp. 166–7; 'E.A. Women's League', *EAS* (2 Oct. 1923), pp. 6, 8.
65 Eve Bache, *The Youngest Lion: Early Farming Days in Kenya* (London: Hutchinson, 1934), p. 132, and see also p. 253.
66 Thos. Raynes, 'The native problem', *EAS* (23 Mar. 1918), p. 6.
67 'Onlooker', 'The native: and how best to deal with him', *EAS* (31 May 1913), p. 24. See also 'Babu sarcasm!' *Critic* (21 Oct. 1922), p. 29.
68 For example, May Baldwin, *Only Pat: A Nairobi School-Girl* (London: W. and R. Chambers, 1930), p. 66; Strange, *Kenya To-Day*, p. 158; Bache, *The Youngest Lion*, p. 28. Indians too learned to use 'boy': E. N. Adamji, 'My journeys to the interior', in Salvadori and Aldrick (eds), *Two Indian Travelers*, p. 44.
69 Huxley, *Out in the Midday Sun*, p. 34.

70 Josiah Mwangi Kariuki, *'Mau Mau' Detainee* (Baltimore: Penguin, 1963), p. 49; Donald L. Barnett and Karari Njama, *Mau Mau from Within: Autobiography and Analysis of Kenya's Peasant Revolt* (New York: Monthly Review, 1966), p. 385.

71 That 'boy' emasculated virile men who worked in such close proximity to white women certainly was not accidental, a topic explored in more detail in Chapter 4.

72 Brett L. Shadle, 'Cruelty and empathy, animals and race, in colonial Kenya', *Journal of Social History* 45 (2012): 1097–116.

73 *Native Labour Commission, Evidence and Report* (Nairobi: Government Printer, 1913), p. 31. Settlers also argued that Africans' treatment of animals revealed their instinctive cruelty and lack of appreciation for kindness. Shadle, 'Cruelty and empathy, animals and race'.

74 'Karatazi', 'The native outlook', *EAS* (13 Mar. 1914), p. 4.

75 When her cook came in, crying over the death of his mother, Eve Bache immediately doubted his story, 'Knowing that such emotion would not be caused by affection for his parent'. Bache, *Youngest Lion*, p. 50.

76 'Empire Day at Eldoret', *EAS* (1 June 1928), p. 9.

77 'Coddling the native', *EAS* (8 Mar. 1913), p. 22. See also 'Tea-table talk', *EAS* (22 Nov. 1913), p. 13; 'Coddling the native', *EAS* (11 Mar. 1914), p. 6; Bronson, *In Closed Territory*, p. 136; Hermann Norden, *White and Black in East Africa: A Record of Travel and Observation in Two African Crown Colonies* (Boston: Maynard, 1924), p. 152. Weakness might also lead an African to question the masculinity of his kind white man. 'The native: and how best to deal with him', *EAS* (31 May 1913), pp. 24–5.

78 'Editor's notes', *Advertiser* (16 Oct. 1908), p. 3. A lesson settlers in Southern Rhodesia had learned in the 1890s, according to some. 'Our native population', *Leader* (20 June 1908), p. 4.

79 *Native Labour Commission, Evidence and Report*, p. 31. See also 'A Colonist', letter to ed., *EAS* (9 Dec. 1911), p. 6; 'Native policy', *EAS* (15 Sept. 1917), p. A. 'Native policy', *EAS* (27 Oct. 1917), p. 12; W. H. E. Edgley, letter to ed., *EAS* (16 Feb. 1918), p. 5; Although one settler, in a letter to a Manchester paper, suggested that 'These boys can be trained to become very efficient servants by a judicious mixture of kindness and firmness'. 'Afric's Sunny Clime', *EAS* (25 Feb. 1911), supplement, n.p. See also Younghusband, *Glimpses of East Africa and Zanzibar*, p. 307.

80 Bronson, *In Closed Territory*, p. 228. McGregor Ross summed up the common thinking: many saw Africans as 'untutored savages, 2,000 years behind us in development and mentality, needing to be treated, like children, with "firmness and justice..."'. *Kenya from Within*, p. 235.

81 When Chief Karanja suggested that, unlike her husband, Mary Strange was 'bad', she wondered 'If I was bad to the natives I would not mix brandy and water and take it to the police station to administer them. I have never refused a native.' She did not directly address his charge that she took shots at Africans passing her property. 'Negligent shooting charge fails', *EAS* (11 Jan. 1928), p. 9.

82 In his Swahili lessons for prospective settlers, Le Breton repeatedly asks his reader to translate sentences that concern injury and illness: 'But Master, I am very ill, all my body hurts me. I must put some antiseptic on your leg, but I shall hurt you.' F. H. Le Breton, *Up-Country Swahili Exercises* (Richmond, Surrey: R. W. Simpson, 1936), p. 28.

83 Huxley, *Flame Trees of Thika*, p. 137, and see also pp. 54–5, 72–3, 110–11, 133–4, 139.

84 The *Standard* even promoted first aid stations, staffed by trained settlers with material supplied from Government, for 'the nett [sic] gain would be a closer tie between settler and native, and the spread of healing and human sympathy to a much greater extent than the Medical Department can afford to-day'. 'Medicine for natives', *EAS* (5 July 1924), p. C. The Convention of Association appears to have originated the idea. 'Medicine for natives', *EAS* (5 July 1924), p. 28.

85 'A Soldier Settler' in Kitale hoped that missionaries 'remember to teach gratitude to the native for his deliverance' from the slave trade, which Britain had extinguished.

RACE, CIVILIZATION, AND PATERNALISM

Letter to ed., *EAS* (22 Oct. 1924), p. 8. Among the sentences Le Breton asked his readers to translate into Swahili: 'When I give you tobacco as a reward you should say thank you'. Le Breton, *Up-Country Swahili Exercises*, p. 51.

86 'A Colonist', letter to ed., *EAS* (9 Dec. 1911), p. 6. See also, for example, Bronson, *In Closed Territory*, p. 137; McGregor Ross, *Kenya from Within*, p. 21. For examples outside Kenya, see Margaret Visser, *The Gift of Thanks: The Roots and Rituals of Gratitude* (New York, Houghton Mifflin Harcourt, 2009), pp. 16–18.
87 *Flame Trees of Thika*, p. 112. Without denying the stereotype, Blixen thought that at least her servant Kamante understood gratitude. *Out of Africa*, p. 36.
88 Bache, *Youngest Lion*, pp. 81, 132. See also the comment of Mr Cunningham in 'Thika gets ready', *EAS* (4 Nov. 1924), p. 5.
89 Bache, *Youngest Lion*, p. 66. See also 'Onlooker', 'The native: and how best to deal with him', *EAS* (7 June 1913), p. 4. 'Usona' taught his servants 'like a father' but they ran off with his money none the less. 'The poor benighted heathen', *EAS* (17 Feb. 1917), p. 22.
90 Georg Simmel, 'Faithfulness and gratitude', in Kurt H. Wolff (ed. and trans.), *The Sociology of Georg Simmel* (New York: Free Press, 1964), p. 392.
91 And, even when the editor of the *Standard* granted that Africans could feel gratitude, it was expressed only through loyal service. 'The squatters' ordinance', *EAS* (5 Jan. 1924), p. 17.
92 Margaret Gillon recalls arriving in Kenya in 1930 as a nurse, and a white doctor turning over to her a domestic servant: 'I gratefully accepted Dr. Massey's kind offer and found myself the proud possessor of an African servant named "Mkita"'. RH: MSS Afr. s. 568, Gillon, 'The wagon and the star', p. 16. See also Huxley, *Flame Trees of Thika*, pp. 14, 53, 58.
93 'Life in Kenya', *EAS* (3 Feb. 1923), p. 8.
94 Alyse Simpson, *The Land that Never Was* (Lincoln: University of Nebraska Press, 1985), p. 69.
95 Arbuthnot, 'Life and prospects', p. 138.
96 Huxley, *Out in the Midday Sun*, p. 102. Similarly, Count Frédéric de Janzé regretted having to leave Kenya, for his 'heart is out here – with my house – my boys – my zoo'. Quoted in Paul Spicer, *The Temptress: The Scandalous Life of Alice de Janze and the Mysterious Death of Lord Erroll* (New York: St Martin's, 2010), p. 87.
97 Judith Thurman, *Isak Dinesen: The Life of a Storyteller* (New York: St Martin's, 1982), p. 74.
98 Blixen to Ingeborg Dinesen, 18 Nov. 1914, in Dinesen, *Letters from Africa*, p. 26.
99 Quoted in C. J. Wilson, *The Story of the East African Mounted Rifles* (Nairobi: East African Standard, 1938), p. 20.
100 'Sir Hasirim', letter to ed., *TEA* (25 Aug. 1906), p. 4. See also 'Editor's note', *Advertiser* (15 Oct. 1909); Native Labour Commission, Evidence and Report, evidence of Rev. C. F. Johnston, p. 20; Simpson, *Land that Never Was*, p. 27. The *East Africa and Uganda Mail* praised whites who inculcated good work habits through their own example, albeit by 'leading the work'. 'Naivasha', *EAUM* (24 Oct. 1903), p. 5.
101 As Huxley remarked of Lord Delamere, feudalism was 'in his bones and blood, and he believed all his life in its fundamental rightness'. *White Man's Country*, vol. 1, p. 6. Delamere instructed Margery Perham that, like all polities, Kenya would have to go through feudalism before attempting democracy. Democracy for Africans, that is; he insisted that whites would soon achieve self-government. Margery Perham, *East African Journey: Kenya and Tanganyika, 1929–30* (London: Faber and Faber, 1976), p. 139. If not feudalism, then the refined, Old South, antebellum, paternalistic Virginia would suffice. Edward Grigg (Lord Altrincham), *Kenya's Opportunities: Memories, Hopes, and Ideas* (London: Faber and Faber, 1955), pp. 205–6.
102 Huxley, *Out in the Midday Sun*, pp. 84–5.
103 Huxley, *Flame Trees of Thika*, pp. 50–1. See also Huxley's description of the near-death of Njombo who was dying (supposedly) as a result of alleged bewitchment:

Nellie 'felt the humiliation personally, especially as Njombo was, so to speak, ours. He was under our protection and we had failed to carry out our part of the implied bargain; this was what stuck in her throat'. Ibid., p. 143.

104 As the *Leader* once editorialized, 'There are few white men indeed who would permit a too arbitrary or drunken native policeman to harry his natives with impunity'. 'Native Askaris', *Leader* (24 Apr. 1909), p. 5. George Nightingale recalled that 'All Africans except your own pet servant were thieves, rogues, liars and bone lazy'. RH: MSS Afr. s. 1951, George Nightingale, 'Memoirs', p. 178. See also Gregory, *Under the Sun*, p. 65.

105 Simpson, *The Land that Never Was*, p. 238, as well as p. 265. See also the comments of Governor Grigg: 'But in spite of their primitive character, I do not think there is anybody who has come into contact with the native in Kenya who has not found him a lovable being'. 'British policy in Kenya', p. 196.

106 Huxley, *Flame Trees of Thika*, p. 47.

107 Huxley, *Flame Trees of Thika*, pp. 48–9, on hectoring, p. 155.

108 For references to servants as friends, see Simpson, *Land that Never Was*, pp. 62, 69. To those familiar with the history of the US South and Jim Crow, this mixing of friendship, paternalism, and domination will be familiar. It is also worth pointing out that debates over the white South's shift from 'paternalistic' to 'modern' relations with African Americans – from vertical, personal domination to horizontal, impersonal domination – is misguided. They can certainly co-exist. Segregation – horizontal, that is, all whites dominating all blacks, whether personally acquainted or not – can be crucial in cities and on transport, while paternalism can operate between employer and employee, land owner and sharecropper. This was the case across the white settler world. On this debate, see George M. Frederickson, *White Supremacy: A Comparative Study in American and South African History* (Oxford: Oxford University Press, 1981); John Cell, *The Highest Stage of White Supremacy: The Origins of Segregation in South Africa and the American South* (New York: Cambridge University Press, 1982); Hale, *Making Whiteness*.

109 Mary S. Lovell, *Straight on Till Morning: A Biography of Beryl Markham* (New York: St Martin's, 1987), pp. 33, 57.

110 Juanita Carberry, with Nicola Tyrer, *Child of Happy Valley: A Memoir* (London: Heinemann, 1999), pp. 39, 128–9.

111 As Knipp points out, in the work of Blixen, as well as that of Huxley and Markham, 'Africans are presented in feudal terms. They are faithful, if sometimes comical and always inscrutable, retainers, as committed as their masters to the same feudal code.' Thomas R. Knipp, 'Kenya's literary ladies and the mythologizing of the white highlands', *South Atlantic Review* 55 (1990): 1–16, quote from p. 6.

112 Her biographer calls *Out of Africa* a 'sublime repair job'. Thurman, *Isak Dinesen*, p. 283.

113 Blixen to Ingebord Dinesen, 19 Dec. 1922, in Dinesen, *Letters from Africa*, p. 140.

114 Blixen to Ingebord Dinesen, 8 July 1923, in Dinesen, *Letters from Africa*, p. 160. It is perhaps not coincidental that Blixen describes Africans' faith in her in terms similar to the way she describes Muslims' faith in God. See also her description of an elderly Gikuyu woman's wailing at the thought of 'her mama' Blixen leaving them: Blixen to Ingebord Dinesen, 28 Mar. 1925, in Dinesen, *Letters from Africa*, p. 231.

115 Kamante, Charles Beard (collector), *Longing for Darkness: Kamante's Tales from Out of Africa* (New York: Harcourt Brace Jovanovich, 1975), ch. 3.

116 Blixen to Mary Bess Westenholz, 1 Apr. 1914, in Dinesen, *Letters from Africa*, p. 4. See also, in the same volume, her letters to Ingeborg Dinesen of 23 Sep. 1914, p. 14; 14 June 1917, p. 49; to Ellen Dahl, 13 Sept. 1917; and to Elle, 2 Aug. 1923, p. 54.

117 Blixen to Ingeborg Dinesen, 4 Feb. 1923, in Dinesen, *Letters from Africa*, p. 146.

118 Blixen might have been less enamoured with the chief had she known his humble background, and how he had parlayed his alliance with British colonizers into a position of great power.

119 Dinesen, *Out of Africa*, p. 156.

120 See, for example, Dinesen, *Out of Africa*, pp. 141–2.
121 Dinesen, *Out of Africa*, pp. 133–4. It did not hurt that settlers accepted Somali protestations of their non-African ancestry. Farah and other Somali resisted being classified as 'natives', whom they considered 'Ushesis, i.e., slaves' or, rather, *washenzi*, uncivilized, savages. When the government proposed classing Somalis with other Africans, Blixen took 'the side of the Somalis, of course, and consider[ed] that they are being unfairly treated'. Blixen to Ingeborg Dinesen, 30 July 1918, in Dinesen, *Letters from Africa*, p. 77.
122 Blixen to Mary Bess Westenholz, 1 Apr. 1914, in Dinesen, *Letters from Africa*, p. 4.
123 Blixen to Ellen Dahl, 13 Sept. 1917, and Blixen to Ingeborg Dinesen, 29 Dec. 1923, in Dinesen, *Letters to Africa*, pp. 54, 181.
124 Blixen to Ingeborg Dinesen, 4 May 1926, in Dinesen, *Letters from Africa*, p. 253; Kamante, *Longing for Darkness: Kamante's Tales*, ch. 7.
125 Blixen's attitudes here may owe much to her father's ideas about Native Americans among whom he had travelled. Thurman, *Isak Dinesen*, pp. 16, 27.
126 Blixen to Thomas Dinesen, 22 Apr. 1914, in Dinesen, *Letters from Africa*, p. 8. She believed Christianity required a spiritual plane which Africans were not yet capable of achieving. Blixen to Ingeborg Dinesen, 27 Feb. 1918, in Dinesen, *Letters from Africa*, p. 62.
127 Blixen to Ingeborg Dinesen, 22 Oct. 1914, in Dinesen, *Letters from Africa*, p. 23.
128 Blixen to Ingeborg Dinesen, 29 Apr. 1923, in Dinesen, *Letters from Africa*, p. 152. See also in the same volume, Blixen to Ingeborg Dinesen, 23 Dec. 1923, p. 177.
129 Blixen to Elle, 2 Aug. 1923, in Dinesen, *Letters from Africa*, p. 163.
130 Blixen to Ingeborg Dinesen, 4 May 1926, in Dinesen, *Letters from Africa*, p. 253.
131 For an early rejection of those who would 'speak for the native', see Jomo Kenyatta, *Facing Mt. Kenya: The Tribal Life of the Gikuyu* (New York: Vintage, 1965), p. xviii.
132 Tabitha Kanogo, *Squatters and the Roots of Mau Mau* (Athens: University of Ohio Press, 1987).
133 Brett Shadle, 'Patronage, millennialism and the serpent-god Mumbo in southwest Kenya, 1912–34', *Africa* 72 (2002), 29–54.
134 Huxley, *Flame Trees of Thika*, p. 50.
135 'Nairobi sessions', *EAS* (20 Jan. 1906), p. 7.
136 Carnegie, *Kenya Farm Diary*, pp. 137–8; Crawford, *By the Equator's Snowy Peak*, pp. 113–4.
137 Brodhurst-Hill, *So This Is Kenya!*, p. 51.

CHAPTER THREE

Prestige, whiteness, and the state

Upon his first visit to the Naivasha home of the Carnellys in the 1920s, the administrator-turned-settler T. R. L. Nestor was 'astonished to find the whole place open',

> with only a couple of house boys left in charge, although our hosts had been away for some weeks. Silver ornaments and other small valuable objects were strewn about on the tables. Anyone could easily have walked in and taken them. It was an illuminating example of the safety of the times, and the high standard of prestige of the white man in Kenya.[1]

Nestor was not the only white who chalked up safety to 'prestige'. This was in fact one of the commonest words of the settler vocabulary, and central to their belief system. Settlers' possessions, their bodies, their standing as a ruling race would all be secure so long as they had prestige. Elspeth Huxley recalled of her childhood in 1910s Kenya that 'respect' – prestige – was all that protected Europeans out on the farms: 'This respect preserved them like an invisible coat of mail, or a form of magic'.[2] Thus in 1919 did the Convention of Associations resolve that 'the maintenance of this country depends entirely on the prestige and force of character of the white man'.[3] Thus did Lord Cranworth brag that 'We govern this territory by prestige alone, not by force'.[4] To have prestige was to have one's word obeyed without question, to have one's body remain inviolate, to have Africans convinced that the prevailing hierarchy was natural and unchallengeable.

Given the importance of prestige to securing whites' bodies and property, they spent an immense amount of time worrying over it. As the Kenya correspondent to *East Africa* put it, 'In the black man's country the European is, generally speaking, obsessed with the desire to maintain his racial prestige'.[5] Or again, Huxley: 'The least rent or puncture [in the chain mail of respect] might, if not immediately checked and repaired, split the whole garment asunder and expose its wearer in all his human vulnerability ... challenged, it could be brushed aside like a spider's web'.[6] Many were the things that could puncture prestige. Most obvious was African 'insolence', a term whites used almost as often as prestige. Should one African roll his eyes at his memsahib, refuse his master's order, not step aside for a white person on a path, or laugh at a white person's foibles, prestige was called into question. As Durkheim explained in another context, 'a sacred thing profaned no longer seems sacred if nothing new develops to restore its original nature. One doesn't believe in a divinity against which the vulgar lift their hands with impunity.'[7] Once the sacred white was profaned by the vulgar African, prestige dissipated. Other Africans, observing from the wings, would realize that whites were not divine, and would do as they liked.

Worse, should *one* white lose prestige, *all* whites lost prestige.[8] A single chain mail of prestige was shared by all whites. Like civilization, prestige had to attach to white skin. It made no sense to permit Africans to pick and choose which settlers deserved prestige, which should be given deference. If some whites did not have prestige, it opened the possibility that whites were not inherently superior. The insistence on race as marker between ruler and ruled appeared shaky. Africans would ask awkward questions, and might no longer be content with white trusteeship. The L. M. Tebajangas of the world could argue that, if not all whites were superior, then perhaps not all superior people were white. Thus did a challenge to any individual white person's prestige expose the vulnerability of all whites.

The need for all whites to have prestige meant that, just as Africans had to be monitored for the least act of insolence, whites had to be policed as well. Whites had to act the role of the superior being. As the administrator G. A. S. Northcote reflected in 1919, 'the Native expects the European to act as his master and superior, is puzzled and takes advantage when the European does not so act, but submits willingly when he does'.[9] So long as whites acted properly, like civilized, superior beings, all was well and good. Yet some whites failed the test. Whites sometimes broke laws, fell into penury and vagrancy, or 'went native'. Afrikaners sometimes seemed closer, in civilizational terms, to Africans than Britons. Eastern European Jews, many settlers thought, were hardly white at all – although Africans could not be expected to know this. At the same time, government officials – seeking to build up the prestige of the state – seemed to favour their African subordinates over settlers. All of this made it difficult, settlers feared, for Africans easily to grant whites prestige. In the interests of their own safety and of the existence of settlerdom, whites had to attend daily to upholding prestige.

Playing prestige

The daily interactions between Africans and Europeans, the acting out of prestige and deference, might be understood as a play, with colonial Kenya the stage.[10] Prestige required all actors to inhabit their roles, execute their lines faultlessly. In the settler version, white men of course played the lead, with Africans in the supporting roles. The settler barked orders and gave soliloquies on his paternalistic care for the African. The African deferred to the settler, called him 'bwana', stepped aside hat in hand as the white man strode across the stage. So long as the African stuck to his role of deferential servant, the play went on smoothly. For various reasons – fear of physical abuse, for example, or loss of employment – Africans often did play their roles as settlers wished. The settler could enjoy his time on the stage.

An ignored order, an insolent glare, a cheeky remark, an uninvited touch – these were not in the script. All these suggested that the African was no longer content to play his part. At that moment, all the actors held their breath. How would the white actor respond? If the African walked away from his mark, the play was done. The white man would be no better, and no worse, than his fellow actors, all of whom would now feel free to break character and do as they wished. The white man stood alone, defenceless among actors resentful of his top billing in the show.

If a challenge to prestige was not answered – generally by violence – then prestige weakened, insolence grew. An employer who lost prestige would find his 'authority over the natives residing on his land ... lessened', and his workers would 'think that they could do just as they pleased'.[11] A loss of prestige could lead to all-out rebellion. White prestige had started a precipitous decline over the past several years, warned J. Drought in 1905 (he had in fact arrived in East Africa only the previous year). Should this continue, 'then it is my honest opinion that it will result in a big native rising and that we may have it within two years'.[12]

Every day, every time an African and a European encountered one another, a scene commenced. If the African played the role of the deferential servant, all was well. The settler could feel confident that the African accepted his place in the social order. Of course, one's actions do not always reveal one's feelings. Europeans sometimes admitted that they could not truly know what thoughts and emotions lay behind Africans' 'inscrutable faces'. One Eldoret farmer suggested that 'Half one's troubles [getting and keeping African labourers] come from the idea, semi-conscious perhaps, that Natives should look upon the white man – and any white man – as a sort of god whose wisdom is infallible and whose word is final. They do not.'[13] All well and good. What mattered was that Africans should at least *act* as if they believed the white man to be a sort of god.

Settlers thus watched Africans constantly for any sign of insolence, any suggestion that Africans were not playing their roles. They regularly found evidence, or at least imagined that they did. Africans near Likoni in 1906 were, according to the *Standard*, 'becoming daily more impudent and obnoxious, we fear there will be trouble in this quarter unless a little discipline is drilled into them'.[14] A story on stone-throwing sheep rustlers came under the title 'Insolent Natives'.[15] 'Boat boys' in Mombasa went on strike and 'defeat[ed] the whole weight of a mighty Government adding the grossest insolence and insubordination to [their] actions'.[16] In and of themselves, none of these acts may have seemed particularly troubling, certainly not a threat to settlerdom. But as affronts to prestige, as examples of Africans no longer accepting their place at the bottom of the colonial hierarchy, they portended doom.

As excellent as they were in their roles, Africans could not carry the show. Settlers had to execute their lines and find their marks as well. They must be the superior people they claimed to be. They must be civilized. They had to make it as easy as possible for Africans to see them as godlike. For how difficult it must be to recite one's lines, to perform deference, when the other actor is clearly one's inferior. How one must struggle to stay in role when the star forgets his lines, when her costume slides to the floor, when he reeks of alcohol.

Just as a civilized African posed a challenge to trusteeship and paternalism, an uncivilized white person posed a challenge to prestige. If a white man became uncivilized, Africans might reconsider the natural superiority of the white race. The majority of settlers themselves had little respect for poor or backward whites. How could Africans be expected to look up to white men who had failed the test of civilization? How could Africans *not* be suspicious of white racial superiority if they saw white men on the streets, or in jail, or living like Africans? Just as allowing one African to challenge a white person could lower the prestige of all whites, so too could allowing one white man to appear uncivilized.

The burdens of whiteness

Observers have often commented on the curious custom of Europeans in the tropical colonies dressing for dinner. No matter how far out in the bush, no matter how difficult and uncomfortable it was, whites insisted that they wear proper, civilized clothing. Often this is explained as a means by which whites made certain that they did not 'go native'. In order to remain civilized, one must carry on the minutiae of civilized life. Yet we might also think of dressing for dinner as an aspect of prestige. Demeanour required it. If Africans were to be humiliated for dressing like Europeans, then settlers must be sure to dress properly themselves. Clothing was but one way in which settlers policed their own demeanour and that of fellow whites. To be civilized meant obeying laws, it meant not falling into poverty. To be white in Kenya was a full-time occupation.

Keeping up appearances

Whites argued that part of Africans' primitive mentality, their lack of progress, was due to their constant fear of the unknown. Those who lived in or near heavy forests feared both wild animals and spirits that inhabited them. Without western science, Africans could not explain eclipses or disease transmission. Instead, they attributed it all to the magic or the witchcraft in which they (supposedly) lived in perpetual fear. Whites, however, could never express similar emotions. Where an African might cower and shake, the white stood strong and unmoved. Michael Blundell, during a terrific thunderstorm in 1926, 'preserved an impassive countenance in front of the boys and gave no indication of the tumultuous feelings inside' him.[17] Exposing oneself as fearful provided an opening for Africans to break through the façade of prestige. James Edward Stocker in 1922 faced some of his workers who had refused to disperse and appeared, to Stocker, to be threatening. He took out his air gun, but 'three Meru gibbered and made faces at the [African supervisor] in reply and did not move'. Stocker took aim at one worker and shot him in the shin. According to the transcript of the resulting court case, Stocker said that 'He had studied natives since 1897, and he knew that if one showed any fear before a native the latter would take advantage of it. Witness did not show fear, but he considered the Merus had adopted a threatening attitude.' To admit fear would only further upset the balance of power.[18]

While part of Kenya's attraction was being waited upon by attentive domestic servants, reliance on African labour also involved prestige. Certainly, whites should never be made to take orders from an African supervisor – and this fear spurred demands for compulsory education for white children, lest they fall behind schooled Africans.[19] It certainly would not do for a white man to engage in dirty, demeaning, unskilled labour. The white man's job was to command. Lady Northey, wife of Governor Northey (1919–22), told a London audience that Kenya was 'a country in which the white man, if he is to keep his dignity, cannot himself do manual labour but must be in a position to employ native labour'.[20] In 1926, early in his anthropological career, Louis Leakey 'somewhat scandalized the European settlers' around Nakuru. His crime? 'I used to carry water side by side with the boys, and the other Europeans considered that in doing this menial work we were lowering "white man's prestige".' The settlers were more ready to overlook his working 'shoulder to shoulder with my men in the excavation work', since that seemed to be more a supervisory role.[21]

More than one settler fled Kenya leaving behind unmet financial obligations, while debts at shops and bars went unpaid for months at a time. Between whites, this could lead to frustration and court cases. When settlers failed to pay their debts to non-whites, however, they threatened racial prestige. The senior commissioner of Coast Province worried over the long-overdue bills left by Col. W. W. Molony. 'This sort of transactions whereby Arabs are kept out of their money through the action of Europeans', he considered, 'is not uncommon and tends greatly to lower the prestige of our race'.[22] Dobbs, Nyanza provincial commissioner in 1928, similarly scolded E. T. Moore for giving an African shopkeeper a bad cheque, and then for over a year failing to settle his debt. 'It has the worst possible effect on the natives when cheques given them by Europeans are dishonoured.' The superintendent of police in Eldoret thought this 'really a most disgraceful thing'.[23] The *Critic* thought even when whites cheated whites it lowered 'the prestige of the British Nation in the eyes of everyone'.[24]

Even fictional representations of uncivilized whites could be dangerous. An African was liable to believe without question everything that appeared on the big screen, or on the pages of a book. The *Standard* in 1910 warned against too quickly teaching Africans to read English: 'Third and fourth class rubbishy novels which we would not put into the hands of our own children are read with avidity by these children of nature who have not the restraining influences of countless generations of moral training to help them.'[25] Without the discrimination that came with civilization, Africans would learn the wrong lessons. The Kericho and Buret Farmers' Association protested against the government's Swahili-language paper *Habari* publishing 'world news dealing with revolutions, uprisings against authority and crimes of violence in general'. It was a question of security: 'there is the feeling that, in a country where the handful of Europeans is outnumbered on a ratio of about twenty to one, it is injudicious to stimulate the Native imagination against organized authority by the dissemination of sensational news'.[26]

Local settler media too was urged to portray whites only in the best light. In 1920, some settlers attacked the *Standard* for publishing names of whites arrested for being drunk and disorderly. The editors turned the accusation back around. '"The prestige of the white man," are no idle words', the paper explained, 'they have a deep meaning, and a deep significance, and more so in a new country like East Africa, where, if from the beginning, the native is taught to look on the white man as a superior being, as one whose example he may safely follow, and to whom he must show respect'. A drunken white man breaching the peace did nothing to preserve white prestige. A public scolding might direct drunkards toward moderation.[27]

Poor whites, vagrants, and 'going native'

Especially in the earliest years in British East Africa, whites lived a frontier existence. Some found themselves isolated from other whites, hunting wild game for food, skins and ivory. They, perforce, lived unsettled lives without the trappings of civilized life. Yet such conditions might be excused by other whites, so long as they on occasion returned to Nairobi or the Coast, cleaned up, and rejoined white society. More worrying were white farmers or pastoralists who took to African ways of life. Such men had homes, but perhaps African-style rather than square, stone structures. They might live near enough to other settlers to trade visits, have tea or 'sundowners', and take part in civilized life, but declined to do so. They instead remained on their farms and interacted primarily with Africans. The worst offenders took African wives and raised mixed-race children. Such men – and they appear always to have been men – severely damaged white prestige. What could more deeply challenge white claims to superiority than to see a white man 'sink' to the level of Africans?

Whites thus constantly watched their fellows for signs of 'going native', and wished only the worst for those who had already gone to the other side. M. H. Hamilton, speaking of her childhood as daughter of an interwar administrator, recalled that

> It was essential that we kept high standards as it was only too easy to go native. There were always examples to warn us of men in the bush on their own. Living in a mud hut with only a camp bed and table, it was all too easy to forget to wash or shave, or even change clothes. If there was no-one to keep you on the straight and narrow, you simply did not bother, took to drink in all probability, and became socially unacceptable.[28]

MacGregor Ross, a government official turned colonial critic, and who poked fun at settler obsession with prestige, none the less had similar opinions on how whites must act.[29] He thought whisky usually led whites down the path of 'going native'. Although he pitied them, they were dangerous none the less. He shed no tears at their early demise from alcoholism or suicide: 'Everyone is relieved when the end comes – however it comes. These people are not maintaining racial standards. They are better out of the way.'[30]

If the bottle or shotgun were too extreme, the Kenyan government could at least control the immigration of 'undesirables' and deport the indigent. The government imposed restrictions meant to ensure that only the financially stable would settle.[31] The 'Restriction of Immigration Ordinance' of 1906 required whites to deposit a surety of 750 rupees upon entering the country, and provided for the deportation of undesirables. The *Times of East Africa* applauded the measure, and urged the police to be liberal using their new powers to summarily arrest people thought to be prohibited immigrants.[32] In 1912, the Vanga assistant district commissioner, perhaps out of a desire to assist fellow whites, sheltered two destitute Germans who crossed from German East Africa. He was reminded by the principal immigration officer, however, that he should 'endeavour in future to keep such persons from entering the Protectorate'.[33] Kenya had no use for destitute whites.

Policing borders could not prevent otherwise upstanding whites from becoming poor. The *Critic* in 1922 warned that 'it is not good for unsophisticated, or partically [sic] sophisticated, natives to know that there are Europeans out of work and scouring the streets of the towns to find it'.[34] Poor whites had either to be quickly uplifted or disposed of. The League of Mercy, a white women's benevolent society, in 1912 asked for contributions to deal with 'the poor white problem', and the Salvation Army joined it in 1922.[35] In fact, the *Standard* thought the League of Mercy one of the most important bodies in a place like Kenya, 'where the misfortunes of the few may react on the influence and the status of the many, where all the conditions are a continual warning against disintegration of the homogeneity which it is necessary to preserve if the burden of the white man is effectively and successfully to be carried'. The League was crucial, for 'it is vitally necessary to give heed to the small and apparently unimportant threats and dangers which exist in the life of the community'.[36]

The alternative to uplift was unattractive. Jail followed by deportation ended the African dreams of unsuccessful, penurious whites. The Vagrancy Ordinance, passed already in 1902, herded failed whites into detention. Administrators might try to find jobs for convicted vagrants, but those with no future were to be deported.[37] The postwar depression landed sixteen in the Nairobi House of Detention. Despite the efforts of the Salvation Army to find employment for them, twelve ended up on steamers leaving Mombasa port in 1922.[38] F. J. Watts, for example, came to Kenya from South Africa during the war, invested in a fishing business, lost all his money, and by 1920 was 'unable to find employment and is in consequence destitute'.[39] He was sent on his way. In 1923, the League of Mercy helped to clothe another 'fifteen impecunious persons' prior to their deportation.[40] Thus the *Standard* in

1923 crowed that 'there is here among the Europeans hardly any of the "poor white" class' that might negatively influence Africans.[41]

Like vagrants, white criminals were a problem. The very presence of whites behind bars could lead Africans to reconsider whether whites were in fact superior. In 1922, the editor of the *Critic* passed along a story from 'Paul', who in his Kenya travels had heard disturbing tales, including this one (allegedly) from an African:

> Sometimes I read in the newspapers of the wonderful things the White man can do. He is very *wakile* (clever). But he is not God. He does bad things just as boys do. How do I know? *Bwana*, I was once an askari in the gaol. I saw *mzungus* (white men) there. They had been stealing – some of them. Some of them had no money and the *sirkali* (Government) put them in gaol. Why should white men steal? Why should they have no money? Why should they be in gaol? The other boys [Africans] think now that the white man is just like the boys. He is no better. That is not good for them to think like that. I know. I hear the boys talking together and they say these things. I like to think that the *mzungu* is better than a boy. He is more clever. Askaris respect and like the white man. But the other boys who do not know think bad things.

White men not godlike, white men no better than Africans – dangerous thoughts. 'Paul' and the editor alike feared the worst if Africans could continue to observe poor or criminal white men. Such men were clearly not superior to Africans. Better: ship out vagrants immediately, and force criminals to serve their sentences in their home countries.[42]

Poor whites and the uses of prestige

White elites tried to eliminate the impoverished and criminally inclined in order to uphold white prestige. Poor whites and their defenders turned the argument around. Rather than excoriation and deportation, in the interest of white prestige they deserved special assistance and consideration. The *East Africa and Uganda Mail* made a point of this in an article titled 'Lowering British prestige':

> One of the most grievous sights in the East African Protectorate, and one that raises the blood of Britons to a boiling point, is the degradation the sons of Britain are subjected to. We refer to the placing of our countrymen in the Mombasa Jail for no crime, save the Crime of Poverty; and we cannot pass this by without an earnest protest ... Our young men of talent, who have come out here, have starved in search of work; whilst we, alas! find billets for hundreds of Portugal's subjects [Goans] and heathens in our Police, Railway, Customs, Consul's Offices, Treasury, and District Offices. Yet there is no work for an Englishman, whether educated or the reverse. His only portion under King Edward, in Mombasa, is prison. Is such lowering of British prestige wise, to say nothing of Right?[43]

Two weeks later, the *Mail* reported that the government had paid for several of the imprisoned to be sent to South Africa. 'It is to be hoped sincerely', the editor wrote, 'that they will secure honest, if not lucrative employment and never again be subjected to the humiliation of earning their living in prisons or work houses'.[44] Humiliation should be the preserve of Africans.

Although the most incorrigible settlers would have to be punished, they remained white behind bars. Surely, even dastardly whites should not be made to rub shoulders with Africans. Thus the *Mail* also complained of 'this crying disgrace, of placing Englishmen to herd with Swahilis, whose crimes cover the whole Decalogue'. In September 1905, Mary Morgan found herself in Mombasa jail on charge of vagrancy. She demanded better conditions and objected 'to any Kaffir people about me and to be locked up all day'.[45] Justice Carter denied not the import of such a complaint but its factual basis.[46] Sometimes jailers appreciated this argument, and more than one white prisoner was given the task of overseeing African inmates.[47]

Two years before Mary Morgan's arrival, W. F. Sinclair had lost his job at Mombasa jail. He was guilty of various failings, including (in his own words) 'a series of miserable bickering and rows, with a Eurasian clerk employed here, who from the very first tried by insolence and insubordination to make harmony impossible, and, by false and malicious reports to my superior officer to undermine my position'.[48] Both ended up getting cashiered, although (according to Sinclair) the Eurasian had committed much more serious infractions. 'Just think Sir!' he implored Donald Cameron, Commissioner of the Protectorate, of the injustice of equivalent punishment for a good white man and an insolent and thieving Eurasian.

Sinclair sheepishly admitted that upon receiving his dismissal he took to the bottle, for which he expressed his regrets. While drunk he ended up in a fight with two African askaris which landed him behind bars. He allowed that the altercation was to be deprecated, but insisted that

> the native askaris had no excuse for treating me in the outrageous fashion in which they did [about which he gave no details] and I am quite sure that had such a thing happened to you or any other self-respecting white man, you also would have been thrown into such an uncontrollable rage and would have cast about for some immediate means of wiping out the insult. Believe me, Sir, when this country experiences its first big native rising people will be sorry, that the principle of 'never allowing a native to raise a hand against a white man', had not been encouraged.

Sinclair had been treated insolently by Africans: in such a case, he argued, his violent reaction was normal, his imprisonment was unjust.

He was defending not just himself but the entirety of white colonial rule. Given the circumstances, he begged of Stewart, he should be granted another job in the administration. Unfortunately for Sinclair, the administration could not countenance an assault on a government employee by a private individual (as just-terminated Sinclair had become). Stewart noted curtly that no offer of employment would be extended.[49]

Those who teetered precariously near the border between upstanding and poor white had their own uses for white prestige. Robertson of the *Critic* regularly championed them. In February 1923, he learned that the Lumbwa Co-operative Society had offered office positions to white men at 300 shillings per month, with no mention of housing or allowances. Insufficient. Commendable enough to offer employment to Europeans, but just 'Because times are bad, that is no reason why employers of labour should endeavour to reduce the standard of living of their European employees to a state not compatible with White prestige in these parts'. Low pay and a lower standard of living lowered white prestige.[50]

Not a month later the issue of pay and prestige emerged on a larger scale with the introduction of the European and African Trades Organisation. The origins and ultimate aims of the EATO were murky even at the time, although Delamere and Northrup Macmillan appear to have founded it.[51] Among its purported aims was the training of Africans in artisanal skills and finding employment for Europeans – the former to prove that settlers were taking trusteeship seriously, and to edge out Indian artisans.[52] Among defenders of the 'small men' – landless skilled and semi-skilled European workers – this project quickly raised eyebrows. 'Suspicious' wrote that white workers feared that 'one of the [EATO's] objects is to import cheap labour to the country and so PERMANENTLY keep down the rate of wages'.[53] The *Kenya Observer* rallied to the defence of the common man. Whatever the aims of the EATO, the white man had to be protected. The paper extended uneasy support to the EATO, but swore to revoke it 'if there is any indication that its operations may produce the result of lowering wages and the standard of living, and by taking advantage of the times and the [economic] crisis, placing white men on the economic level occupied by Indians'.[54] Conventional wisdom held that Indian workers and merchants, content with lower standards of living, could handily undercut whites. If whites had to compete fairly with Indians, they would either fail or be forced to live like Indians – clearly not permissible in the interests of white prestige. The constant lowering of wages in Nairobi, which 'A Democrat' associated with the EATO and its kind, could only force workers into ruin. 'It is said that poor Europeans are not wanted in Kenya', he moaned, 'yet here one sees them being created every day. There is no sense of proportion where profit-making is concerned. It is "get as much as you can" and "give as little wages as you can" and "d--- the under-dog."'[55] If Kenya must be cleansed of poor whites, then elite settlers would do well to not create poor whites.

Afrikaners and Jewganda

From at least the early nineteenth century, derogatory stereotypes of Afrikaners circulated freely among English-speaking South Africans. They were said to be particularly violent toward Africans. They were insular and backward.[56] According to Francis Younghusband, who toured Natal in the late 1880s, Afrikaners were 'deficient in honesty and veracity, ignorant, unprogressive and in most respects two centuries behind other European nations'. Among their saving graces was their excellence at pioneering.[57] The stereotyping of Afrikaners only increased with the South African War (1899–1902). Jingoist anti-Afrikaner accounts harped on them as 'ignorant peasants'. Millicent Fawcett reported that the 'horrors' Afrikaner women imposed on ill children 'could be found in old-fashioned English family receipt books of 150 or 100 years ago'.[58] That is, Afrikaners were a century or more behind Britons on the ladder of civilization. British media described the war as necessary to 'civilize the Boer'.[59]

At the end of the war hundreds of Afrikaners sought fresher fields abroad, including East Africa. Reactions of administrators and established settlers in Kenya toward Afrikaners was decidedly mixed for some years.[60] Afrikaners were celebrated for their skills as frontiersmen. Indeed, in certain respects they outstripped Britons in their abilities to tame the African wilderness. 'The Afrikaner is an ideal pioneer', gushed the *Leader*. '[H]e has a natural eye for country; he is a born "selector"; he could live in comfort and even grow wealthy on a farm in this country where the ordinary English farmer from Home would starve and pine away.'[61] They were famed for their ability to handle oxen.[62]

Observers also commented on what they saw as Afrikaners' special skills in dealing with Africans. After generations of commanding African labour on isolated farms, their closest neighbours most likely black, Afrikaners (it was claimed) had developed an intimate knowledge of Africans. The *Leader* believed that Afrikaners 'understand the native better than the Englishman – even better than the trained Englishman – even better than the average Native or Provincial Commissioner – and their presence in the midst of the native tribes can trend but for good'.[63] One writer to the *Times of East Africa* praised Afrikaners, who were not taken in like 'certain type of raw Englishman [to whom the African] delights to tell pretty tales which are greedily swallowed'.[64]

Yet the frontiersman culture had a darker side. While Afrikaners were white, they remained 'less modern' than other whites.[65] Many were quite poor and had been granted admittance into British East Africa without posting bond. Their clothing, food, housing, and ways of earning a living were not always comparable to other settlers'. Huxley speculated that their 'wildness had not quite been bred away'.[66] Ethel Younghusband told of a British lady who 'took one of their girls on as a nurse, to try if they were any use as such'. It was a failure.

> [T]he girl was one of few words, and soon got home-sick (?), and ran back to her wagon; but evidently they did not receive her back with open arms, as she reappeared again in the course of a few days. One day she offered to take the children out for a walk, but my friend said she was too untidy, her hair especially, and asked her if she had not a brush and comb; the girl replied that she had not. But nothing daunted, presently her mistress missing her, she hunted her up and found her doing her hair in her lady's bedroom, using her glass and brush and comb![67]

Afrikaners lived not in houses but in wagons; the girls lacked the tools to render themselves presentable in public; they did not understand that a lady's toilet was not to be shared.

Even Afrikaners' celebrated agricultural skills went only so far. The district commissioner at Uasin Gishu in 1914 compared the Briton, an often itinerant but modern farmer, with the Afrikaner, who 'may not be in the main of much use of developing the land but on the land he is and will remain'.[68] As one critic pointed out in 1916, 'there are quite a large number of Dutch children growing up on the Uasin Gishu with little more knowledge than how to drive a team of oxen or shoot a buck, accomplishments which any native will soon be able to do as well or better'.[69] As important as Afrikaners' skills were, if they did not progress they would soon be at the level of Africans. White would no longer equate with superiority and civilization.

Just as whites had to train up Africans, Britons would have to do the same with Afrikaners. If the goal of settlement and colonialism was to apply modern methods to extract all that could be had from the earth, Afrikaners were at best a first step, one soon to be eclipsed. Even the *Leader* in 1908 admitted that Afrikaner farming was important, but only for a certain stage of development: 'If the present [Afrikaner immigrant] addition to the farmer element will not tend to more scientific principles, it will break the virgin soil for the adoption of these principles'.[70] Ewart Grogan welcomed stolid, hardworking Afrikaners who would be even more valuable settlers once they had been introduced to the 'leaven' of British progressivism.[71]

Stereotypes of Afrikaners' semi-civilized – not-quite-white – nature continued into the 1920s. May Baldwin's children's novel *Kenya Kiddies* revolves around a settler family's struggle to civilize a young white man apprenticed to their farm.[72] Baldwin, born in 1862 in India where her father served as chaplain, lived with her brother in Kenya for several years in the 1920s. She authored dozens of novels featuring British girls in Britain and abroad, often in places she had close friends or where she had travelled. The entry on her in *The Encyclopedia of Girls' School Stories* asserts that her 'open-mindedness means that she never boosts the upright, honourable British at the expense of nasty foreigner'.[73] The nasty young man in *Kenya Kiddies*, however, is clearly not British. He is, at least in temperament, Afrikaner.

Pat Evans, sixteen years as the story unfolds, has been placed with Mr Frobisher to be trained in the operation of a modern farm. Pat had his own set of skills, closely associated with the Afrikaner farmer: 'He had a certain rough manliness of manner, and had been made to work on his father's farm ever since he was old enough to hold a panga (spade), and could command natives and plough well'.[74] His mother was a socialite, his father unwilling to rein in her excesses. Pat had never been to school, had been neglected by his parents, and lacked the refinements expected of a white person. He was cruel to children and animals, he was illiterate, he lacked 'any ideas about the chivalrous treatment of women and girls'.[75] Pat lied and stole, and to take revenge against Frobisher he encouraged Africans to strike for higher wages. Not the type of civilizing influence expected of white men. Frobisher finally, through patience, shaming, and forgiveness, turns Pat around. 'A polished member of society he could not be called', Baldwin wrote, 'but he was no longer the ignorant Boer he had been a year ago, and his devotion to Mr Frobisher, at any rate, was sincere.'[76]

It is difficult to believe that Pat was in fact an Afrikaner. 'Pat Evans' is certainly not a typical Afrikaner name, and Afrikaner women were not known for frequenting fashionable parties and the Nairobi races. Short of being an actual 'ignorant Boer', Pat was the next worse thing: a Briton who had fallen to the level of the Afrikaner. Pat's tale is both a comment on the uncivilized Afrikaners and a warning to English-speakers of the colony. Everyone knew the dangers of 'going native'. They should also be aware of the dangers of 'going Afrikaner'. Only a strong father, a doting mother (or mother figure: Mr Frobisher was a widower with a governess dedicated solely to the children), and a proper education could ensure the continuity of a civilized white population.[77]

Those who represented the best of the Afrikaners (according to Britons) were those who spoke proper English and sought to integrate their community into the dominant British class.[78] As the *Leader* noted, many Anglo settlers disparaged Afrikaners as unprogressive, but had their attitudes turned upon realizing that 'among those so-called "Boers" many men of Dutch patrynomic were men of substance, men of education, and men of considerable political promise'. Perhaps the highest praise such setters could give: 'In close contact they were "quite English you know" though of a provincial-colonial type'.[79] The larger white community was more welcoming once Afrikaners had moved from being strictly Afrikaner – and all the roughness, violence, and backwardness that implied – to being a 'colonial'. But in the meantime, they posed a danger. According to Brevet-Major Lloyd-Jones, 'The natives also had not the same respect for [Afrikaners] as they had for Englishmen, and called them "Washenzi Wazungu" (uncivilised white men)'.[80] This should have been a logical impossibility.

If Afrikaners did not always live up to the standards expected of them, Anglo settlers could at least welcome them as fellow whites. Not all immigrants from Europe found outstretched hands awaiting them, for not all were recognized as white. Joseph Chamberlain, Secretary of State for the Colonies, toured Kenya in 1902 and thought he had found a solution to a trying political problem: Zionism. Cool, fertile, and (supposedly) unoccupied, the hills of central Kenya would make an ideal home for persecuted Jews of Russia. Plans to resettle Jews in the Levant had come to nought; perhaps East Africa might serve as an acceptable half-way point. Sir Charles Eliot, Commissioner of British East Africa, had reservations about the plan. His solution was to offer the Uasin Gishu plateau in the west to potential Zionist settlers, segregating them from the bulk of settlers.[81] Uasin Gishu had previously been part of the Ugandan Protectorate, hence much mistaken reporting called it the Uganda scheme. Settlers, most unwelcoming to the proposal, took this one step further and dubbed it 'Jewganda'.[82]

As word circulated of Chamberlain's proposal, settlers quickly called a public meeting in Nairobi to condemn it. Lord Delamere fired off a telegram to the *Times* reporting that 'Feeling here very strong against introduction of alien Jews'. Some of their resistance was simple anti-Semitism, but many settlers took pains to downplay this.[83] In fact, Jews were well represented and largely accepted among the earliest settlers as merchants, artisans, farmers, members of various professions, and the Colonist Association.[84]

The real complication with the Zionist plan was that the Jewish immigrants were poor and non-Anglo.[85] These Russian and Romanian peasants or ghetto-dwellers would not have the financial wherewithal, the status, and the bearing that whites in Kenya must have. As impoverished, downtrodden victims of pogroms, the Jews would not appear civilized. Delamere explained that Jews were not necessarily unwanted in Africa.[86] English-speaking Jews, who served the British Crown and contributed to the development of the colony, these Delamere approved of.[87] What mattered more to Delamere than the immigrants' Jewishness was their ways of living, their character. Poor, eastern European Jews were not of the mettle to rule. Africans would not see them as superior, would not respect them, and would refuse to be ruled by them. A single Briton (it was said) could stare down hordes of African warriors simply by his force of personality. In contrast, the editor of the *African Standard* sneered, the Nandi would forever remain unconquered if confronted by 'the Jewish warriors'.[88]

The *African Standard* linked its anti-Semitism with the threat these Jews would allegedly pose to the status of all white men. The editor, Tiller, dredged up stereotypes of the dirty, miserly, foreign Jewish merchant: 'The long-greasy-frock-coated gentlemen, who "vould sell you a coat" or anything else – who drop into a bar and produce from the manifold pockets of their rags anything from a comb or piece of soap – for neither of which have they any use – to a watch or a revolver'.[89] Such types were white – or at least would be considered such by undiscerning Africans – and would only lower the prestige of all whites. Tiller drew on the history of South Africa: 'What has been the history of the South? Simply this: that the natives absolutely distrust the white men, thanks to the swindling practices of these itinerating "Peruvians" [Polish Jews].'[90]

It is not clear if anyone paid attention to settlers' rhetorical violence. In the end, the Zionist World Congress rejected Chamberlain's proposal. The commission sent out to East Africa presented an unfavourable report in 1904; the plan's champion, Hertzl, had died; and a majority of congress delegates refused to accept any schemes that did not lead directly to Palestine. With the passing of 'Jewganda' and the threat of non-Anglo Jewish mass immigration, so too went doubts about Kenya as a home for Jews – or, rather, for proper whites, whites who could uphold prestige, and who happened to be Jews.[91]

Serikali's prestige, settler prestige

Serikali – government – had more means that did settlerdom to ensure its continuity. Low-level violence and imprisonment could extract compliance, as could extending benefits to loyal Africans. Opening new lands for African settlement and new markets for cash crops, and providing material and social benefits to state employees, could help convince Africans that colonial rule was not a pure evil.[92] But on a day to day basis, colonialism was thought (by its practitioners) to be based on prestige. The state, via its representatives, must be known by its 'permanence, omnipotence, and infallibility'.[93] Not unlike the prestige settlers lived by. As much as administrators believed in racial superiority and racial prestige, their first order of business was advancing serikali's prestige. When the two forms of prestige came into conflict, settlers usually lost out.

Serikali's prestige

Colonialism in Kenya, especially in its messy first few decades, found itself caught between an older, personalized style of government and a modern bureaucracy in which office was of more importance than its holder. Officials relied on prestige as much as did settlers.[94] Thus could Captain C. Heywood recall with good humour a dangerous spot he had once been in:

> Here were we, a small force of sixteen rifles all told, close to a crowd of hostile Somalis, between fifty and a hundred strong, most of whom had firearms, the remainder being armed with spears – and their women had run to us for protection when attacked by a hostile tribe! How wonderful is 'prestige'! Good old British flag! May it long fly dauntless even in the most adverse breezes![95]

Yet their personal prestige must not make them Kurtzian gods of the bush. It must instead build the prestige of government and the Crown. Their personal superiority must represent (to Africans) the superiority of all government officials; Africans' willingness to defer to a particular officer must be transferable to all officers.[96]

What complicated serikali's prestige: serikali was not pure white. The bulk of the men on the colonial payroll were Africans who filled the ranks of policemen, interpreters, chiefs, and headmen. They, too, must have some prestige if they were to carry out the routine business of colonialism. If government was to be respected, its laws followed, then all those affiliated with it must be respected, their orders obeyed. The district commissioner of Kikuyu proposed in 1910 that the 'strengthening of the authority and prestige of the sub-Chiefs, Headmen and Native Councils should be one programme for the next few years'.[97] At the same time, the most powerful African subalterns had to be reminded that they always remained a step below the most junior white officer.[98] Where exactly non-official whites fitted into this scheme was less clear.

Serikali prestige and white prestige

Unfortunately for white settlers, whatever prestige the government earned was not transferable; prestige accorded only to government and the administrative order that stretched from the lowest cadet to the Crown. Settlers did not act in the name of the queen or king. Worse, settlers charged, administrators' dedication to serikali's prestige meant a lessening of *white* prestige. Settlers often charged administrators with open hostility towards fellow whites and favouritism towards Africans.[99] This, they felt, was not only unfair – after all, settlers argued, they had been invited to help the civilizing mission in East Africa – but empowered Africans to challenge any non-official. The *Standard* in 1914 recalled earlier days when 'The official class was, as it were, the "elect of God" while the settler class was relegated to the position of "shenzi" or much inferior white beings'. Africans had learned to address officers, but not settlers, with respect. Administrators, not settlers, received deference. 'By a simple process of reasoning, therefore', the *Standard* argued, the African 'is able to relegate the [non-official] white man to the position of an ordinary, if a more advanced, mortal. The teachings of the official are, in short, having a salutary effect, and the fruits of insolence, independence, and even defiance, are fast springing from those early seeds of discord'.[100]

Particularly galling to settlers was the possibility of African subalterns being given authority over whites. The Colonists' Association in 1905 warned that 'The employment of blacks by the Government as soldiers and police to deal with white settlers is absolutely fatal to the maintenance of white prestige among natives and must seriously hasten the day of black rebellion. We stand practically on the edge of a human volcano.'[101] That an African could arrest a white, the *Standard* editorialized again in 1913, broke a 'cardinal principle' of white prestige and 'racial superiority'. A black policeman would not understand that it was the law, not the individual, that was 'doing the arresting', and would arrogantly conclude that 'The big white man has given me power over the lesser white man. I shall take every opportunity to use that power now I have the chance.'[102] Often whites thus ignored or threatened African police who tried to do their jobs. In 1922, Eva Bloem pointed a (holstered) revolver at an askari who stopped her on suspicion of possessing stolen goods, and told him that 'he was a black man and could not arrest her'.[103]

Eva Bloem had a kindred spirit in John Finnie. Early in 1905, Finnie came upon two Africans walking a mule near Mikindu River in Fort Hall. According to Mzee bin Ali, who witnessed the confrontation, the first African stepped aside to let Finnie pass. The white man grabbed him 'by the throat, gave him a punch in each of the sides' and kicked him. The second African received a slap. According to Ali, no words were exchanged.[104] While Finnie may well have said nothing, much was communicated. Finnie later claimed that the Africans had not intended to move, and stepped off the path only when they realized Finnie would not surrender it. MacLellan Wilson, Secretary of the Colonists' Association, later acknowledged that Finnie had indeed, and rightfully, assaulted the Africans. The importance of controlling public space, Wilson argued, could not be overestimated. 'The white man's prestige', he tutored the commissioner of the protectorate, 'is upheld only by an assumption of superiority whether real or fancied, which is, even in the Government method, attained only by a show of force and power.'[105] Assaulting an African who refused immediately to grant right of way to a white was not only excusable but necessary.[106]

Certainly Finnie was not the only settler to slap or choke an African who failed to understand path etiquette. This time, however, the two Africans were government askaris. Finnie refused to admit that an African in government employ deserved any special consideration. A uniform and fez did not alter Africans' skin colour, nor their duty to prostrate themselves to every white man they encountered. MacLellan Wilson granted that perhaps an askari could command a sliver of respect, as a government representative, but not enough to trump race: 'whilst realizing that the *askari* being a Government servant must be treated with the amount of consideration which his uniform entitles him to, it seems a pity if he be not taught sufficient respect to white men to stand aside when a white man is passing on a narrow path'. He predicted danger if government officials did not rein in their black subordinates. 'I can only hope', he wrote the commissioner, 'that you will take some steps to have such an unfortunate state of things remedied, as there is sure to be trouble in the future if natives intend to dispute the right of way with white men and are supported by certain Government officials in such an impertinence?'[107]

Government officials might agree that black should give way before white, but not that civilians could assault a representative of the state. As much as officials shared ideas of racial prestige with white settlers, their first concern was the establishment and perpetuation of the state. Just as settlers feared that any act of 'insolence' or 'cheek' threatened white prestige, and thus white rule, officials feared that any challenge to the state, or state representatives, would expose its weaknesses and make it out to be a sham. The prestige of serikali had to be preserved. As Judge Barth later commented, Finnie had to be punished when the importance 'of maintaining the authority of a native police is considered'.[108]

PRESTIGE, WHITENESS, AND THE STATE

Soon after the incident on the path, Fort Hall Collector R. W. Humphrey arrested Finnie for interfering with government servants. As Humphrey was on safari, he intended to try Finnie the next day back at the government station. That night, the collector set up camp and placed Finnie in a tent atop a small hill. Finnie was given free rein of the hilltop, but was placed under the armed guard of an African askari. During the night Finnie stepped into the bush, apparently to relieve himself. The askari, Mabuki Mkamba, thought he was attempting to escape, and grabbed his arm. True to his nature, Finnie hit the askari, took his rifle and threw the cartridges into the bush. Told that Finnie had again assaulted a government servant, Humphrey marched up and 'told [Finnie] that I thought that he had behaved like a fool which apparently annoyed him and he stepped up to me in a very threatening manner whereupon I thought he was going to strike me and [I] knocked him down'. Finnie spent the rest of the evening in a tent near to Humphrey's, his guard now under orders to shoot the settler should he emerge.[109]

Cowed for the night only, Finnie later refused to consider any of his actions unwarranted. The askari on the hilltop, he later explained, 'gave me a lot of cheek and tried to catch me by the breast but I threw him but did not touch him further'. When taken before Sub-Commissioner Tate for trial, Finnie 'said that I had no time for a case such as this would entail[.] I admitted throwing the askaris off the path and was fined 48 rupees.' John Finnie still believed himself the wounded party. Humphrey had assaulted him. An armed askari had been put in supervision of him. Racial prestige remained the root of the issue: 'I believed the case would turn around the question of whether a white man or a black should get off the path.'[110]

Settlers continued to act on the assumption that racial prestige trumped all else. In January 1914, Provincial Commissioner Hobley had reserved a carriage on the Uganda Railway for a cross-colony journey. Stopping at Nakuru, he asked a nearby African constable to protect his property while he disembarked for a meal. When Hobley returned, he discovered three unknown Europeans occupying his carriage. Among them was C. E. Smith, a settler heavily invested in timber farming and stock raising. Smith asked Hobley, as the administrator later reported, 'what I meant by telling a nigger to stop a European from getting into the train'. After a 'somewhat heated conversation' the two finally came to an understanding. Although Smith may have shaken hands with Hobley, he still harboured resentment with the constable for daring to prevent a white man from doing what he wished to do, and he lodged a complaint with the constable's superiors in Nairobi. Hobley defended the constable, who undoubtedly was 'doing what he considered to be his duty'.[111] For Smith, the constable's primary duty was never to challenge a white man.

Serikali never seemed entirely sure what to do with racial prestige. Missionaries who taught Africans to defer to all whites were applauded, and administrators may have sometimes given similar lessons.[112] They understood the sting a white man must feel to be arrested by an African. Yet magistrates often sought to deliver justice in their courts, with less regard for race, and the number of white police would never be sufficient to dispense with African askaris.[113] Certainly, Humphrey never asked Finnie to bow and scrape before the soldier, but neither could the white man be allowed to undermine Government's prestige.

Conclusion

Even as they celebrated their prestige, settlers constantly worried over its decline. Indeed, it seemed that the heyday of prestige was always just a few years ago. As early as 1908, the *Advertiser* warned that 'the fact is obvious that the native in contact with our civilisation is becoming more insolent and daring'.[114] In 1914, an 'old timer' would say that the current houseboys were insolent compared to the 'old days'.[115] In 1918, the *Standard* commented on 'the increasing insolence and defiance displayed by the majority of the [house] boys'.[116] Two years later W. M. Hudson complained that African criminality was increasing 'and the native has become cheeky and arrogant'.[117] Prestige kept settlers safe and sound, but it was constantly on the verge of dissipating. Anything that might threaten prestige – from insolent houseboys, to white vagrants, to alien Jews – had to be eliminated.

Notes

1. RH: MSS Afr. S. 1086, T. R. L. Nestor Papers, p. 82.
2. Elspeth Huxley, *Flame Trees of Thika* (New York: Morrow, 1959), p. 16.
3. Quoted in W. McGregor Ross, *Kenya from Within: A Short Political History* (London: Frank Cass, 1968 [1927]), pp. 322–3.
4. 'Lord Cranworth on the Kenya problem', *EAS* (4 June 1923), pp. 3–4.
5. 'Our Kenya letter', *EA* (4 Dec. 1924), pp. 274–5.
6. Huxley, *Flame Trees of Thika*, p. 16.
7. Emile Durkheim, *Moral Education: A Study in the Theory and Application of the Sociology of Education* (New York: Free Press, 1961 [1925]), p. 165.
8. Thus as the Royal Commission into Papua concluded in 1906, 'No matter how little a particular white man may deserve the respect of the native, it is still necessary in the interests of all white men that the native should not be in a position where respect for the ruling race will be jeopardised'. Quoted in Chilla Bulbeck, *Australian Women in Papua New Guinea: Colonial Passages, 1920–1960* (Cambridge: Cambridge University Press, 1992), p. 164.
9. KNA, Ukamba Provincial Annual Report, 1918–19.

10 The idea draws on James C. Scott, *Domination and the Arts of Resistance: Hidden Transcripts* (New Haven: Yale University Press, 1990).
11 *Native Labour Commission, 1912–13: Evidence and Report* (Nairobi: Government Printer), p. 4.
12 Evidence of Drought, *Native Labour Commission*, p. 182.
13 'Eldoret', letter to ed., *EA* (20 Aug. 1924), p. 963.
14 'Occasional notes', *EAS* (1 Sep. 1906), p. 7.
15 *Advertiser* (17 July 1908), p. 5.
16 'The native', *EAS* (25 May 1912), p. 14.
17 RH: MSS Afr. s. 746/1, Michael Blundell, 'Diary, 1925–26', entry of 21 Dec. 1925. Selous, the famed white hunter of east and central Africa, once remarked 'it is very foolish [diving] in a river full of crocodiles, especially ... when the water is warm, but one cannot help it, if only to show the natives that a white man will do what they dare not attempt'. Quoted in Harriet Ritvo, *The Animal Estate: The English and Other Creatures in the Victorian Age* (Cambridge, MA: Harvard University Press, 1987), p. 262. See also Alyse Simpson, *Red Dust of Kenya* (New York: Crowell, 1952), p. 228.
18 'Stocker case', *EAS* (10 March 1922), p. 5.
19 'A believer in education', letter to ed., *EAS* (2 Feb. 1924), p. 28; 'Climatic influence', *EAS* (20 Sept. 1924), p. 7; 'European education in Kenya', *EAS* (19 Nov. 1924), p. 7.
20 'Women in B.E.A.', *EAS* (14 Feb.1920), p. 16.
21 Louis Leakey, *White African: An Early Autobiography* (Cambridge, MA: Schenkman, 1966 [1937]), p. 190. Leakey enjoyed casting himself as an outsider among whites in Kenya, regularly commenting that he was more Gikuyu than European. Yet his paternalism would not have been that alien to other settlers. Note his use of 'boy'. Note his claims that after his time in England, 'loving [the Gikuyu] as I did, a part of me was exceedingly keen to go back and devote myself entirely to them and their needs'. *White African*, p. 161.
22 KNA: PC/Coast 1/10/117, Senior Commissioner Coast to CNC, 18 Apr. 1922.
23 KNA: PC/NZA 3/17/2, Dobbs to Moore, 22 Oct. 1927, and Superintendent of Police to Dobbs, 12 Jan. 1928.
24 Spectator, 'Stiffs and the stiff's paradise', *Critic* (18 Nov. 1922), p. 29.
25 'Evils of civilization', *EAS* (18 June 1910), p. 13. See also 'Poisonous literature', *EAS* (23 Feb. 1923), p. 5.
26 'Our Kenya letter', *EA* (19 Mar. 1925), p. 572.
27 'Checking an evil', *EAS* (29 May 1920), p. 22.
28 M. H. Hamilton, *Turn the Hour: A Tale of Life in Colonial Kenya* (Sussex: Book Guild, 1991), p. 66. See also Elspeth Huxley, *The Mottled Lizard* (New York: Penguin, 1981), p. 77; *Kenya: Its Industries, Trade, Sport and Climate* (London: Kenya Empire Exhibition Council, 1924), pp. 33–4. In describing a pet cat which turned feral in a matter of weeks, Alyse Simpson seems also to point out how easy it would be for a European to 'go native': 'The influence of thousands of generations of purring house-cats had been of no avail – she had "gone native"'. *The Land that Never Was* (Lincoln: University of Nebraska Press, 1985 [1937]), pp. 198–9.
29 MacGregor Ross, *Kenya from Within*, p. 168. In the index of the book, white prestige is placed in quotes.
30 MacGregor Ross, *Kenya from Within*, p. 120. An administrator in India explained that 'The sight of Europeans in the lowest depth of degradation brought on by drinking and profligacy must tend to degrade our race in the eyes of all who see them, and must go far to weaken our prestige amongst a nation avowedly ruled by the respect and fear in which they hold their conquerors'. Quoted in Kenneth Ballhatchet, *Race, Sex and Class under the Raj: Imperial Attitudes and Policies and Their Critics, 1793–1905* (New York: St Martin's, 1980), pp. 124–5.
31 Thus debates surrounding the Soldier Settlement Scheme repeatedly returned to the question of how much capital was necessary to prevent a farmer from becoming a 'poor white'. C. J. D. Duder, 'The Soldier Settlement Scheme of 1919 in Kenya' (Ph.D. diss., Aberdeen University, 1978), pp. 163, 183, 199, 300.

32 'Restriction of immigration', *TEA* (25 Aug. 1906), p. 4. See also Evelyn Brodhurst-Hill, *So This Is Kenya!* (London: Blackie, 1936), p. 2; 'Our Kenya letter', *EA* (30 Oct. 1924), p. 160. Other 'undesirables' included Bolshevist agitators sent to cause unrest among Africans. 'Police man hunt in Kenya', EAS (30 Aug. 1924), p. 2C.
33 KNA: PC/COAST 1/3/85, Waller, Principal Immigration Officer, to ADC Vanga, 10 July 1912.
34 'Now then ladies!', *Critic* (22 July 1922), p. 25. That year saw as many as 128 white men unemployed in Nairobi. Duder, 'The Soldier Settlement Scheme of 1919 in Kenya', p. 285.
35 'Occasional notes', *EAS* (26 Oct. 1912), p. 15; 'Charity organisation', *EAS* (4 Mar. 1922), p. 4; KNA: PC/COAST 1/1/367. Some vagrants found shelter at the Salvation Army Hostel in Nairobi. 'General Colville and his servant', *EAS* (4 Dec. 1924), p. 1. The directors of the hostel were even 'continually confronted with the demand for second-hand clothes'. Maud Peat, letter to ed., *EAS* (15 Dec. 1924), p. 5.
36 'The League of Mercy', *EAS* (7 Jan. 1928), p. 6.
37 'Vagrancy laws', EAS (9 Sept. 1922), p. 3; J. R. Gregory, *Under the Sun: A Memoir of Dr. R. W. Burkitt of Kenya* (Nairobi: self-published, 1952), p. 32; and the following files in the KNA: AP 1/108; AP 1/115; AP 1/547; AP 1/1105; PC/COAST 1/17/130; PC/COAST 2/3/3. Some down-on-their-luck Europeans came forward voluntarily for imprisonment and deportation. V. M. Newland, 'The romance of settlement', *Kenya Graphic* 1 (1922), p. 66. The *African Standard* condemned imprisonment for the indigent, preferring the Rhodesia model in which the poor were engaged in public works 'to earn enough to enable him to go away'. 'The retardation of East Africa', *AS* (7 Nov. 1903), p. 4. The Distressed British Subjects' Act allowed for the deportation to India of criminals or the indigent. W. Robert Foran, *The Kenya Police, 1887–1960* (London: Robert Hale, 1962), p. 21. For similar solutions elsewhere in the colonial world, see Mrinalini Sinha, *Colonial Masculinity: The 'Manly' Englishman and the 'Effeminate' Bengali* (Manchester: Manchester University Press, 1995), p. 49; Ann Laura Stoler, 'Rethinking colonial categories: European communities and the boundaries of rule', *Comparative Studies in Society and History* 31 (1989): 134–61.
38 'Vagrancy laws', *EAS* (9 Sept. 1922), p. 3.
39 KNA: PC/COAST 1/3/174, A.D.C. Mombasa to PC Coast, 13 July 1920, and Ag. PC Coast to Chief Secretary, 13 July 1920.
40 'The League of Mercy', *EAS* (23 Feb. 1924), p. 35.
41 'Native welfare', *EAS* (20 June 1923), p. 4. For a similar comment, 'Our capital', *Kenya Graphic* 2 (1923): 73–80, p. 78. By 1928 reports surfaced of over 150 unemployed Europeans in Nairobi alone, and the Convention and the *Standard* alike called for tightening immigration restrictions to keep out the poor and unemployable. 'Convention of Associations', *EAS* (7 May 1928), p. 5; 'Undesirable immigrants in Kenya', *EAS* (31 May 1928), p. 1; 'An immigration problem', *EAS* (31 May 1928), p. 8.
42 'An open letter', *Critic* (28 Oct. 1922), p. 16. Earlier, the editor had called for the elimination of imprisonment for vagrants, a point which the Nairobi Municipal Council supported. 'Prison is your home!', *Critic* (12 Aug. 1922), p. 19, and 'Prison is your home', *Critic* (2 Sept. 1922), p. 10.
43 'Lowering British prestige', *EAUM* (14 Nov. 1903), p. 4.
44 'Local notes', *EAUM* (28 Nov. 1903), p. 7.
45 KNA: PC/COAST 1/12/29, Complaint by Mary Morgan, Vagrant, Sept. 1905. The *Standard* later promoted the need for segregated jails. 'Nakuru notes', *EAS* (6 Feb. 1909), p. 17. See also 'Habitual jail birds', *EAUA* (15 Aug. 1903), p. 4.
46 KNA: PC/COAST 1/12/29, Remarks by visiting justice, 12 Sept. 1905.
47 This was because the 'prestige of the White man having of necessity to be upheld'. Simpson, *The Land that Never Was*, p. 139. See also Foran, *The Kenya Police*, p. 41. In this latter case, the alcoholic cheque-bouncer and noted horticulturalist Pelham-ffooks was also allowed to leave Fort Jesus during the day, unguarded, to tend to officials' gardens.

48 The following draws on KNA: PC/COAST 1/12/29, W. F. Sinclair to Donald Stewart, Feb. 28, 1905.
49 KNA: PC/COAST 1/12/29, Donald Stewart, minute to Senior Commissioner, Mombasa, 21 Feb. 1905. Sinclair's loss of temper may have been a factor as well, for self control was another measure of white superiority. See Chapter 5.
50 'Letters of credit – and debit!' *Critic* (24 Feb. 1923), p. 13. See also 'Remember the unemployed', *Critic* (3 Mar. 1923), p. 23.
51 'The European and African Trades Organisation', *KO* (28 Mar. 1923), p. 1; 'Doing my bit', letter to ed., *KO* (30 Mar. 1923), p. 8; 'European and African Trades Organisation', *KO* (16 May 1923), p. 3; 'E&ATO', *KO* (28 July 1923), pp. 4, 8; D. Goldworthy, *Tom Mboya: The Man Kenya Wanted to Forget* (Nairobi: Heinemann, 1982). The first listings of even partial membership I have discovered is in 'European & African Trades Organisation', *EAS* (30 Dec. 1924), p. 1, and 'Annual Report of the E. & A. T. O.', *EAS* (31 Dec. 1924), p. 5; Vice-presidents were Northrup McMillan and Kenneth Archer, with Col. R. B. Turner the Organizing Secretary. Other notables included Rev. and Mrs J. F. G. Orr, Mrs Monkton (the latter two both of EAWL), Capt. J. Coney, Hon. Conway Harvey, Hon. R. B. Cole, Capt. F. O. B. Wilson, MacLellan Wilson, S. Jacobs, and R. F. Mayer.
52 'The E. & A. T. O.', *EAS* (26 Apr. 1924), p. 13.
53 Letter to ed., *KO* (26 Apr. 1923), p. 6.
54 'Labour and wages', *KO* (20 Mar. 1923), p. 3.
55 Letter to ed., *KO* (14 June 1923), p. 4.
56 Hermann Giliomee, *The Afrikaaners: Biography of a People* (Charlottesville: University of Virginia Press, 2010), pp. 149–50, 194–6, 202–3. Rhodes was rather less critical of Afrikaners, if nothing else as a political ploy. Ibid., p. 240.
57 Quoted in Giliomee, *The Afrikaaners*, p. 189.
58 Quoted in Paula M. Krebs, *Gender, Race, and the Writing of Empire: Public Discourse and the Boer War* (Cambridge: Cambridge University Press, 1999), p. 75.
59 Krebs, *Gender, Race, and the Writing of Empire*, p. 75.
60 See also A. S. Mlambo, *White Immigration into Rhodesia* (Harare: University of Zimbabwe, 2002), pp. 53–9.
61 'Will he do it?' *Leader* (9 July 1904), p. 4.
62 Huxley, *Flame Trees of Thika*, pp. 49–50.
63 'The Boer trek', *Leader* (18 July 1908), p. 3.
64 'An old fallacy', *TEA* (20 Jan. 1906), p. 4.
65 Although one traveller found much to admire in Boers' antiquated ways, stuck as they were somewhere between savage Africans and modern Britons: 'We went our way with pleasant memories of grandsire, fathers and sons dwelling together on the family lands. Though we had jumped centuries since Mount Elgon [where they met Africans supposedly living in the stone age] we seemed not yet to have quite reached the present. The patriarchal household belong to an older day than ours. Older and sturdier and simpler.' Hermann Norden, *White and Black in East Africa: A Record of Travel and Observation in Two African Crown Colonies* (Boston: Small, Maynard, 1924), p. 149.
66 Huxley, *Flame Trees of Thika*, p. 177.
67 Ethel Younghusband, *Glimpses of East Africa and Zanzibar* (London: John Long, 1910), p. 179.
68 KNA: Uasin Gishu DAR 1913–14. Similarly, in 1912, the *Leader* recalled that 'the first British settlers looked somewhat askance at the apparent influx of the Afrikaner element, which to them spelt agricultural and intellectual stagnation and not progress'. 'C. J. Cloete', *Leader* (13 July 1912).
69 Quote from 'ESTE', in *Leader* (Sept. 1916), quoted in Brian M. Du Toit, *Boers in East Africa: Ethnicity and identity* (Westport, CT: Bergin and Garvey, 1998), p. 86. The problem of poor white Afrikaners had not improved by 1924, when Afrikaner preacher Loubser predicted that 'The poor white condition is approaching on horseback in East Africa, not on foot. In ten years' time this ugly monster is going to rear its head.' Quoted in Du Toit, *Boers in East Africa*, p. 106.

70 'The Boer trek', *Leader* (18 July 1908), p. 3.
71 Ewart Grogan, letter to ed., *The Times*, reprinted in *Leader* (8 Aug. 1908), p. 5
72 May Baldwin, *Kenya Kiddies: A Story of Settlers' Children in East Africa* (London: Lippincott, 1926).
73 'May Baldwin', in Sue Sims and Hilary Clare, *The Encyclopedia of Girls' School Stories* (Aldershot: Ashgate, 2000), pp. 47–50, quote from p. 49.
74 Baldwin, *Kenya Kiddies*, p. 65.
75 Baldwin, *Kenya Kiddies*, p. 66.
76 Baldwin, *Kenya Kiddies*, p. 283
77 And education was considered crucial for preventing the emergence of a poor white class. Michael Gordon Redly, 'The Politics of a Predicament: The White Community in Kenya, 1918–32' (Ph.D. diss., Cambridge University, 1976), pp. 184–7.
78 C. J. Cloete, for example, served on the Colonists' Association and was well respected among non-Afrikaners, settlers and administrators alike. Du Toit, *Boers of East Africa*, pp. 83, 102; KNA: Uasin Gishu DAR, 1912–13.
79 'C. J. Cloete', *Leader* (13 July 1912).
80 Brevet-Major W. Lloyd-Jones, *Havash!: Frontier Adventures in Kenya* (London: Arrowsmith, 1925), p. 46.
81 M. P. K. Sorrenson, *Origins of European Settlement in Kenya* (Oxford: Oxford University Press, 1968).
82 For a detailed history of the scheme, see Robert G. Weisbord, *African Zion: The Attempt to Establish a Jewish Colony in the East Africa Protectorate, 1903–1905* (Philadelphia, Jewish Publication Society of America, 1968); Mwangi wa Githumo, 'Controversy over Jewish ante-chamber in Kenya: British settlers' reaction to the proposed Jewish settlement project in Kenya, 1902', *Transafrican Journal of History* 22 (1993), 87–99.
83 'Planters and farmers', *AS* (5 Nov. 1903), p. 5.
84 Julius Carlebach, *The Jews of Nairobi* (Nairobi: Nairobi Hebrew Congress, 1962), p. 24; Somerset Playne (compiler), F. Holderness Gale (ed.), *East Africa (British): Its History, People, Commerce, Industries, and Resources* (London: Foreign and Colonial Compiling and Publishing, 1909), pp. 185–7; www.oldafricamagazine.com/blog/christine-nicholls%E2%80%99-blog-20-july-2013 (accessed 2 Jan. 2014). As best can be garnered from archival sources, Kenya Jews appear to have remained (publicly) silent about the 1903–4 Zionist programme, perhaps so as not to endanger the relatively welcoming reception they enjoyed. The commission sent out to examine the land met with at least one Jewish farmer. Eitan Bar-Yosef, 'Spying out the land: the Zionist expedition to East Africa, 1905', in Eitan Bar-Yosef and Nadia Valman (eds), *'The Jew' in Late-Victorian and Edwardian Culture: Between the East End and East Africa* (New York: Palgrave Macmillan, 2009).
85 A rumoured plan to settle some half-million Russian Jews in Australia sparked similar reaction: it was not Jews per se who were unwanted but Jews of this particular class. See J. Stratton, 'The color of Jews: Jews, race, and the white Australia policy', in Sander L. Gilman and Milton Shain (eds), *Jewries at the Frontier: Accommodation, Identity, Conflict* (Urbana: University of Illinois Press, 1999), pp. 320–1.
86 Elspeth Huxley, *White Man's Country: Lord Delamere and the Making of Kenya* (New York: Praeger, 1935), Vol. 1, p. 120.
87 Carlebach, *The Jews of Nairobi*, p. 24.
88 'To colonize East Africa', *AS* (5 Dec. 1903), p. 4; 'Men and matters', *AS* (28 May 1904), p. 7. See also Moreton Frewen, 'The dominion of palm and pine (notes on East Africa)', *The Monthly Review* 69 (1906): 43–73, esp. p. 51. Elspeth Huxley either agreed or simply repeated conventional wisdom of 1903. In her 1935 biography of Delamere, she wrote that 'Ghetto-bred Russian Jews, whatever their virtues, industry and misfortunes, were unlikely to command respect among, say, Masai warriors, or among the even less tractable Nandi, whom the King's African Rifles and Indian troops had failed to daunt and on whose country the Jewish settlement was apparently to impinge'. *White Man's Country*, Vol. 1, p. 121.

PRESTIGE, WHITENESS, AND THE STATE

89 'The threatened Jewish invasion', *AS* (12 Sept. 1903), p. 4. For further stereotypes from the pages of the *African Standard*, see 'Stranger', letter to the ed. (19 Nov. 1903), p. 4.
90 'The threatened Jewish invasion', *AS* (12 Sept. 1903), p. 4; Huxley, *White Man's Country*, Vol. 1, p. 121. In South Africa itself, many whites classed less well-off Jews with Indians, Chinese, and Africans. According to one report, Jews did nothing to elevate themselves in white eyes: 'Cape Town at the present time is full of those Polish Jew hawkers who live in a dirtier style than kafirs'. Quoted in Marcia Leveson, 'The enemy within: some South African Jewish writers', in Sander L. Gilman and Milton Shain (eds), *Jewries at the Frontier: Accommodation, Identity, Conflict* (Urbana: University of Illinois Press, 1999).
91 On the acceptance of Jews by other settlers, see 'A Resident', 'Nairobi and Kenya colony', *Scottish Geographical Magazine* 37 (1921): 99-103, esp. pp. 102-3.
92 For these processes, see Gavin Kitching, *Class and Economic Change in Kenya: The Making of an African Petite-Bourgeoisie* (New Haven: Yale University Press, 1980); Bruce Berman, *Control and Crisis in Colonial Kenya: The Dialectic of Domination* (London: James Currey, 1990); Bruce Berman and John Lonsdale, *Unhappy Valley: Conflict in Kenya and Africa* (Athens: Ohio University Press, 1992).
93 Berman, *Control and Crisis*, p. 204.
94 Berman, *Control and Crisis*, p. 205.
95 Capt. C. Haywood, *To the Mysterious Lorian Swamp: An Adventurous and Arduous Journey of Exploration through the Vast Waterless Tracts of Unknown Jubaland* (London: Seeley, 1927), p. 157.
96 The reverse was also true. The moral failings of an individual officer damaged the prestige of serikali. So too, however, did publicly rebuking a wayward officer. How could Africans – or anyone, truly – understand that a district officer was at once both the law (to be obeyed without question) but not above the law (liable to removal for his failures)? How could an administrator be both divine and fallible? Thus, as Berman explains, 'Neither the Provincial Administration nor any individual officer could ever admit to miscalculation or failure, even in reversing previous policy'. Berman, *Control and Crisis*, p. 206. For examples, see Richard St Barbe Baker, *Men of the Trees: In the Mahogany Forests of Kenya and Nigeria* (New York: L. MacVeagh, 1931), p. 49; Baker, *Africa Drums* (London: Travel Book Club, 1945), p. 78.
97 KNA: Kikuyu DAR, 1909-10. See also, for example, A. Hardinge to Ainsworth, 20 Mar. 1896, and Gov. Girouard, Memoranda for Provincial and District Commissioners, 10 May 1910, both in G. H. Mungeam, *Kenya: Select Historical Documents, 1884–1923* (Nairobi: East African Publishing House, 1978), pp. 77, 99–103. Chiefs, like white government officials, must not be corrected in front of their subjects for fear that their prestige be lessened. KNA: PC/NZA 3/32/2, DC South Kavirondo to Senior Commissioner, Nyanza, 5 June 1925.
98 KNA: PC/NZA 3/32/2, Assistant DC Rimmington to SC, Nyanza, 7 Oct. 1925.
99 Reading the words of virtually any settler provides examples of such thinking. For an extended litany, see 'Mr E. S. Grogan and the "Standard": an interview', *EAS* (25 Jan. 1908), p. 5.
100 'Coddling the native', *EAS* (11 Mar. 1914), p. 6. The Convention of Associations in 1925 issued a blanket condemnation of district commissioners as 'anti-white' and 'a menace to the prestige of the white man'. Quoted in McGregor Ross, *Kenya from Within*, p. 174.
101 Colonists' Association to Secretary of State, 23 Aug. 1905, in Mungeam, *Historical Documents*, p. 458. See also McGregor Ross, *Kenya from Within*, p. 99; 'The Colonists' Association', *EAS* (5 Jan. 1907), p. 9; 'Exodus' [writing from Zanzibar], letter to ed., *EAUM* (7 Mar. 1903), p. 3.
102 'Our police system', *EAS* (15 Nov. 1913), p. 25. See also Sorrenson, *Origins of European Settlement*, pp. 236–7; Lord Hindlip to Secretary of State, 2 Sept. 1905, quoted in Martin Wiener, *An Empire on Trial: Race, Murder, and Justice under British Rule, 1870–1935* (Cambridge: Cambridge University Press, 2009), p. 200;

'Nairobi Sessions', *TEA* (6 Oct. 1906), p. 3, C. A. Hindlip, *British East Africa: Past, Present, and Future* (London: Unwin, 1905), pp. 49–50; 'The police strike', *TEA* (12 Jan. 1907), p. 4. See also, for example, Carol Summers, *From Civilization to Segregation: Social Ideas and Social Control in Southern Rhodesia, 1890–1934* (Athens: Ohio University Press, 1994), p. 102. On white resistance to indigenous police arresting white men, see Edward P. Wolfers, *Race Relations and Colonial Rule in Papua New Guinea* (Sydney: Australia and New Zealand Book Company, 1975), p. 18.

103 'The theft case', *EAS* (15 Nov. 1922), p. 5. The abortive settler coup gained some strength on the basis of the belief that the state would not call out African troops to fight Europeans. The truth of this will never be known. One European subaltern later recalled that he would not have hesitated to order his African troops to fire on white rebels, who included his cousin. Earl of Lytton, *The Desert and the Green* (London: Macdonald, 1957), pp. 114–15. Read in the Colonial Office rejected the idea, however: 'I am satisfied that any use of the native troops in suppressing organised action on the part of the Europeans is unthinkable. It would be disastrous to the discipline of the troops; it would be fatal to British prestige throughout Africa; and it would mean that in the whole of the continent the life of a European would not be safe in any area of native population. Further, it may be taken as certain that such action would be bitterly condemned in Parliament.' 'Indians in Kenya', Cmd. 1922 (1923). Governor Bowring agreed. Duder, 'Soldier Settlement Scheme', p. 687. There was surprisingly little talk of the effect on prestige of the use of African troops during the East African campaign in the First World War. Settlers agitated for the Soldier Settlement Scheme as a way to bolster white prestige, damaged by the war, but Duder argues this was directed primarily to metropolitan audiences. Duder, 'Soldier Settlement Scheme', p. 157.

104 KNA: AG 1/489, Statement of Mzee bin Ali, 2 Feb. 1905, taken down by Ag Sub Commissioner Tate.

105 KNA: AG 1/489, MacLellan Wilson, Secretary, Colonists' Association of BEA, to Commissioner, 23 Jan. 1905.

106 This was true on roads as well as paths. Simpson, *Land that Never Was*, p. 197.

107 KNA: AG 1/489, Wilson to Commissioner, 23 Jan. 1905.

108 KNA: AG 1/489, Comment by Judge Barth, 8 Feb. 1905. See also 'Assaulted an askari', *EAS* (7 Oct. 1924), p. 5.

109 KNA: AG 1/489, R. W. Humphrey, Collector Fort Hall, to H. R. Tate, Ag Sub Commissioner, Kenya Province, 2 Feb. 1905, and Statement of Mr Elder and Mr Swift, taken by Tate, 2 Feb. 1905.

110 According to Finnie, Tate had agreed that black must step aside for white. If true, Tate none the less would not allow a government servant to be assaulted. KNA: AG 1/489, John J. Finnie to Mr Wilson, 17 Jan. 1905.

111 KNA: PC/COAST 1/17/79, Commissioner of Police, Nairobi to Hobley, PC Coast, 21 Feb. 1914, and reply, 26 Feb. 1914.

112 KNA: Machakos DAR, 1916–1917; Simpson, *Land that Never Was*, p. 177; Felix Oswald, *Alone in the Sleeping Sickness Country* (London: Kegan Paul, 1915), p. 152.

113 And, as South Kavirondo DC Campbell noted in regard to Chief Okoth, accused of not always respecting non-official whites, 'it should be remembered that [such individuals] are probably sometimes themselves difficult persons!' KNA: PC/NZA 3/32/2, DC Campbell to SC Nyanza, 6 Jan. 1926.

114 'A rumour', *Advertiser* (26 June 1908), p. 3.

115 'Coddling the native', *EAS* (11 Mar. 1914), p. 6.

116 'Control of natives', *EAS* (16 Feb. 1918), p. 11.

117 W. M. Hudson, letter to ed., *EAS* (15 May 1920), p. 2.

CHAPTER FOUR

Chivalry, immorality, and intimacy

It was difficult for settlers to describe African society without condemning African men for virtually enslaving their womenfolk. The image settlers drew was of African men daily drinking themselves into a stupor while their wives prepared their food, collected their water, retrieved their firewood, then toiled in the fields for hours in blistering sun.[1] African men protected their cattle from exhaustion, but treated their wives as beasts of burden.[2] One could easily find a 'strapping young man swinging a cane leading his women to market, bent and deformed beneath 80 lbs. loads of firewood and produce'.[3] Olive Grey awaited the day when 'chivalry and the tenderness begotten of Christian training' would reform African men.[4] 'Wife of a Settler' in 1931 explained the implications of mixed-up African gender relations: 'till the men of black or other coloured races admit their own women to equality of status with themselves, it is useless to preach equality with the white man. The position is too anomalous altogether.'[5]

This meant, in turn, that settlers had to be specially attuned to proper gender roles. According to prevailing bourgeois gender norms in Britain and elsewhere, men had a duty to defend their female dependants (mothers, sisters, wives, daughters). Men must protect women's bodies, their honour, their sensibilities. Even in Kenya, a white man's insult to a white woman would be answered with violence from her male protector. Insult, insolence, or bodily harm from an African man against a white woman had more disturbing implications. If no white man came to her defence, then all white men would be humiliated – they had not lived up to their self-proclaimed duties as men, and, in a racialized context, all white men must defend all white women. Moreover, an insulted white woman would be reduced to the level of an African woman, the only other being an African man could treat with disdain. Again, 'Wife of a Settler': 'How can the white woman be the equal of the black man if she is on the same level as the black man's chattel, his wife?'[6] No white woman could feel secure if, in the eyes of her houseboy, she were no better than his enslaved wives. Her prestige as a special being dissipated, she would be subject to greater and still greater indignities.

Just as a white vagrant or criminal injured white prestige, so too did public displays of white carnality and immorality. Granted, British men and women were in some serious debates over sexual morality and women's rights. In front of inquiring African eyes, however, these discussion must be muted, and whites should appear to be paragons of the Christian civilization that marked the boundary between white and black. Public scolds and film censors took it upon themselves to regulate public displays of white sexual immorality, just as they did displays of white criminality or revolution. Despite the image of the bed-hopping and wife-swapping 'Happy Valley' set, most settlers condemned such profligacy – at least that which might come to the attention of always-watching Africans. A bit of quiet adultery might go unremarked upon. At least within the race. Sex across the colour line caused more worries. White women should have only the most limited contact with African men's bodies, lest their reputation as semi-divine be sullied. Many white men, however, believed sex with African women to be something of a perk of empire. Others, particularly white women, argued such intimacy destroyed the boundaries that preserved white prestige. If African men knew that carnality could exist between the races, and saw their own women taken by white men, certainly they would decide that they could cross the colour line as well. The result: black peril.

Threats to settler women

With all the worry over African women weeding in the sun and toting loads, one might imagine that settler women were tucked away inside while their menfolk boldly strode across farm and town. Certainly, some white women in Nairobi and Mombasa passed their days exchanging visits and planning dinners with those who matched their class standing. Yet the settler project would have been far different without settler women. This is not to harken back to the old trope that the arrival of white women destroyed some imaginary golden era of friendly inter-racial relationship.[7] Nor is it a question of white women having 'civilized' the frontier by hanging curtains and redirecting white men's passions from the brothel or bush to the marital bed. Settler women in Kenya were deeply involved in farming, charity work, and politics. Labour, but not the kind that would degrade them to the level of African women.

White men admitted that settler women's labour was crucial for the perpetuation and growth of white civilization in Africa.[8] Especially in the earliest years of settlement, white farms had to be built from scratch. Women often found themselves taking on roles to which they had been unaccustomed back home: overseeing labour, for example, or dreaming up schemes to bring in more money.[9] In August 1914, immediately the news of war reached outlying areas, settler men in their hundreds rode into Nairobi to volunteer. Had they neighboured German Southwest Africa, or Kamerun, they would have been back at their farms within months. Kenya settlers had the poor fortune to face General Paul von Lettow-Vorbeck, who kept his enemies tied up until after the guns had fallen silent in France. Although some women returned to England for the duration, many others stayed and tried to keep their farms running.[10]

Pointing to their role as pioneers, settler women argued for a greater voice in public affairs. Their pleas could not be ignored. As early as 1916, four men running for Nairobi Municipal Council advocated for women's enfranchisement at the 'earliest possible opportunity, in view of the full share of the burden of settlement thrown upon the shoulders of the women in this pioneer land'.[11] The East African Women's League was formed in March 1917, with its first order of business promoting the franchise for white men as well as white women.[12] (Since the Legislative Council's establishment in 1907, the governor had appointed settler representatives.) The EAWL emphasized women's special abilities to address matters concerning women, the family, and the home.[13] The *Standard* further argued that their service during the war made theirs a compelling case.[14] Partly because the League did not follow the more vociferous methods of suffragists in Britain, there was relatively limited opposition to its founding.[15] On 10 July 1919, all Europeans – men and women – over the age of eighteen gained the right to elect members to the council.[16]

Women's role outside the home did not go without negative comment. During the debate over the franchise this was apparent. 'Disgusted' challenged the manhood of councillors who supported women's franchise:

> Why not let us have done with this humbug and let us be men, more of the type of our fathers and not pander to every silly whim of the women folk! It seems to me, if the time has arrived when men must submit their opinions to women, that women have progressed and men have retrogressed. I say again, let us be men and not listen to such silly fads and the women may think the more of us.[17]

In the postwar economic downturn, 'Observer' chastised men whose wives kept 'some deserving man out of a job'. Indeed, simply working outside the home threatened to bring white wives to the level of those African 'beasts of burden'. Such labour 'is lowering the status of their wives, and bringing them to the level of the Swahili women, who labour and support their lords and masters'.[18] Contributing to the advancement of the colony was one thing. Blurring distinctions between civilized and savage was another.

Yet filing papers in an office, raising brooders, and directing labour was a far different thing from toting firewood, being traded for cattle, and tugging at weeds. Few settlers, male or female, condemned all public roles for white women. Indeed, women's franchise in Kenya was more liberal than in Britain, where full suffrage was not achieved until 1928. The goal was not that white women should be restricted to the domestic sphere but that they should not be mistaken for African women.

Chivalry: white women and non-African men
White women created civilized homes and gardens – their carefully tended flowers marked off the home from the bush – but they also stood beside their menfolk surveying their fields and their herds and their maturing racial civilization. Yet white women remained women, emotionally sensitive, physically weak, their honour among their most prized possessions. It was men's duty – and this was a point agreed upon by most whites of both sexes – to protect women.[19] Elite settler men had gone through the homosocial, hypermasculine furnaces of public schools and the military, where they had been taught the virtue of chivalry. Gentlemen treated women properly, or, at least, women of their own class.[20] (Thus supporters of the British White Slave Traffic Act of 1912 used the language of chivalry – of men regulating other men to protect women – to assure its passage.)[21]

In Kenya, too, settlers believed that white men had the duty to protect white women, no matter the race of the offender – for more than once, white men acted unchivalrously. Alyse Simpson recalled that the only time she felt threatened on her Kenyan farm was when a drunken, pistol-wielding white man showed up to demand all her whisky, and her husband was not home. Simpson's husband never retaliated, perhaps satisfied by the buckshot their African cook sprayed across the intruder's buttocks and legs.[22] (Simpson portrayed her cook as a loyal servant protecting his memsahib, not as a man protecting a woman.) More often, should a white man feel that a white woman had been insulted, he answered with violence. Thus when a woman was chased off from her flower-picking by a white farm manager (although the owner had given her permission), her husband took out his kiboko. The manager received 500 rupees in compensation for his injuries.[23]

Similarly, several white men of the Kaimosi district came to blows on 11 January 1928, over injudicious language used in front of white women.[24] On that day, Lt. Col. L. I. C. Schwaiger, of Kaimosi Saw Mills, and his wife Marjorie were standing near their home. Mr K. Gough passed in an automobile, and Schwaiger called out that the chairs he had ordered were ready for delivery. As Schwaiger related in an affidavit, Gough yelled back: 'Balls to you!' A few minutes later, Gough's car came to a stop opposite Schwaiger's house. He stomped up and asked 'what [Gough] meant by using such expressions before my wife'. Schwaiger then noticed that there were three white women in the car, and so asked Gough to step out of the automobile to continue their discussion. Gough refused, Schwaiger slapped him, and received a slap in return.

Gough drove off and reported to friends that, although ill, he had been insulted and struck. Fifteen minutes later, Gough drove up with Mr Mathews and three men of the Jolly family – father, F. H. Jolly, and his sons, Reginald and Pat.[25] Schwaiger, now standing on his doorstep with several other men, ignored Gough's challenge to step forward. Reginald Jolly repeated the invitation: he yelled either 'Come out you bloody fucking bastard' or 'son of a bitch'. Schwaiger then demanded an apology from Jolly, as his wife had been inside but well within hearing of the cursing. Jolly refused, and they came to blows. Marjorie Schwaiger entered the fray, wielding a piece of wood. At that point (her husband claimed) Pat Jolly approached Marjorie 'with arms upraised [until] someone shouted "Do not hit a woman"'. After more violence and impolite language, the parties went their way.

The mêlée reveals that, whatever the need to keep intra-settler disputes indoors, the code of chivalry had to be upheld. Whatever Schwaiger may have thought of being insulted, what brought him to violence was the use of vile language in front of his wife. On the other side, one of the women in the automobile claimed that Schwaiger had first used 'bad language', at which point Gough said 'I am not going to stop and listen to such language I have ladies present we will have this out another day'. If Africans were watching, the fight would have done little for white prestige. But defending white women was more important.

The injudicious language of Gough and Jolly paled next to that of Sitaram Achariar, editor of *Democrat* in Mombasa. A firestorm from the coast to the lake greeted an editorial in the 25 January 1923 issue of the *Democrat* – in the midst of the Indian crisis. The insult was grave: Achariar questioned Englishwomen's morality, asserting that most 'had to procure an abortion before being finally led to the altar'.[26] The *Standard* would have dismissed Achariar's 'efforts to vilify the [male] British settler in Kenya', but involving white women was too much:

when he descends so low as to attempt to sully the fair fame of the white women of Kenya, by stating obvious lies, by suggesting immodest behaviour, or improper motives, then indeed, it is high time for the law to step in and lay its hand on the perpetrator of the infamy.[27]

The *Critic* agreed that the *Democrat* had crossed a line, and action was required.[28]

Under pressure, local officials carted off Achariar ('bareheaded and dishevelled') to the jail at Fort Jesus.[29] White Mombasans agreed to allow the law to take its course. As the *Standard* noted, 'The good [white] people of Mombasa are in general easy-going and averse to extreme measures'.[30] The *Critic* hinted that other reactions were equally plausible. In some countries, men 'whose women had been so grossly and cruelly insulted would have taken very summary steps indeed without waiting for the issue of a warrant for arrest. And we hardly think we should have condemned them.'[31] Accused of acting in a way likely to cause breach of the peace, Achariar was recommended for deportation by Judge Sheridan.[32] The *Critic* recommended St Helena or some other equally lonely island where the Indian could do no further harm.[33]

St Helena would have to wait, for the colony's law books knew nothing of white women's reputations. 'Easy-going' white Mombasans girded themselves for vigilantism upon discovering that the state had failed them. The governor and his council determined that the deportation ordinance 'was intended to deal with political offences of a more or less secret and dangerous nature; and the letters His Excellency has received from Mombasa all state that no political issue is involved'.[34] Of course, this was interpreting 'political' quite strictly. For the settlers, printed attacks on white morality certainly constituted a political issue. The good white people held a mass meeting, at which they proposed 'organised steps to prevent the recurrence of such an incident' and warned of the possibility of 'direct action'.[35] John Delvin, editor of the *Mombasa Times*, later swore (perhaps not entirely convincingly) that 'To the best of his recollection he had never used such words as "Achariar ought to be lynched"...[36]'. The governor did his best to defuse the situation – violence would do the colony no good, especially if directed at an Indian, especially given the larger crisis. By mid-March calm had begun to prevail. Achariar promised to eschew any further insults, and was rather anxiously looking to flee Mombasa.[37]

Chivalry: white women and African men

Insults to white women by Indians and fellow Europeans were disturbing to settlers, but it was African men who posed the gravest threat.

Whites tried to civilize the areas they claimed as their own – their farms, homes, neighbourhoods, business districts, and public conveyances. In those civilized realms, the naked body of an African was jarringly out of place. As early as 1903, the administrator John Ainsworth issued an order that all Africans in Nairobi 'be decently clothed'.[38] Enforcement, as Olive Grey discovered, did not apply outside the town. As her train pulled up to the station in Kibogori, she found 'the real, live, Noble Savage'. 'No clothing', she choked, 'not even the vaunted fig-leaf. There they stand at the side of your carriage until the horror creeps into your blood, gets into your brain and you feel like yelling out. Spare us such revolting sight.'[39] It took some time for African men in Nairobi to appreciate the need to cover themselves to European standards. In 1914, the Municipal Committee member Beaton felt compelled to revisit the issue for, as the *Standard* explained, 'The nakedness of the native in our towns has been an insult to modest women and a danger to impressionable children'.[40] Throughout the years, the display of African women's breasts posed a danger to no one.

White women also required special protection from what they found to be the malodorous bodies and unsanitary homes of non-whites. White women were said to be tender, easily offended by untoward bodily smells, and too precious to be subject to commingled, riotous crowds. Some might have amended this: it was true of proper bourgeois women. Hence a complaint about the lack of segregation for individuals welcoming the Duke of Connaught in 1906: 'That respectable European men and worse still – women should have been forced to elbow their way in among and be jostled by Indians and even Natives is one of these things over which even the most punctilious of mortals is apt to overstep the language of courtesy'.[41] Despite the reference to 'respectable' women, it had to be presumed that all white women in Kenya deserved protection. Thus when whites had to contend with Africans at the Post Office, the *Times of East Africa* thought it 'a disgrace that [white women] especially should be pushed about by greasy and odoriferous (!) natives'.[42]

When the question went from naked and malodorous bodies to insulting language, blood would be spilt. A female columnist in the *Standard* praised a white man who had defended a white woman's honour:

> A man told me that pushing his bicycle up a hill in Parklands [a Nairobi neighbourhood], he found himself behind a lady in a rickshaw, and upon her giving some orders to the men, one of them made a foul remark to her in his own language. [The remark was so foul] that the cyclist seized the man and thrashed him, but refused to tell the lady what he had said.

The author worried that the colony's lawmakers demonstrated less commitment to the protection of white women than did the cyclist. White men would not 'allow us to so protect ourselves [in what manner, she did not say] and yet will do but little to control the growing dangerous native'. As such, women's erstwhile protectors 'must not complain if out here we refuse to live again'.[43]

For an African man to strike a white woman? This was too much for whites to bear. In March, 1920, an African man took issue with a reprimand he received from his supervisor – a white woman – at a government school. He slapped her and called her a 'shenzi' (savage). When word leaked out of the incident, and the fact that the 'boy' had not been fired, settler reaction was severe. 'A European Woman' warned that 'Such incidents tend to inculcate disrespect for white women in the minds of the natives, and become a distinct menace to their safety'.[44] Robert Nixon charged that 'No [white] person capable of condoning an offence of the nature described should be allowed to remain in this country' while 'A Settler' wondered if whites were going 'to stand by with arms folded in the face of ... the outrageous insult to a white lady teacher by a nigger at the European School?' This was particularly a matter for white men: 'The very idea of a white lady being made to suffer such an indignity is enough to make the blood of any white man boil who has an inch of manhood in him'.[45] 'A White Woman' similarly deplored the assault

> which calls for immediate and drastic remedy. Otherwise, no white woman is safe in this country. She is already menaced by a grave danger – she always has been – but the gravity of her danger has been increased by this scandalous incident and its more than scandalous treatment. Can nothing be done even yet to put a stop to this kind of thing, once and for all? Are we to stand by and look on and say nothing, while one of our own sex is put to shame by a black brute?[46]

As it turns out, the offender had been 'thoroughly thrashed' by school officials and, finally, relieved of his position.[47] His supervisor could continue her employment, the insult – to the woman, and to white prestige – avenged.

Black peril

Editorials warning that settler women were in danger of being ravished by African men. Letters predicting that soon enough not a white woman would be safe in the colony. An illegal flogging of three Africans in a magistrate's courtyard for insulting white women. Repeated demands that rape be made a capital crime. Thinly veiled threats of 'strange fruit' hanging from Nairobi's lamp posts. Many have marvelled at these 'black peril' episodes – weeks or months during which settlers seemed to think and speak of nothing else but the alleged sexual threat African men posed to white women. They seem less strange once we understand the settler soul.

Kenya's periods of great alarm – particularly 1907, 1920–21, and 1926 – were exceptional only in their intensity. Between these periods, warnings of African-on-white rape constantly spilled from settlers' lips. Already by 1903, the *African Standard* warned that lack of effective policing in Mombasa had led to increased African crime, which would inevitably lead to inter-racial rape. Changes had to be made, or Kenya would become Rhodesia where (the *Standard* claimed) 'native outrages on white women and children are so frequent'.[48] A month later it was necessary to make the point yet more clear: 'From burglary (in Mombasa) and murder (in Nairobi) to the unnameable crimes perpetrated in Rhodesia is but a question of time'.[49] All manner of things could be linked to black peril. Insolence, especially towards white women, led to indecent remarks, led to black peril.[50] Educating

4.1 Russell Bowker

Africans was dangerous, as was treating any African as an equal.[51] In 1909, Sidney Fichat claimed that, owing to the failure of the government and the law to protect settlers, one could witness murder, robbery with violence, 'many cases of insolence to white women, and at least one case of attempted rape'.[52]

The stage was always set, then, the powder always dry. When an assault did take place the settlers found all their terrible prophecies come true. And, in fact, some African men did commit sexual violence against white women and children. One must be careful not to exaggerate their numbers – compared to intra-racial and white-on-black assaults, 'black peril' cases were extremely rare. But such assaults did occur, perhaps more commonly against white children. Not all were publicized. White parents were unlikely to file police reports, the Women's League stated in 1920, fearful of the mental anguish that inquiries and trials might cause to their daughters. Some families emigrated, hoping to bury horrific memories with their farms and gardens.[53] On a few occasions, however, police charged African men (or boys) with committing sexual violence against a white female. This is not to say that the accused were guilty, but evidence suggests that crimes had been committed – a mother finds sperm on the panties of her crying daughter, a woman raped beside a path by a man panting *Nataka kuma* (I want cunt), an elderly widow brutally beaten and raped in her home.

Vile acts, ones we surely all would condemn. To white settlers, the rape of one white woman by one African man was more than vile. It was a portent of a larger evil, it was the sign of the apocalypse captured in a single act. It was that sinking feeling in the pit of the stomach, as if one's vitality had drained away. The blank stare, the sudden deep breaths that do not seem the fill the lungs. The realization that life can never be as it was, that life will never again be good. The grievous assault or even the murder of a white man by an African could not shake settlers as deeply as could black peril. As the *Leader* put it in 1908, 'the mere suggestion of native outrages on white women moves the citizen more strongly than any other epidemic of crime'.[54] As much as they might sympathize with the victim, settlers dwelt more on what the rape meant for themselves, and for settlerdom as a whole.

Settlers saw themselves as doting parents, with settler women 'mama' to the childlike Africans. The black rapist was the boy grown into a man, ungrateful, violently acting out his Oedipus complex. If the victim were a white child in his charge, he had savagely repudiated the trust and beneficence of her parents, of his 'parents'. Settlers humiliated Africans as a tool of dominance. The black rapist humiliated his victim by treating her as a body, a target for his urges, a thing to be used and discarded. He degraded the white woman, put her at the level of the black woman. He ended the innocence of the white child, he prematurely sexualized her, he made her the equal of African girl-brides. He humiliated his victim's male protectors by showing European chivalry to be no match for his brawn. All those cuffs on the head, all those stripes with the kiboko, all those demonstrations of white dominance, the black rapist answered with violence against the one who was most delicate, the one who was to be protected. The white body – the one he must not touch, must not see unclothed, must not offend with his smells – the black rapist brutalized. The rapist was a being who would no longer be dominated. His act would inspire other Africans to rise from their knees and stare straight into those blue eyes. In those eyes, Africans would see fear. The rape of a white woman or girl by a black man sounded the death knell of the settler soul.[55]

Perhaps the most telling explanation of the meaning of black peril came from the pen of an aggrieved father. In November, 1911, an African had assaulted a white girl on a farm just outside Nairobi. The *Standard* jumped on the story, reporting that the girl had suffered serious injuries. The editor placed the assault in a narrative of other rapes and of rising insolence. Similar cases from 1908 and 1909 had ended in comparatively light sentences, the article went, emboldening African men.[56] Little else might have come of the incident had not the girl's father, J. Kerslake Thomas, gone public. On 18 November, the *Leader* published a long letter in which Thomas described the psychological and physical injuries his five-year-old daughter had suffered. Jaguna wa Kamau, his ostrich herd about thirty-five years old, had, according to the girl, held her down and covered her mouth. Jaguna lifted her skirt even as she continued to struggle, leaving several scratches on her legs. A call from the 'houseboy' stopped Jaguna from going any further. He threatened to kill her should she tell anyone of the assault. When he first learned of the assault from his wife, Thomas – an enraged and chivalrous man – resolved to shoot Jaguna. His wife had prudently hidden his rifle. Instead, Jaguna was arrested and the girl went under medical care.

Thomas came forward, he explained, both to ensure justice was served in this case and to alert other whites to the peril that faced them. In his letter, Thomas laid out precisely how African ingratitude, government laxity and ignorance of 'the native', the failure of the law, restrictions on violence, and the need for chivalry, all came together:

> I am one of the oldest settlers here and have with my wife and children endeavoured to develop this country as much as any one man could do by roughing it in the foreground for the past eight years. The natives have

received thousands of pounds in wages and food from me, and *where are we?* They in return steal our cattle and sheep, kill our ostriches and stock, and are encouraged to do so, being cuddled and patted on the back by the officials. So now there is no reason why they should not advance further under the smiling protection of the Barak [the blessed one, i.e. government official] and rape our children and wives. The Baraka will see they are not hurt, and the Shamba Bwana dare not shoot or piga [hit] them with the kiboko. I do assure you though that it was no guilt of mine that this brute was not shot, and God help him if his sentence allows him to come out while I am alive.

I call on every man that has a wife and children to protect, to protest against the official way of dealing with the native. We know the native better than they, we are the ones hear [sic] that have to handle them, and we have the commonsense to know how to do it. All we hear is the country can't afford the proposition. Are we to sacrifice our more-than-lives on this low-down excuse.[57]

The *Leader* and Thomas both demanded that rape immediately be elevated to a capital crime.[58] Within the week, Governor Percy Girouard met with a delegation of 'parents of children of the Nairobi district' and the Convention of Associations. The governor assured them that he was giving the issue his considered attention.[59] But so long as the settler soul existed, the threat of black peril never dissipated.

Dangerous intimacies

Whites in Kenya, and across the empire, spent many hours thinking about their bodies. They gloried in the bracing air of the highlands, but feared the allegedly debilitating effects of the equatorial sun. They planned on tutoring their Africans for centuries, but worried that third-generation white Kenyans would be sterile degenerates. Settlers also reflected on whom their bodies could come into contact with, and for what reasons. Some touching of different coloured skin was permissible, even celebrated – such as medical care. Some other types of touching, ones that suggested equality, were to be deplored. The *Leader* worried over American missionaries who were known to 'hail a native, educated or otherwise, with a shake of the hand as a sign of equality and good-fellowship, even have him eat at the same table, this with missionaries of both sexes'. The paper dared not believe reports of missionaries kissing African 'women and babies' when meeting at the railway station.[60]

Such tenderness was worrisome enough. Other kinds of intimacy, and immorality, compounded the problem. White vagrants hurt white prestige; so too white criminals and those 'gone native'; so too whites who lacked sexual self-control. Settlers preached white civilisation and superiority, they condemned African men for their failure to treat their women with care and consideration. Yet whites ignored their wedding vows, film houses showed lascivious white women, and white men sought intimacy with African females. Surely Africans could not esteem whites who brazenly ignored their own moral codes. Surely Africans would struggle to show deference to sexually degenerate Europeans. White sexual immorality emboldened Africans, and from that confidence was born sexual danger.

White sexual impropriety

'Back home', Britons were titillated by stories of bed-hopping settlers, men and women marrying, taking lovers, divorcing, and starting the whole process over again with new partners. The contemporary joking query: Are you married, or do you live in Kenya? Fuelled by alcohol and narcotics, the 'Happy Valley' crowd lived blissful days and nights of sex, safaris, and servants. Or at least that was the colony's reputation. Granted, married couples seeking to re-establish trust after adulterous affairs would have done well to avoid Kenya. The sexual escapades of settlers have been well attested by celebratory biographies of Beryl Markham, Denys Finch Hatton, Bror and Karen Blixen, and the rest. The love triangle between the owners-operators of the *Standard* in the 1910s was an open secret, while C. T. Todd recalled being greeted by his friend's wife clad only in her pyjama bottoms, embarrassing no one but Todd.[61] Long before emerging as a settler politician, a young Michael Blundell fell in love with Flora Russell. 'Tis a pity', he confided in his diary, 'she's already married ... but after all, that does not apparently matter in Kenya'.[62] If he did follow up on his yearning for Dr Russell's wife, it certainly did little to harm his public reputation.

Undoubtedly, however, the majority of settlers saw Kenya as more of a hunter's than a lothario's paradise. Many looked down on the Happy Valley smart set.[63] It was a question not of prudery but of prestige. Promiscuity and pills set a bad example for Africans. Lord Francis Scott thought Idina Gordon 'behaves more like a barmaid than a lady'.[64] What would be more likely to lower white women's prestige? The government in 1928 tried to keep out Alice de Janze and Raymond de Trafford, lately reunited after her attempt to kill him, and then herself, on a French train rather than surrender his love.[65] London refused to consider that immorality necessarily marked an immigrant as 'undesirable', although the governor's wife, Lady Grigg, finally prevailed.[66]

Two years later, Mabel Murray petitioned the EAWL to find a means of denying re-entry to the newly remarried Earl of Errol, lord of Happy Valley: 'The "Happy Valley" or "Hot Stuff Corner," as the district of

Gilgil in which the Errols and other of their kidney lived was called, was a disgrace to any country, and the behaviour of the residents was not of a kind to add to the prestige of the white man, or to cause the native to have any respect for white women, rather the reverse'.[67] Alyse Turner informed the governor's private secretary that the League regularly received settler women's complaints of blatant and dangerous immorality in Kenya; Errol's was a 'particularly serious matter'.[68] Given the Colonial Office's inability to understand the consequences of white high life in an African context, the government could do nothing.[69]

Better than the Colonial Office, newspaperman Robertson understood the need to keep settlers to a high moral standard. In the *Critic* he served as the public scold, shaming whites into keeping the public arena clear of romantic impropriety. Among the things the paper 'wanted to know' on 5 August 1922:

> The name of the gay old party who always leers at respectable married ladies in the streets of Nairobi.
> ...
> What the gay young blood said when he was found climbing out of the bedroom window.[70]

And on 9 September:

> Why the married lady and the married gentleman always go off together for a motor joy ride on Sunday afternoon.
> And if it is because the married lady and the married gentleman (who are married respectively to another gentleman and another lady) know that this particular day is 'all clear'.
> ...
> If the 'wrecker of homes' is still up to his old games.
> And if his latest escapade has sickened even his hardened satellites and admirers.[71]

And on 7 October:

> If the gentleman with the large family who winked at the pretty lady in the rickshaw will do so again.[72]

In a series of poorly written 'Nutshell novels', the *Critic* condemned colonial 'types', such as the young man who dances with other men's dates, sleeps with other men's wives, drinks too much, evades his debts, and ignores his doting mother 'back home'.[73] It shamed the woman who marries a man for his title and, once in Kenya, drops him to spend her time with a string of lovers.[74]

The *Critic* knew its audience, a gossipy bunch. Undoubtedly, readers wiled away the hours trying to identify the 'gay young blood' and the 'wrecker of homes', and speculating if characters in the 'Nutshell Novels' were not based on actual settlers. But Robertson had more in mind than titillation and sales. Kenya newspapers were nothing if not dedicated to shaping the colony's society and political future. Sexual impropriety harmed white society. Africans could hardly be expected to respect white people who lustily jettisoned the Christian morality upon which western civilization was based.

Images of immorality

Settlers' improprieties were bad enough when carried out behind closed doors, worse when performed in Nairobi streets. Perhaps worse still was for white immorality to be reported in the papers, where literate Africans could learn dark secrets. In 1920, a lawyer asked that a divorce case be held *in camera* to prevent it being reported in the press, an argument 'solely made because of the mixed population in the Colony'. The *Standard* replied that they had no desire to 'dish up, unless it serves a useful purpose, sordid details that may tend to lower the European's prestige in the eyes of the Asiatic and the native'. At the same time, it was essential to alert whites about the immoral ones in their midst who 'lay themselves open to ostracism' – that is, to punish those who lowered white prestige.[75] Given the rather lax morality of the owners of the *Standard*, one might question this dedication to policing white behaviour. But in Kenya, the argument had merit.[76]

An article, in English, with relatively dispassionate and circumspect language, might reach a few literate Africans. Immorality in the cinema was less abstract, and was intelligible regardless of the viewer's linguistic abilities. And thus after the franchise, the EAWL's next order of business was censorship.[77] While censors in Britain sought to protect the morality of children and the lower classes,[78] Kenyan settlers wished to protect white prestige. Films which lowered white women's prestige were particularly unnerving. 'C.A.S.' complained of one picture he saw in February 1917. 'The film', he reported, 'depicted a white woman being maltreated by natives, which, judging by the exclamations in the gallery, greatly pleased the coloured audience. There is no need to dilate on the mischief this type of film might cause.'[79] When the EAWL took up the issue, Robert Nixon cheered them on:

> I am most emphatically of opinion that natives should not be allowed to see films which tend to cheapen their opinions of white women, and therefore they should not be permitted to attend the screening of films intended for Europeans. Let the natives see films by all means but see to it that they are educational and fun pictures only. If the present state of affairs is allowed to continue only harm can result, and very serious harm I think.[80]

Early on, film censorship was a haphazard affair, with a police officer (sometimes acting on advice of the Women's League) determining whether a film should be screened in the colony.[81] Guidelines lacked specificity, but any film 'depicting in any appreciable extent the victory of black over white, the nude or lewd is strictly censored, curtailed or cut altogether'. (Local satirists Davis and Robertson sent up such thinking: a fictional letter from 'A Purist' complained that some Africans had dared laughed at a white man – Charlie Chaplin.)[82]

In part as a result of agitation by the Women's League, in 1922 the Legislative Council took up the issue. None the less, despite the importance of film censorship – none doubted it, including cinema owners[83] – the Legislative Council did not manage to take further steps until 1927. A select committee concluded that censorship must continue, lest Africans come 'to entirely erroneous conclusions from the picture shown and may be unduly influenced by the false conclusions so obtained'.[84] Conway Harvey, coffee planter and member of the Council, warned of the effect of Africans viewing a film on the French Revolution, or another that had been advertised as 'a thrilling story of the debauchery of King James I court'. 'The prestige of the white man', he argued, 'must inevitably suffer from the exhibition to natives of ... men rioting with women in night clubs and various phases of domestic infidelity.'[85] The 1929 Committee on Film Censorship explicitly recommended the barring of any film which 'is likely in a wide sense to bring white women into disrepute'.[86]

Throughout discussions over film censorship, the Women's League took a leading role, and men rarely disputed that at least one woman should sit on a censorship board.[87] Alisa Turner, president of the EAWL, insisted that white women's input was essential on the censorship of films, for 'the European woman's point of view is one that needs to be kept constantly in mind'. She suggested that any woman on the board should be either employed by the government or compensated for her time. Otherwise, she warned, 'it will be extremely difficult to obtain the services of any *suitable* woman who would be able and willing to attend meetings' several times a week.[88] The need to find 'suitable' white women to identify films unsuitable for Africans points to that key fissure among settlers: not all whites kept to civilized standards as they should.

Inter-racial intimacy

Among the most intimate types of physical contact, of course, is sexual intercourse. More than a few white men took African women to bed. The prevailing sexual double standard in Britain and Kenya meant that men often suffered no real repercussions for adultery. Since rarely were tender emotions involved, the sex might be dismissed as nothing more than satiation of a carnal need. Not all whites were so sanguine. If prestige did not permit a white man to share a railway car with a black man, then surely it did not permit him to share a bed with a black woman. Africans discovering that white men were carnal and bestial was as bad as them discovering a white man imprisoned. Worse was sexual intimacy between a white woman and a non-white man. Despite some loosening of sexual restrictions in the 1920s, the language of sex still suggested a battle: a man's lovers were his conquests, while a woman surrendered her chastity to her husband. Thus even consensual sex between a white woman and an African or Indian man suggested an inversion of the racial hierarchy.[89] No African could consider a white woman to be a higher being if she submitted to the carnal desires of a mere mortal.

Many white men in Kenya had no interest in limiting their sexual freedom. Men of all races helped African prostitutes in Nairobi prosper.[90] Alfred Anderson, sometime editor of the *East African Standard*, took regular trips to Thika to buy timber, which gave him opportunities to have sex with Somali women in a hotel (while his son awaited him in the lobby).[91] Llewelyn Powys saw sex with African girls ('great Gilgil trots' or prostitutes) on his brother's farm as among the few benefits of his labour.[92] When in 1924 the Legislative Council took up a bill on marriage and divorce for whites, Captain J. E. Coney balked. He spoke sympathetically of the man forced

> to go for long periods into the country, out of contact with civilization, right out into the 'blue'. I have no great opinion of the morals of any man and know perfectly well that we are all human. I do realise that, and I think therefore it is a very great hardship if that man, having made a mistake because perhaps his wife would not or could not come out to him in this country, that that mistake should give her the chance to break up a home.[93]

The *Standard* chastised Coney (who, they pointed out, was a bachelor) for favouring inequality against women, and the bill was passed into law.[94] Nevertheless, many white men had made, and continued to make, 'mistakes'.

While whites in other times and places often portrayed black women as hypersexualized, white stereotypes of African women in Kenya focused more on their exploitation by African men. Rather than a temptress of loose morals, the African woman in Kenya was a slave sold off as a girl to some toothless old man, the rest of her life a monotony of childrearing and field work. The narrative of asexual African women traded among men in fact provided white men with an ideological cover for their own sexually exploitative acts. If African women expected, indeed, accepted, being sold off for sex and labour, then why should white men hesitate to engage in similar practices? If chiefs sometimes offered women to warm the beds of passing white men, who were they to reject local custom?[95]

Not all whites excused the sexual escapades of administrators and their settler brothers.[96] Some administrators overlooked the amorality of their fellows, but others insisted that they must lead by example and keep to a higher morality.[97] Prestige, again. The *Critic* wondered about

> The names of certain European young men about town who frequent certain houses of ill repute in the ... River Road area.
> And if a sense of self-respect (apart from the prestige of the White Man) should not deter them from so doing.[98]

If white men demanded urban segregation, then sharing a bed should be unthinkable. If white men shrunk from rubbing shoulders with Africans at the Post Office, then unclothed intimacy should be revolting. In her fiction based on time spent as a Kenya settler, Florence Riddell conjured up such emotions in her male heroes. Coming upon another white man sharing a room with an African woman, 'a feeling of nausea and utter disgust flooded David's soul, and his manhood revolted at the degradation so palpably displayed in all its bestiality'.[99] To indulge in inter-racial sex meant giving in to one's base instincts – to show oneself to be no better than the Africans one was supposed to civilize. Inter-racial sex, like being a drunkard or vagrant, lowered the prestige of *all* whites. Thus M. H. Hamilton recalled that 'No white women would marry a man who, even if it was only a rumour, had lived with a black woman. He, it was considered, was letting the side down.'[100]

Evidence of white women engaging in sex with African men is much harder to come by. Indeed, it is virtually absent from the records for the early decades of colonial rule. An unusual case involved sex between a white woman and Indians. On 20 January 1911, Colonial Secretary Hollis prepared a report for the Secretary of State for the Colonies about a Swedish woman in Mombasa. Hollis termed her a prostitute, and the Colonial Office opened a file titled 'Prostitution by White Women'. As Hollis pointed out, she had committed no crime. None the less, he wrote, 'you will realise that she is lowering the prestige of Europeans in the eyes of the natives'.[101] What could more damage white prestige, especially white women's prestige, than to see a white woman sharing a bed with multiple non-white men? Godlike, indeed.

If the Swedish woman (her name was never mentioned) had not broken a law, then the legal code itself was in need of repair. Hollis asked the Colonial Office to approve a law along the lines of the 1903

Transvaal ordinance which made 'it an offence for a white woman to permit a native to have unlawful carnal connection with her, the punishment for such an offence being Five years hard labour for the woman and Six years hard labour for the native'.[102] Such a law would 'prove a most salutary warning' against any attempt on the part of a white woman to bring into contempt her fellows'.[103] Officials in London expressed mixed feelings. Read, a long-time official in the Colonial Office, minuted that 'promiscuous intercourse to a community like that of the E.A.P. might have most drastrous [disastrous] results and I think that we ought to do what we can to prevent it'. The Secretary of State supported 'the view expressed by Mr Hollis that such practices must be attended by serious consequences, and that it is important that they should be prevented'.[104]

Yet the Colonial Office was sensitive to blatantly racial legislation. Despite the obvious racial thinking that attended colonialism, London hesitated to approve laws that too obviously drew distinctions between races. The fact that the powerful India Office defended the Indian diaspora – and it was Indians, not Africans, who were the non-whites involved – was not forgotten. Officials thus recommended a law that would deport white prostitutes, overlooking Hollis's admission that the Swedish woman was not, in fact, a prostitute – she had only been cohabitating with a series of Indian men. Governor Girouard sheepishly pointed out that such a law would not solve the problem at hand. He reiterated the need for the criminalization of sex between white women and non-white men.[105] The Colonial Office remained unpersuaded, but the 'Swedish prostitute' seems to have disappeared. The potential for white prestige to be damaged by similarly immoral women remained.

A Swedish prostitute active in early 1911, an assault on young Kerslake in November 1911. In 1912, Nairobi asked the Colonial Office for advice on a proposed ordinance 'to amend the Criminal Law in relation to Rape and other Sexual Offences'. The Colonial Office demurred from allowing the death penalty to be attached to rape, but sentences were increased.[106] The 'other' sexual offences? 'Sex between a white woman and a native.' Apparently because of the 'black peril' threat that followed the assault on the Kerslake girl, the Colonial Office now agreed to criminalizing inter-racial sex – although white men, and their propensity for 'making mistakes', remained immune.[107] The law was either unnecessary or utterly intimidating, for it was rarely used.[108]

Immorality, bad mothers, and black peril

White men having sex with African women lowered white prestige. More worryingly, some white women argued, it served as an invitation to African men to rape settler women.[109] Edith Cecil-Porch was convinced of this. Born Edith Money in India, in 1882 she married Fred Maturin, an Australian serving the imperial army in the subcontinent. By 1902 they had separated, and the next year she joined her enlisted son in South Africa. She briefly worked as a journalist, but spent more time exploring the possibilities of communal living with other unattached whites, reflecting on the inanity of wedding vows, going off on long safaris, and speculating on how one might speak with the dead through séance. She cohabitated with a Mr Cecil-Porch prior to her 1911 divorce from Maturin.[110] By 1914 she was in East Africa. An unusual woman in some ways, but in others entirely conventional. In an article for the *Standard*, she explained why intimacy across the colour line endangered white women.

> Another terrible cause of trouble to women in the colonies is the degradation of the whole white race in the eyes of natives by the actions of men themselves. Between the white and the black race a great gulf is fixed. He who lays a plank across this gulf, and himself crosses it, leaves the plank then for the black man to cross in turn. Why should the black man respect your women when he finds that you do not respect and hold sacred his?[111]

White men caused black peril: 'At your door, men, lies the tragedy of outraged white women – every one of them!'

Cecil-Porch was not alone. It was more than 'letting the side down' that worried M. H. Hamilton. White men cohabitating with African women was deplored, 'diminishing as [settler women] felt it did, the white man in African eyes, and making white women more vulnerable to assaults by black men'.[112] Grace Orr, wife of the Director of Education and President of the Women's League, similarly accused white men of putting white women in danger. If whites desired female African domestic workers who were 'wholesome, chaste, clean of body and mind' then African women must be treated properly: 'to the men of my own race I feel compelled to say "Hands off the black woman"'. To threaten African men with annihilation should they touch a white woman rang hollow coming from 'so-called white men' who sexually exploited Africans. 'Example', Orr wrote, 'is always stronger than precept'.[113]

White women too carried a heavy responsibility to act properly, to keep up white prestige. Vagrancy, criminality, and the like were of course bad form, and sex with a non-white should have been inconceivable. White women had also to comport themselves properly around their male African servants. Here was the difficulty of paternalism. As much as whites called African men 'boys', as much as they thought of Africans as their children, the domestic servant nevertheless remained physiologically a man. Whites might be tempted not to see a servant, to treat him as simply a labour-saving device. But he remained a man with eyes and ears, thoughts and desires. White women might praise their ayahs (male and female) for their goodness in performing the boring, routine work of caring for white children. Yet they remained humans capable of all kinds of evil. The home – which should have been the freest of spaces, the domestic idyll where whites could be themselves – was for women the most fraught with potential danger.

Jane Elliot, married to an interwar administrator, had little good to say about white women who did not act as they should. Recalling the colonial days during an interview in the 1990s,

> My husband's point of view was that the white women, and there weren't all that many of them, who did get themselves raped were asking for it. Some of the women used to walk about in the house when their servants were doing the cleaning, washing, or cooking, or whatever, dressed in a nightie or pair of shorts, or a bath towel half draped around them, or even just in their skin. Those were the sort of people who got raped. It wasn't fair on the African to behave like that.[114]

It is perhaps also worth noting that Elliot was the daughter of Ewart Grogan.

At the conclusion of the 1921 black peril, some white women were made to shoulder blame for sexual assaults on children. The courts had recently heard several cases of 'houseboys' who had assaulted young white girls. As it turned out, these 'boys' were, in fact, boys, all aged between ten and fifteen years. According to the official Report of the Special Committee on Sexual Assaults of Natives upon Europeans, this was the age 'at which sexual instincts are beginning to develop'. Could one really condemn young men, the implication went, for exploring their sexuality with whoever was closest at hand? The men on the committee may have empathized with a young man who, brimming with new sexual curiosity and overwhelming urges, failed to control his baser instincts when opportunity presented itself.

If the African youth could not be wholly blamed, who else bore responsibility? Mothers. Sexually amoral whites, low-class whites, whites who failed to comport themselves properly – lax white mothers should be added to these groups who threatened white society. Thus the committee noted that in two recent court cases 'the learned Judge expressed the opinion that there had been grave negligence on the part of the parents concerned in leaving their female children in the sole charge of *totos* little older than themselves'.[115] Somewhat chagrined, the *Standard* admitted that given the evidence the commission had to conclude that no peril was at hand. Like the committee, the paper charged that the laxness of white women in watching their children and allowing African servants too much familiarity was a major factor behind whatever inter-racial assaults had occurred.[116] 'It must be remembered at all times', it warned, 'that a native is human, possessed of the ordinary instincts and passions, and should be treated accordingly'. White women who did not properly mother their white children were placing them, and by extension all white women and children, at risk.[117]

The Women's League too argued that white women – *some* white women – must share the blame for assaults on white children. In a July 1920 'Appeal' to white women, the League urged people to step forward to give evidence to the Committee, but also offered advice on how to protect children:

> Unfortunately it has been the deplorable custom for newcomers here to believe that the natives are merely some kind of irresponsible animal, with neither guilt nor guile, neither thought nor feeling, whereas to the contrary they are full of cunning, and possessed with most unhealthy passions. Through ignorance, white women, even when half dressed, have been known to allow these savages to enter their bedrooms and even to bath and dress their baby girls as if the natives had no more thought nor feeling than a machine. It is not to be wondered at then that such familiarities led first to lack of respect, and later by easy stages to the horrors which have been occupying our Law Courts lately.[118]

Their advice: find a reliable ayah, and 'see yourself that the natives respect you as they should'. Demeanour and deference would prevent black peril.

Hildegard Hinde, an administrator's wife, also blamed whites – primarily white women – for black peril. Sidney Langford Hinde, a Canadian medical doctor, had been sent by the Foreign Office in 1895 with a brief to deal with Maasai affairs, and took up a position at Machakos in 1896. Three years later he returned from a leave in Britain with his English wife, the former Hildegard Beatrice Ginsburg. At a time when officials in London and Mombasa discouraged state employees from bringing their wives to the Protectorate, she was certainly one of a very few white women in the country.[119]

In 1921, after the black peril had receded, Hildegarde Hinde wrote an article in *The Empire Review*.[120] In the earliest days of British East Africa, she reported, white women were so rare, they differed so greatly from Africans and from white men, that Africans believed them to be 'a special creation: they were looked on as something infinitely higher and more remote than white men'. Just as one could not desire or even imagine raping an angel, 'it was entirely beyond [African men's] physical desires [and their] mental imaginings' to assault a white woman: 'neither their minds nor their bodies could have evolved such ideas'. This situation would continue 'as long as the white women and their men-folk kept the standard on the high levels.' Indeed, African men proved to be good men and good retainers: they not only did not assault white women but protected them. The height of prestige.

Unfortunately, Hinde wrote, things had not progressed well. White women seemed to have special antipathy toward 'coloured people' and failed to learn local languages that could encourage a 'sound relationship' between the races. White men encouraged this distance between their wives and Africans – African women especially, for fomenting relationships between their current wives and their former lovers was nothing white men wished to do. Thus African *men* entered white homes as domestic servants. In this way white women's status as a 'special creation' was proved false. The white woman would 'call the boy into her bedroom to fasten her dress', and the garments worn on the equator tend toward 'scantiness'. Mothers too often turned their children over to African ayahs, which was 'a fatal mistake'. Women failed to remember that their 'boys' were not boys at all.

Things had only got worse, Hinde continued, with the introduction of bad whites as masters and ignorant Africans as servants. The 'recent influx of Europeans' – presumably of low class or bad character – tended to militate against the 'high standards and straight dealings of the old days'. The result: 'lowered' prestige. Swahili servants – 'faithful, efficient and honest' – had been replaced by upcountry, untrained, and easily impressionable Africans. After a couple of 'bad masters' such an African was ruined. And thus any lowering of white prestige, any tendency of African men no longer to see white women as a higher being, must be largely the fault of whites.

In a single, extraordinary paragraph, Hinde lays out a charge against settler women:

> The lack of privacy in the lives of their employers, the acts the natives not infrequently witness, the fact that they themselves are brought into close contact with the physical aspect of white women, and the further fact that these women are often careless of the proprieties of life, have had a most disastrous effect on the characters and morals of the native servants. It is no excuse for woman to say she regards her servant as a piece of wood, and doing this to call him into her disordered bed-room when she herself is practically nude. The question is not how she regards him, but how he regards her, and there is much to be said in extenuation for the boy who, having been invited by his mistress to attend her in such circumstances, loses his bearings and his head. [Cases of African males abusing white

children or attempting to rape white women] must be regarded as the outcome of the conduct and the attitude of the Europeans themselves, for had more decorum been observed on the part of white women, they would have been in no danger of physical assault from the natives. They have themselves lowered their standard – the native mind is incapable of placing any other construction on their actions than that which his eyes and senses show him. Control cannot be demanded of him beyond a certain point; he is very much a human being, and all animal. Even so, white women and children would have been quite safe in his proximity had the former not failed in the high task it was theirs to fulfil.

Rape still was rare, regardless settler claims of black peril. But things could get worse. Only if *all* Europeans recommitted themselves to high standards and building up distance could prestige be rebuilt. Settlers needed to cease their agitating against hard-working officials, and white women had to show some character and mother their offspring as white women should.[121]

Conclusion

The enslaved African woman, the bovine African woman, toiling for her layabout man. The delicate white woman, the colony-building white woman, protected by her chivalrous man. Such were the pictures settlers drew. Like all pictures, it captured only a part of the truth. Despite the many impositions by African and white men, 'meekness' would describe few African women. And not quite all whites measured up. And their fellow whites continued to point out those shortcomings. There was the lazy white mother, who dropped her child into the arms of a 'boy', a curious adolescent young man. There was the depraved white man, who fell into the arms of any African woman who would have him. (And took some of those who would not have him.) There were the white couples who found that their wedding vows wilted under the equatorial sun.

This was the reality, and the one Africans paid attention to. Kenya's white settlers held to dominant moral standards just as much, or as little, as did whites elsewhere. The difference was the importance they attached to upholding those moral standards. What settlers said, what settlers did – and with whom they did certain things – mattered more in a place like Kenya than it did in Europe. A high-profile divorce in Britain might create a scandal, and an elite man visiting a brothel might bring home shame and a disease. In Kenya, such things were dangerous; dangerous for the safety of white women and for the existence of white settlement.

Notes

1 Elspeth Huxley, *The Flame Trees of Thika* (New York: Morrow, 1959), pp. 25, 66, 114.
2 A. A. Grieve, letter to the ed., *Advertiser* (17 July 1908), pp. 7–8. See also 'Our Kenya letter', *EA* (5 Aug. 1926), p. 993.
3 'Kenya's Critics', *EAS* (11 Feb. 1921), p. 2. See also 'Coverdale's meeting', *EAS* (28 Feb. 1920), p. 14A.
4 'Local notes', *EAUM* (2 Jan. 1904), p. 7.
5 'Wife of a Settler', 'Kenya: a few reflections', *The English Review* (Mar. 1931): 360–4, quote from p. 362.
6 Wife of a Settler, 'Kenya: a few reflections', p. 362.
7 For a review and rejection of this historiography, see Claudia Knapman, *White Women in Fiji, 1835-1930: The Ruin of Empire?* (Sydney and London: Allen and Unwin, 1986).
8 Thus in 1909, the Ulu Settlers Association voted to allow (white) women landowners admission as full members. RH: Uncatalogued, Ulu Settlers Association Papers, General Meetings Minutes Book, 1908–22, Minutes of 31 Dec. 1909. The Njoro Settlers Association, at least by 1924, also admitted females. RH: MSS Afr. s.1506, Njoro Settlers Association, Minutes of Aug. 1924.
9 Perhaps the most well-known example is Nellie, Elspeth Huxley's mother. See Huxley's *Flame Trees of Thika* and *Nellie: Letters from Africa* (London: Weidenfeld and Nicolson, 1980). See also Huxley, *White Man's Country* (New York: Praeger, 1935), Vol. 1, p. 280; W. S. Bromhead, 'Kenya highlands', *EAS* (21 June 1923), p. 3; H. K. Binks, *African Rainbow* (London: Sidgwick and Jackson, 1959), p. 61.
10 Edward Grigg, 'British policy in Kenya', *Journal of the Royal African Society* 26 (1927): 193–208.
11 'Municipal election', *EAS* (30 Dec. 1916), p. 17.
12 'The Women's League', *EAS* (17 Mar. 1917), p. 12; 'E.A. Women's League', *EAS* (17 Mar. 1917), pp. 25–6; 'Votes for Women', *EAS* (23 June 1917), p. 19C; 'East African Women's League', *EAS* (5 May 1917), p. 19.
13 'E.A. Women's League', *EAS* (17 Mar. 1917), pp. 25–6. This was the argument Olga Watkins used when running for Nairobi Municipal Council in 1920. 'Mrs Watkins', *EAS* (2 Mar. 1921), p. 5; Elizabeth Watkins, *Olga in Kenya: Repressing the Irrepressible* (London: Pen, 2005). For a similar argument, see 'A mere man', *EAS* (21 Aug. 1920), p. 26.
14 'The Women's League', *EAS* (16 Mar. 1917), p. 12; 'The Women's League', *EAS* (17 Mar. 1917), p. 12; 'The vote for women', *EAS* (29 Sept. 1917), p. 12. This argument was made in Britain as well. Carolyn Spring, 'The political platform and the language of support for women's suffrage, 1890–1920', in Angela John and Claire Eustance (eds), *The Men's Share? Masculinities, Male Support and Women's Suffrage in Britain, 1890–1920* (London: Routledge, 1997).
15 'The Women's League', *EAS* (17 Mar. 1917), p. 12; 'Women's world', *EAS* (17 Mar. 1917), p. 18.
16 Support in the LegCo was not universal. Government officials on the LegCo were given a free vote – they could vote with their consciences rather than follow the governor's order – and the vote split, eight to eight. Governor Northey cast the deciding vote in favour of women. 'Governor's deciding vote', *EAS* (12 Apr. 1919), p. 5; LegCo debates, Second Session, 1919, p. 23.
17 'Disgusted', letter to ed., *EAS* (3 May 1919), p. 4. See also 'Barbaros', letter to ed., *EAS* (26 Apr. 1919), p. 21.
18 'Observer', letter to ed., *EAS* (26 Apr. 1921), p. 5. See also 'Make them if they won't!', *Critic* (25 Nov. 1922), p. 13; 'Sticking to our guns', *Critic* (2 Dec. 1922), p. 23; 'Nutshell Novels No. 11: Humanity –!', *Critic* (16 Dec. 1923), p. 11. Although in an earlier contretemps, employed women insisted they filled otherwise empty

jobs. In any event, proposed 'One of Them', 'surely we cannot be usurping men's billets? I cannot believe that manly men, who support their wives comfortably, want to sit in an office all day doing such strenuous work as typing.' 'One of them', letter to ed., *EAS* (23 Oct. 1920), p. 19. See also Isabel Ross, letter to ed., *EAS* (30 Oct. 1920), p. C.

19 Hence a 1928 debate in Mombasa as to the propriety of women witnessing boxing matches. 'Should women witness boxing bouts?', *EAS* (21 Mar. 1928), p. 11.
20 Paul R. Deslandes, *Oxbridge Men: British Masculinity and the Undergraduate Experience, 1850–1920* (Bloomington and Indianapolis: University of Indiana Press, 2005), p. 43; J. A. Mangan, 'Social Darwinism and upper-class education in late Victorian and Edwardian England', in J. A. Mangan and James Walvin (eds), *Manliness and Morality: Middle Class Masculinity in Britain and America, 1800–1940* (Manchester: Manchester University Press, 1987), p. 45; Kelly Boyd, *Manliness and the Boys' Story Paper in Britain: A Cultural History, 1855–1940* (Basingstoke and New York: Palgrave Macmillan, 2003).
21 Angus McLaren, *The Trials of Masculinity: Policing Sexual Boundaries, 1870–1930* (Chicago and London: University of Chicago Press, 1997), pp. 17–26.
22 Alyse Simpson, *The Land that Never Was* (Lincoln: University of Nebraska Press, 1985 [1937]), pp. 96–100.
23 'In the Sessions Court, Nairobi', *EAS* (25 Jan. 1908), p. 7.
24 The following draws on an affidavit by Schwaiger, taken by Col. Copeman, JP, 11 Jan. 1928, and transcripts of the resulting court case, 20 Jan. 1928, all in KNA: NZA 15/8.
25 The senior Jolly, formerly an administrative officer in India and unwell mentally as a result of the war, was well known to the administration as someone unable to get along with either fellow whites or local Nandi. See KNA: PC/NZA 3/18/5/1 and PC/NZA 3/17/2.
26 Quoted in C. S. Nicholls, *Red Strangers: The White Tribe of Kenya* (London: Timewell, 2005), p. 136.
27 'Poisonous literature', *EAS* (23 Feb. 1923), p. 5.
28 'Scurrilous Indian journalism', *Critic* (24 Feb. 1923), p. 23.
29 Hermann Norden, *White and Black in East Africa: A Record of Travel and Observation in Two African Crown Colonies* (Boston: Maynard, 1924), p. 42.
30 'Poisonous literature', *EAS* (23 Feb. 1923), p. 5.
31 'Scurrilous Indian journalism', *Critic* (24 Feb. 1923), p. 23.
32 NA: CO 544/26, Minutes of an Extraordinary Meeting of the Executive Council, 24 Feb. 1923; 'Libel suit between newspapers', *EAS* (26 Apr. 1924), p. 27.
33 W. McGregor Ross, *Kenya from Within: A Short Political History* (London: Frank Cass, 1968 (1927), p. 370); 'Scurrilous Indian journalism', *Critic* (24 Feb. 1923), p. 23.
34 KNA: PC/COAST 1/12/217, E. A. Dutton, Governor's Private Secretary, to Senior Commissioner, Coast Province, 9 Mar. 1923; Ross, *Kenya from Within*, p. 370.
35 Quoted in KNA: PC/COAST 1/12/217, E. A. Dutton, Governor's Private Secretary, to Senior Commissioner, Coast Province, 9 Mar. 1923.
36 'Newspapers in libel cases', *EAS* (3 May 1924), p. 28.
37 KNA: PC/COAST 1/12/217, Senior Commissioner, Coast Province, to the Governor's Private Secretary, 13 Mar. 1923. It appears that by April he was in Nairobi, and had again entered journalism. 'The Critic cake', *Critic* (14 Apr. 1923), p. 17. In 1924, he charged the *Standard* with libel, claiming that an article had sullied his reputation. The opposing lawyer, Mr Figgis, queried, 'What reputation have you got?' and asked Achariar to confirm that he had been the one to besmirch 'the moral character of English women'. The Magistrate allowed the question. 'Libel suit between newspapers', *EAS* (26 Apr. 1924), p. 27.
38 'The clothing of natives', *AS* (15 Aug. 1903), p. 2.
39 'A trip to Lake Victoria', *EAUM* (6 Feb. 1904), p. 3. See also George McDonnell, letter to ed., *TEA* (13 Jan. 1906), p. 3; letters to ed. from 'Southerner' and 'Shame', both in *TEA* (20 Jan. 1906), p. 3; 'Clothing for natives', *Advertiser* (3 July 1908),

CHIVALRY, IMMORALITY, AND INTIMACY

p. 9; 'Colonists' Association: native nakedness', *EAS* (20 Feb. 1909), p. 8; 'Wanted: moral healthy natives', *EAS* (14 May 1910), p. 8.

40 'Municipal Committee', *EAS* (18 June 1914), p. 5; 'Municipal Committee', *EAS* (25 June 1914), p. 4; 'White and Black in East Africa', *EAS* (26 June 1914), p. 4. Another six years passed, and problem was again raised. 'Native clothing', *EAS* (18 Dec. 1920), p. A. Again in 1924, the *Standard* could complain of 'disgracefully underclothed' rickshaw 'boys'. 'The ricksha nuisance', *EAS* (2 Oct. 1924), p. 25.
41 'Unpleasant but necessary', *TEA* (24 Mar. 1906), p. 4.
42 No title, *TEA*, (23 Dec. 1905), p. 9
43 'An angel in the House: Women's position and ultimate place in the protectorate', *EAS* (1 Apr. 1914), p. 6.
44 'A European woman', *EAS* (27 Mar. 1920), p. 6.
45 Letters to ed. from Robert Nixon and 'A Settler', *EAS* (27 Mar. 1920), p. 6.
46 'A white woman', letter to ed., *EAS* (27 Mar. 1920), p. 6.
47 Note by editor, *EAS* (27 Mar. 1920), p. 6. See also 'Assault and theft', *EAS* (22 Jan. 1921), p. 2; 'The Hockley case', *EAS* (20 June 1922), p. 5; 'Things we want to know', *Critic* (5 Aug. 1922), p. 15; 'Attempted stabbing', *KO* (28 Sept. 1923), p. 8. In an earlier incident in which an elderly African man knocked down a white woman, the *Standard* recommended 'The cat, and plenty of it'. 'Attack on a European lady by a native near Nairobi', *AS* (18 Apr. 1903), p. 3. See also 'Assaulted European lady', *EAS* (22 Mar. 1924), p. 36; 'Alleged assault on a European lady', *EAS* (28 June 1924), p. 14.
48 'Police and robberies', *AS* (22 Jan. 1903), p. 4. See also the article which directly follows, 'How are we to protect ourselves?'
49 'The want of police protection', *AS* (12 Feb. 1903), p. 4. See also 'Native passes', *EAS* (18 Aug. 1917), p. 9.
50 The *Standard* explained the stance of Convention of Association representatives who warned of black peril in 1911: 'These members, the majority of whom have spent their lifetime amidst native races, could well read the signs of the times, and by the increased insolence to, and morally careless behaviour in the presence of white women, realised that deterrent steps were necessary should the persons of their wives and children remain inviolate in the natives' eyes'. 'Black peril', *EAS* (18 Nov. 1911), p. 5. See also 'The angel in the house: women's position and ultimate place in the protectorate', *EAS* (1 Apr. 1914), p. 6; 'White and black in East Africa', *EAS* (26 June 1914), p. 4; W. M. Hudson, 'Crime and punishment', *EAS* (15 May 1920), p. 2.
51 'Occasional notes', *EAS* (15 June 1912).
52 Sidney Fichat, Secretary, Colonists' Association, to Governor, 5 Mar. 1908, in 'The white book', *Leader* (29 Aug. 1908), supplement. See also 'The native menace', *EAS* (15 Mar. 1919), p. 15; 'An open letter', *Critic* (30 Sep. 1922), p. 14.
53 KNA: AM/1/1/5, 'The black peril', *Leader*, July 1920, clipping.
54 'Notes and comments', *Leader* (8 Aug. 1908), p. 5.
55 None of this, of course, tells us anything about rapists' intentions, only settlers' reactions.
56 'Black peril', *EAS* (18 Nov. 1911), p. 5. After one incident in 1909, both the *Leader* and the *Standard* called for rape being made a capital crime. The former warned that Judge Lynch might take matters into his own hands. 'Protect the children', *Leader* (20 March 1909), p. 4; 'Occasional notes', *EAS* (20 Mar. 1909), p. 9.
57 J. Kerslake Thomas, letter to ed., *Leader* (18 Nov. 1911), p. 4.
58 'The native peril', and J. Kerslake Thomas, letter to ed., both in *Leader* (18 Nov. 1911), pp. 8 and 12.
59 'Occasional notes', *EAS* (25 Nov. 1911), p. 13. Judge Pickering in December convicted Jaguna of attempted rape or indecent assault with violence on a child of five years, as well as criminal intimidation (for threatening to kill the girl if she reported the assault). Jaguna received a total of twenty-four lashes, eleven years', rigorous imprisonment, and a 500 rupee fine; he likely served a further one year in default of paying the fine. 'Prisoner convicted', *Leader* (9 Dec. 1911), p. 2.

60 'Notes and comments', *Leader* (13 Nov. 1909), p. 4.
61 Juanita Carberry, with Nicola Tyrer, *Child of Happy Valley: A Memoir* (London: Heinemann, 1999), pp. 51–4; RH: MSS Afr. s. 917, C.T. Todd, 'Kenya's red sunset', p. 103.
62 RH: MSS Afr. s. 746/1, Blundell, 'Diary, 1925–26', entry of 5 Feb. This infatuation is notably absent in his memoirs. Michael Blundell, *A Love Affair with the Sun: A Memoir of Seventy Years in Kenya* (Nairobi: Kenway, 1994), p. 13.
63 According to a character in settler-turned-author Florence Riddell's novel, Nairobi was 'Ten years behind the times in everything except morals!' Florence Riddell, *Kismet in Kenya* (Philadelphia: Lippincott, 1932), p. 144. Such portrayals of Kenya, by Riddell and others, were not looked kindly upon by the *Standard*. '"Kenya Mist"', *EAS* (2 Aug. 1924), p. 27.
64 RH: MSS Brit. Emp. s. 349, Lord Francis Scott, 'Diaries', entry of 21 Jan. 1920.
65 NA: CO 544/26, Executive Council, Minutes, 3 Feb. and 15 Sept. 1928.
66 KNA: GH 7/24, A. D. A. Macgregor, AG, to E. A. T. Dutton, 28 Feb. 1930. In fact, upon order of Queen Mary herself, no divorced person was invited to Government House during the governorship of Sir Edward Grigg. Her Majesty warned Lady Grigg (Sir Edward later recalled) of 'the irresponsible group in Kenya which disregarded all convention and restraint'. Edward Grigg, (Lord Altrincham), *Kenya's Opportunities: Memories, Hopes, and Ideas* (London: Faber and Faber, 1955), pp. 73–4.
67 KNA: GH 7/24, Mabel Murray to Alyce Turner, 13 Feb. 1930.
68 KNA: GH 7/24, Alyce Turner to Major Dutton, 19 Feb. 1930.
69 KNA: GH 7/24, A. D. A. Macgregor, AG, to E. A. T. Dutton, 28 Feb. 1930.
70 'Things we want to know', *Critic* (5 Aug. 1922), p. 15.
71 'Things we want to know', *Critic* (30 Sept. 1922), p. 15.
72 'Things we want to know', *Critic* (7 Oct. 1922), p. 15.
73 'Nutshell novels: The Waster', *Critic* (18 Nov. 1922), p. 23.
74 'Nutshell novels, No. 8: Lady Angela's Divorce', *Critic* (25 Nov. 1922), p. 23. See also 'Nutshell novels, No. 10: A Kenya Drama', *Critic* (9 Dec. 1922), p. 11.
75 'Courts and press', *EAS* (9 Oct. 1920), p. 10.
76 Similarly, proprietors of the Stanley Hotel took seriously their self-appointed role of regulating the sexual affairs of European women on their staff. 'Stanley Hotel assault case', *EAS* (26 June 1915), p. 21, and 'High Court: Brundsen v. Tate', *EAS* (23 Oct. 1915), p. 29. On concerns over metropolitan papers imported into Kenya, see 'Undesirable pictures in advertisements', *EAS* (24 Mar. 1928), p. 9.
77 Isabel Ross, President, EAWL, letter to ed., *EAS* (5 Jan. 1918), p. 15.
78 D. R. Rapp, 'Sex in the cinema: war, moral panic, and the British film industry, 1906–1918', *Albion* 34 (2002): 422–51.
79 C.A.S., letter to ed., *EAS* (17 Feb. 1917), p. 6.
80 Robt. Nixon, letter to ed., *EAS* (21 Dec. 1917), p. 6. See also letter to editor from Harold E. Henderson, *EAS* (20 Dec. 1917), p. 4. Davis and Robertson sent up such attitudes, pointing out that some Luomen – whose own womenfolk covered only a small area in front and behind – had witnessed images of white women in tights. And what to do with domestic servants, who brought white women morning tea in bed, being exposed to 'screen pictures of giddy girls rudely reclining on couches, clad only in pyjamas!' A. Davis and H. G. Robertson, *Chronicles of Kenya* (London: Cecil Palmer, 1928), pp. 236–7. Advertisements in settler media also provided line-drawings of white women in slips. See, for example, the ads for 'Holeproof Hosiery' in *EAS* on 12 Jan. 1924, p. 9, and 9 Feb. 1924, p. 38.
81 KNA: AG 42/7, Memorandum of interview held at the Secretariat on 29 Oct. 1929; LegCo debates, 10 Sept. 1924.
82 Davis and Robertson, *Chronicles of Kenya*, p. 235.
83 Some films were censored even when scheduled to be screened only for Europeans. For example, in 1924 the Theatre Royal cancelled the screening of *House without Children* due to 'local censorship'. 'Under the Standard clock', *EAS* (9 July 1924), p. 2; LegCo debates, 11 Sept. 1924; Cecil Davis, Director, Theatre Royal, letter to

ed., *EAS* (20 Sept. 1924), p. 8. For Davis's support of censorship for African viewers, see his letter to the ed., *EAS* (14 July 1928), p. 11.

84 NA: CO 533/37/11, Report of the Select Committee on Film Censorship, 29 July 1927. There were ongoing debates over how censorship would be carried out, and if films for Europeans should be pre-screened. NA: CO 544/26, Executive Council, Minutes, 9 May 1928; KNA: AG 42/5; RH: MSS Afr. s. 594 1/7, Convention of Associations, Minutes, 28-30 May 1928, p. 27; 'Film censorship', *EAS* (11 July 1928), p. 8; LegCo debates, 22 Aug. 1928, and 7 Dec. 1928.
85 LegCo debates, 22 Aug. 1922.
86 Report of the Select Committee on Film Censorship, 1929, copy in KNA: AG/42/7. This time legislation was passed with minimal opposition. Minutes of the Film Censorship Committee Meeting, 8 Apr., 1928, KNA: AG 42/4; LegCo, debates of 16 July 1929, pp. 218-29. Kenya settlers and police were not alone in their concern over white sexual immorality being screened in colonial filmhouses. It was an imperial problem. See KNA: AG/42/5; KNA: AG/42/7, Report of the Colonial Films Committee (London: HMSO, 1930).
87 KNA: AG/4/27, Report of the Select Committee on Film Censorship; Alisa Turner, President, EAWL, to Gov. Kenya, 14 Aug. 1929; 'Film Censorship', *EAS* (11 July 1928).
88 KNA: AG/42/7, Alisa Turner to Colonial Secretary, n.d.
89 As an attorney in Fiji argued in 1915, 'A woman who goes about with natives, making love to them – a woman like that is an absolute danger to the community ... she is ... acting in a way that is a disgrace to her colour'. Hence in Rhodesia in 1916, the Legislative Council criminalized sex between white women and African men. Their reasoning, according to one member of the council: 'It was a law really to preserve the prestige of the white race in this country and to prevent anything being done which might endanger the existence of the honour of white women in this territory'. In New Guinea, white observers believed voluntary and forced sex between indigenous men and white women to be 'injurious to the colonial social order'. On Fiji, see James Heartfield, '"You are not a white woman!": Apolosi Nawai, the Fiji Produce Agency and the trial of Stella Spencer in Fiji, 1915', *Journal of Pacific History* 38 (2003): 69-83, quote from p. 79; on Rhodesia, see Mindy Hohenstein, 'Between Black and White: Ideology in the Southern African Black Peril Scares' (M.A. thesis, Department of History, University of North Carolina, Chapel Hill, 2002), and NA: DO 119/38; on New Guinea, see Wolfers, *Race Relations and Colonial Rule*, p. 99. Mohanram suggests that all white women in India were considered (by white men?) to be lower on the evolutionary scale, perhaps near to non-whites. Her evidence points to this being the case only for white prostitutes. Thus it is not that white men thought all white women to be nearly black, but that a certain class of white women threatened to reduce the value of whiteness for all white women. Radhika Mohanram, *Imperial White: Race, Diaspora, and the British Empire* (Minneapolis: University of Minnesota Press, 2007), ch. 2. Similarly, in the Fiji case examined by Heartfield, a white woman who entered a romantic relationship with a local man was told that she was not white.
90 The standard work on African prostitution is Luise White, *The Comforts of Home: Prostitution in Colonial Nairobi* (Chicago: University of Chicago Press, 1990). On Japanese prostitutes, see W. Robert Foran, *The Kenya Police, 1887-1960* (London: Robert Hale, 1962), p. 22.
91 Carberry, *Child of Happy Valley*, p. 54. Anderson's wife, owner of the *Standard*, later filed for divorce, at which point his adulterous actions with an African domestic servant were revealed. 'A local divorce', *EAS* (25 June 1914), p. 5.
92 Letter to John Cowper Powys, 7 Nov. 1915, in Llewelyn Powys, Louis Marlow, and Alyse Gregory, *The Letters of Llewelyn Powys* (London: John Lane, 1943). For other evidence of sex between white men and African women, see W. Robert Foran, *A Cuckoo in Kenya: The Reminiscences of a Pioneer Police Officer in British East Africa* (London: Hutchinson, 1936), p. 331; Anton Gill, *Ruling Passions: Sex, Race and Empire* (London: BBC Books, 1995), p. 85; Errol Trzebinski, *The Lives of Beryl*

Markham: Out of Africa's Hidden Free Spirit and Denys Finch Hatton's Last Great Love (New York: Norton, 1993), p. 20; 'Veritas', letter to ed., *EAS* (8 Dec. 1906), p. 7; RH: MSS Afr. r. 126, E.A.P. Audit Office 'Funny Book', 'The Official's Lament on Circular B'; NA: CO 533/384/9, Kikuyu Central Association to SS, 14 Feb. 1929; Elspeth Huxley, *The Mottled Lizard* (New York: Penguin, 1962), pp. 165–6.

93 LegCo debates, 11 Sept. 1924.
94 'The divorce debate', *EAS* (31 May 1924), p. 2.
95 For refusals of such offers, see Alyse Simpson, *The Land that Never Was*, p. 253; R. Gorell Barnes, *Babes in the African Wood* (London: Longmans, Green, 1911), p. 164. Perhaps more often, white men simply took African females by force. Llewlyn Powys seemed to believe it his right to have sex with whichever African girl he wished. 'I see in the background three Kikuyu girls who have come from far', he wrote in a letter home in November, 1915. 'I shall perhaps select one when I come back from dinner tonight'. Letter to John Cowper Powys, 14 Nov. 1915, in Powys, Marlow, and Gregory, *Letters of Llewelyn Powys*, p. 81. See also Daniel Nyaga, *Customs and Traditions of the Meru* (Nairobi: East African Educational Publishers, 1997), pp. 143–8.
96 Scholars of Kenya will note the lack of references to Colonel Richard Meinertzhagen, whose diaries often comment on the sexual adventures of his fellow Britons in Kenya. It would appear that Meinertzhagen was an inveterate liar and composed parts of the diary years later. The diaries perhaps tell us more about Meinertzhagen's personality than about early colonial Kenya. See Brian Garfield, *The Meinertzhagen Mystery: The Life and Legend of a Colossal Fraud* (Dulles, VA: Potomac, 2007).
97 Henry Seaton, *Lion in the Morning* (London: Murray, 1963), p. 44. Similarly, the Indian wives and mistress of earlier decades were condemned by the Raj in the later part of the nineteenth century, on grounds of prestige. The Chief Commissioner, Burma, in 1894, thought that an officer with a local mistress 'not only degrades himself as an English gentleman, but lowers the prestige of the English name, and largely destroys his own usefulness'. The High Commissioner in South Africa in 1910 dismissed a Northern Rhodesian official for 'having habitually practiced concubinage' which was 'most degrading to a white officer ... and incompatible with the maintenance of the prestige of the British Government'. On India, see Kenneth Ballhatchet, *Race, Sex and Class under the Raj: Imperial Attitudes and Policies and Their Critics, 1793–1905* (New York: St Martin's, 1980), p. 147; on Northern Rhodesia, see Karen Tranberg Hansen, *Distant Companions: Servants and Employers in Zambia, 1900–1985* (Ithaca and London: Cornell University Press, 1989), p. 93.
98 'Things we want to know', *Critic* (12 Aug. 1922), p. 15. See also the comment by Reverend Harry Leakey during a Legislative Council debate over licensing and regulating brothels: 'This would be disastrous. I am perfectly certain it would lower the prestige of the white man in the eyes of the native. What we want to-day is the teaching of morals by example and precept ...' LegCo debates, 20 Aug. 1928. The *Standard* reprinted a column from the *Natal Witness* which called for action to prevent officials in South Africa and British East Africa 'who are paid to defend and uphold the honour of the Empire from rotting it at the core, and from secretly undermining the prestige and respect in which its members should be held'. 'A protection league', *EAS* (22 July 1922), p. 16.
99 Jane Rodner, *Datura: A Romance of Kenya* (London: Hutchinson, 1928), p. 134.
100 M. H. Hamilton, *Turn the Hour: A Tale of Life in Colonial Kenya* (Sussex: Book Guild, 1991), pp. 151–2.
101 NA: CO 533/85/4722, Hollis, for Ag Gov. Kenya, to SS, 20 Jan. 1911.
102 NA: CO 533/85/19019, Hollis to SS.
103 NA: CO 533/85/4722, Hollis, for Ag Gov. Kenya, to SS, 20 Jan. 1911.
104 NA: CO 533/85/4722, note in file by Read, 17 Jan. 1911, and SS to Gov. Kenya, 17 Mar. 1911.
105 NA: CO 533/85/19019, Girouard to SS.

106 Imprisonment for rape was increased from ten to fourteen years, attempted rape from five to ten years, and assault with intent to offend modesty from two to seven years.
107 Arabs in Mombasa protested – they had been included in the definition of 'native'. If such a law were passed, they argued, the government 'should take steps to prevent white prostitution' as well as prevent white men using Arab girls 'for carnal purposes'. Their requests were denied, although they were thanked for their willingness to draw official attention to white prostitutes soliciting Africans. KNA: PC/Coast/1/10/72; NA: CO: 533/118/19308; NA: CO 533/120/27871, SS to Gov. Kenya, 14 Aug. 1913.
108 I have found evidence of it being used only once, involving an Afrikaner and a Gikuyu. She was acquitted, and the case against him was dismissed. KNA: Nyanza Province Intelligence Report, Nov. 1930.
109 The *Leader* republished a column from *African World*, published in Portuguese East Africa, which blamed a South African black peril in part on whites 'permitting the existence in their midst of evils associated with colour of which delicacy forbids description'. 'The "black peril"', *Leader* (20 July 1912), p. 10.
110 For her marriage and divorce, see www.maturin.org.uk/7.html (accessed 27 Apr., 2012). On her time in South Africa, see Mrs Fred Maturin (Edith Money), *Petticoat Pilgrims on Trek* (London: Eveleigh Nash, 1909).
111 Mrs Fred Maturin (Edith Cecil-Porch), 'The angel in the house: women's position and ultimate place in the protectorate', *EAS* (1 Apr. 1914), p. 6.
112 Hamilton, *Turn the Hour*, p. 151.
113 Grace Orr, letter to ed., *EAS* (6 Sept. 1924), p. 28. Three weeks later, Mr D. Sparrow applauded Orr for linking white men's sexual immorality with black peril. D. Sparrow, letter to ed., *EAS* (30 Sept. 1924), p. 8. 'Indignant Mother', however, believed that African women were 'invariably' consenting partners, while black peril cases involved an 'innocent victim'. Letter to ed., *EAS* (11 Oct.1924), p. 5.
114 Quoted in Gill, *Ruling Passions*, p. 105.
115 KNA: AM/1/1/5, 'Report of the Special Committee on Sexual Assaults of Natives upon Europeans', July, 1920.
116 'Black peril', *EAS* (31 July 1920), p. 21.
117 In Southern Rhodesia, such women were a matter of police concern, while a judge there sentenced an African leniently for assault on a white woman, for she had ordered him to serve her in bed during an illness. 'I think we must seriously consider', the judge explained, 'how much her conduct may have conduced his conduct'. Similarly, in 1938, an Australian administrator in Darwin damned two white women, victims of attempted assault, for they had '"encouraged" an Aboriginal worker by treating him as a "pet pussy-cat" and being scantily clad in his presence'. On Rhodesia, see DO: 119/38, Jos. C. Brundell, CID, BSAP, to Chief Staff Officer, BSA Police, enclosed in Administrator, Salisbury, to High Commissioner, South Africa, July 1920; on Australia, Julia Martinez and Claire Lowrie, 'Colonial constructions of masculinity: transforming Aboriginal Australian men into "houseboys"', *Gender and History* 21 (2009): 305–23, esp. p. 317. See also Edward P. Wolfers, *Race Relations and Colonial Rule in Papua New Guinea* (Sydney: Australia and New Zealand Book Company, 1975), p. 57.
118 KNA: AM/1/1/5, 'The black peril', *Daily Leader*, July 1920, clipping.
119 See Sidney Langford Hinde and Hildegarde Hinde, *The Last of the Masai* (London: Heinemann, 1901), p. x; Stephen North, *Europeans in British Administered East Africa: A Provisional List, 1899–1903*, 2nd ed. (Wantage: S. J. North, 2000), p. 164.
120 H.B.H. [Hildegard B. Hinde], 'The "black peril" in British East Africa', *The Empire Review* (1921): 193–200.
121 For other comments linking bad mothering and black peril, see 'Parents' responsibilities', *EAS* (16 Aug. 1924) p. 15; Hilda M. Peirson, letter to ed, *EAS* (30 Aug. 1924), p. 26; 'Unanxious', letter to ed., *EAS* (13 Sept. 1924), p. 3.

CHAPTER FIVE

The law and the lash

Turn-of-the-century Britons prided themselves on their legal system. The impartiality of the law, combined with procedures developed over centuries, added up to a legal order in which any person, regardless of station in life, could expect justice. Granted, as in any endeavour, practice did not always reach this ideal state. None the less, for Britons few things demonstrated their superiority more than their dedication to law and justice. Indeed, few things better justified their colonial expansion than how it served to spread law and justice.

Despite their pride in British justice, administrators and settlers alike concluded that it just did not fit all that well in a colonial context. District officers, who held varying levels of magisterial power, saw the law as a means of rule. In every case they heard, officers struggled to balance their knowledge of the parties and the politics involved with adherence to the impartiality of the law.[1] Quite commonly, officers preferred to follow what they felt to be justice, rather than be constrained by the letter of the law. Impersonal, impartial British justice served settler interests even less. When courts attended to 'technicalities' in inter-racial cases, Africans sometimes won. This settlers could not abide. Should a magistrate or judge favour an African, it meant nearly by definition that injustice had prevailed. Worse, it humiliated the white person. Only when a settler bested an African in court could justice be said to have been served, and white prestige to have been preserved.

Many settlers thought it easier, and proper, to take the law into their own hands. Whites regularly employed extra-judicial punishments against Africans. This often involved punishment on the person. Whites in Kenya came from places where corporal punishment was not uncommon. Although it was fading in some contexts, parents, teachers and military officers in Great Britain, South Africa, and elsewhere used violence to correct their charges. Such violence also helped remind everyone of the particular hierarchy involved: parent over child, teacher over student. Settlers and administrators alike attached great value to the lash as a way to inculcate certain habits in Africans, and break them of others. It also was the quickest way to answer African insolence and shore up prestige.

The sticking point was how much lash was too much. Virtually all whites would have agreed with C. W. Hobley, when in 1912 as Coast Provincial Commissioner he expressed his aversion to 'an excessive amount of whipping and whipping for trivial offences'.[2] But, especially in the earlier years, few settlers could imagine what number of stripes could be excessive, and what was too trivial for the lash. Debates ensued, among settlers and between settlers and the state, over the proper use of violence toward Africans. Settler juries trivialized white brutality against Africans Settlers continued to push for the use of corporal punishment – by the courts and by private individuals – to secure white rule. Violence would (settlers fervently believed) create the kind of African they desired: docile, subordinate, attuned to settlers' expectations. And only violence – the taking of an African life – could wipe clean any black peril that might besmirch the settler soul.

Settlers and the law

Most settlers – whether from the United Kingdom or Anglo South African – shared a common attachment to British justice. Yet early Kenya was a frontier, where 'law and order' could be fragile. Lord Delamere once bought two baskets of oranges, then invited those drinking in his Nakuru hotel to come outside and shatter the glass in all the windows.[3] At least the destroyed property was his own, if only on that occasion. He also took part in a ritual common in the early years: drunkenly shooting out lamps and glass insulators along the streets of Nairobi.[4] Delamere encouraged rugby playing inside pubs, while others rode their horses directly through them.[5] One man often ordered dozens upon dozens of glasses to be set upon the bar, only to sweep them all to the floor for no reason other than to watch them shatter.[6] The police ignored most of this, either through lack of resources or because of the knowledge that it would do little good to interfere, or because they sometimes took part.[7] Perhaps, growing up as the son of a peer, Delamere's boyhood pranks had also been ignored by constables. In Kenya, every white man, peer or not, felt emboldened to act out their juvenile fantasies of living in a world without pesky adults and constraining laws.[8]

Inebriated carousing aside, settlers knew that a colony must have laws. They knew that British legal traditions required one to respect those who applied the law. Unless racial prestige was at stake, which brings us to the Rainbows, Arthur and Patrice. Arthur Rainbow first arrived in Kenya in 1900 from Johannesburg.[9] Not surprisingly, given what we know of him, Rainbow had a falling out with a fellow immigrant with whom he had expected to partner in business.[10] By 1907 he had turned to ostrich herding, and in 1910 married Patrice Dooner, the sister of a business associate.[11] In 1914, the ostrich business broke up, and the Rainbows established a mill on a plot in Narok.[12] Over the next decades, it appears the Rainbows' financial situation continued to be strained, as did their relations with government officials.

Arthur Rainbow's first (recorded) dispute with the state arose in 1919. Police corporal Oyula lodged a complaint with Assistant D. C. Ogilvie, alleging that the corporal's wife had been assaulted by Rainbow. (The details were never clear, but Arthur claimed the woman had insulted Patrice.) Ogilvie posted three notes to Rainbow before the settler responded. 'If you do not know your position', Rainbow scolded, 'and how to write a European it is about time you spared a few moments and learn how to do so'. Rainbow also recommended that Ogilvie learn a few things about the law.[13] Hemsted, Officer in Charge of the Masai Reserve, chastised Rainbow for his 'grossly insulting letter' to a representative of the Crown. Some ten days later, Rainbow finally 'apologized' to Ogilvie:

> I am extremely sorry and must apologize [sic] to you for my action in having struck the native women the other day. I was not aware at the time that one of them filled the position as your wife. I think it would be better if you explained matters telling her when coming near European houses not to insult a White lady. As an A.D.C. wife with colour attached to her has no social standing in the Country.[14]

Ogilvie and Hemsted, both incensed, inquired of the attorney general if libel proceedings could be undertaken.[15] Rainbow had posted the letter directly to Ogilvie, so no charge could be preferred against him.[16] Rainbow could smile, the prestige of a white woman upheld, government servants reminded of the primacy of race.

Alas, government would not yet be over the Rainbows. In early March 1923, after a successful civil case, G. D. Macintosh gained a warrant of attachment for some of Mr Rainbow's property. Sergeant Songoro and another askari proceeded to the Rainbow farm. What exactly transpired is not clear. According to Songoro, Mrs Rainbow brandished a shotgun and suggested he continue his mission only 'If you want to lose your life'.[17] Charges were filed against her for obstructing an officer. Not unlike John Finnie (who was fined for his assault on a government askari), Rainbow thought the matter came down to a question of white prestige. She had told Songoro (he stated under oath) that 'he was a black man and could not execute a warrant on a white person'.[18] Indeed, when she came before the magistrate (District Commissioner C. E. V. Buxton), she stated, 'Mr Buxton, do you know what you are doing. I am a white woman and being charged by a black man with a crime which I don't suppose was ever brought against a white woman before.' Such a fundamental miscarriage of justice, Rainbow believed, outweighed the respect otherwise due the court. 'You will not give me a chance nor listen to reason', she berated Buxton, 'so I must commit some action in this court to emphasise it'.

Commit an action she did, and a criminal one at that. A correspondence basket sat within reach on a nearby table. Rainbow struck Buxton with it three or four times before storming out of the courtroom. During her subsequent trial for 'intentional insult or interruption to a public servant sitting in judicial proceedings', Rainbow did not deny the assault. Her justification: 'There were a number of natives outside, all taking the keenest interest in a white woman being insulted in court.'[19] With this admission of guilt, the jury convicted her.[20]

Few settlers, of course, assaulted a magistrate. The Rainbows' actions were chalked up to class. Hemsted noted that Arthur Rainbow was 'a somewhat poor type of European'.[21] They certainly were not financially well-off: unable to pay her 600-shilling fine, Patrice served one month in jail. Granted, even poor people could act respectably, but the Rainbows were not that type. Ogilvie's district commissioner, T. J. A. Salmon, thought Arthur Rainbow's insolent letters reflected 'ill breeding'.[22] Persons of a certain class background knew how properly to address a representative of the King.

Class issues aside, in some ways the Rainbows were utterly representative of white settlers.[23] They deeply believed in the majesty of the law. Indeed, Patrice Rainbow in 1926 dredged up her vendetta against Buxton. She warned settlers in Fort Hall (where Buxton was appointed DC) that he did not deserve the post of magistrate, which required 'a man with a sense of *Honour* and *Justice*'. He had run his court 'in a manner which presents a travesty of the elements of British Justice and fair play'.[24] The Rainbows honoured British justice and fair play. But in Kenya, these could not be isolated from the pragmatic concerns of white prestige and security. If the law allowed an askari to attach white property, what good was the law? If a magistrate permitted a white woman to be dragged to court only on the basis of a black man's word, and tried her while Africans leered from the windows, then surely that magistrate ought not to receive the respect his position demanded.[25]

Settlers saw themselves as above the law, and indeed the law itself. Administrators, as magistrates, must not impede settlers. The duty of a white man was to defend white men. 'Many Europeans take objection to the most elementary principles of the law', reflected the district commissioner at Kikuyu in 1912,

> scarcely a case is finished without severe if inexpert criticisms being passed. Little or no evidence is expected to procure certain conviction and mere suspicion is taken to suffice so long as a European is the complainant, in the reverse case however, or if the accused happens to be a favourite of the European, no amount of evidence will appeal to them. On the other hand when convenient the Europeans often recognize no law at all. Every man wants to be a law unto himself, fines are freely extorted, stray stock confiscated and private punishment practised without regard to the law.[26]

If a settler wished to ride his horse in a bar, so be it. If a magistrate dared to promote impartiality over racial unity, then bang his head with a basket, the majesty of the law be damned.

Africans and the law

British legal traditions did not always apply to themselves, settlers argued, and rarely should they apply to Africans. For settlers – and many administrators alike – civilized English law and legal norms were supremely ill-adapted to a savage African setting. After all, they reasoned, the law could not be separated from British civilization. Civilized law should be applied only to civilized people. Africans would neither understand nor appreciate English legal procedures. Captain Edwards, Inspector General of the Police, explained in 1911 that English law 'was unsuited to the character of native peoples in stages of infantile thought and primitive conception'.[27] A letter writer contrasted how a white observer would 'view [a legal] case from the standpoint of 2,000 years of Christian and legal evolution [while] the native views the case from the standpoint of primitive man'.[28]

Whites insisted that all of the niceties of English law, ones which ensured justice to whites, only confused Africans. Protecting the rights of the accused and equality before the law – central to English legal traditions – were simply incomprehensible to an African man.[29] Standing perhaps for the first time before a room of white men; trying in vain to follow evidence, objections, and rulings translated once, sometimes twice, from English into his own language; ordered to leave out supposedly irrelevant background and inadmissible hearsay that he considered essential; all this, many white observers argued, left Africans more befuddled than reassured by the majesty of the law.

Of greater concern was the effect English legal procedures would have on African minds. Civilized men understood why certain evidence must be excluded from a court. Whites could agree that a man must not be convicted on the basis of a confession extracted under duress. Africans would only see a guilty man walk free. With their misplaced attachment to 'technicalities', white judges scandalously allowed this to happen.[30] Settlers, and administrators as well, railed against 'technicalities' and judicial revisions. Too-strict attention to 'technicalities' meant acquittals of guilty Africans. The result, wrote the London *Times* Nairobi correspondent, 'has been to create a firm belief in the native mind that the Courts exist to protect him from the Europeans, and to inculcate a sense of antagonism which is to be greatly deplored'.[31] According to the Convention of Associations, it produced 'increasing truculence, insubordination and crime'.[32] Africans, the argument went, felt invincible: crime paid.[33]

Administrators were as much to blame as the judges, according to settlers. Settlers complained incessantly of government officials being too 'pro-African'. These pompous members of a 'black partizan [*sic*] administration', according to the *Advertiser*, ensured that settlers never found justice in the colonial courts.[34] How could administrators and judicial officials take the word of a raw heathen against that of a civilized European? Africans, to settlers' minds, had no notions of truth, honour, or integrity. They did not respect the majesty of the law. They invested no meaning in courtroom oaths. Unlike whites, Africans felt no compunction about lying in court. The result, Brodhust-Hill wrote: 'the proceedings of the courts are thus turned into farce – only that is far too mild a word to express the harm that has been done'.[35] The editors of the *Standard* in 1913 railed against the government and 'law and justice' in the colony: 'We are not romancing when we state that the word of even the most ignorant and sunken of our native population is taken against that of even the most educated and trustworthy of our white community'.[36] Injustice, pure and simple.

In a vile bit of doggerel published in the *Standard*, the Nairobi businessman A. B. Mortimer portrayed official discrimination as making the African life an enviable one:

> White people all, whoever you may be,
> You imagine you've got a supremacy –
> But so long as High Officials hold a nigger's word
> To a white man's statement is to be preferred,
> Well – every time I score, you see! –
> It's fine to be a nigger in this country.[37]

Mortimer, the Rainbows, and their fellow settlers felt themselves oppressed should a white magistrate or judge doubt a white man or women in front of Africans.[38] Allowing African lies to trump the word of a gentlemen did not teach Africans to respect the law. Neither did it protect whites. Not incidentally, it did nothing for white prestige.

Settler justice

Rather than rely on magistrates and judges, settlers clamoured for the legal authority to deal with Africans as they wished.[39] In practice, few settlers worried about the niceties of the law before punishing their workers.[40] If the logistics and logic of the colonial legal system failed them, settlers had to take the law into their own hands.[41] Going to court was simply impracticable for busy people.[42] Fines and corporal punishment at the hand of the settler was quicker. Penalty could follow crime much more rapidly, the two more clearly linked in the sufferer's mind.[43] In fact, many whites were convinced – or tried to convince themselves – that Africans themselves fully accepted the legitimacy of extra-judicial violence.[44]

Norman Leys, a government doctor and later a harsh critic of white rule in Kenya, explained how whites had subverted the legal system:

> The broad fact is that every European in the country uses the powers of a magistrate over his native employees. The ordinary European has indeed more power than a magistrate. His judgments are never revised and never appealed from. Though illegal, the power to fine and flog is supported by public opinion. Natives of course are rarely aware that such practices are illegal and practically never take a European to Court. While the punishments are presumably always regarded as just by the employers they are frequently otherwise regarded by natives.[45]

Fines and beating were favourite punishment, while Beryl Markham's father had his own jail in which to lock up workers 'for however long he felt fair and just'.[46]

Crime and punishment

Despite what settlers saw as the 'farce' of courtroom procedures, magistrates and judges convicted more than a few Africans. Even then, settlers never seemed satisfied with the sentences imposed on Africans. Allegedly insufficient punishments led directly to increased African criminality. 'Rickshaw boys' in Nairobi were 'getting out of hand' in 1911 due to insufficient punishments. Such complaints were echoed over a dozen years later by Kiambu farmer Henry Tarlton, an Australian who had arrived in Kenya in 1903 after serving in the South African War. 'To-day', he fumed, 'most of the sentences are merely a farcical travesty of justice and in my opinion are directly responsible for the natives being so out of hand as they undoubtedly are'.[47] The *Standard* concurred: 'In plain words, if the Native is being spoilt by a consistent leniency which is leading to undue licence, we must ask that matters should be so regulated as to ensure a proper discipline.'[48]

What African law-breakers needed was less coddling and more lashes. The settlers' refrain: courts operated on the mistaken assumption that fines and imprisonment could reform African criminals.[49] Jail, the conventional wisdom went, was nothing but a rest home to Africans.[50] After all, asked W. M. Hudson, 'What native objects to very little work, plenty of food and a comfortable place to put his head at night and he is a hero with many of his kind for having been clever enough to thieve something'.[51] Corporal punishment had far better effect.[52] 'A little *physical* pain', the *Standard* noted, 'is a greater deterrent to the Native than imprisonment for long periods'.[53] Even better: lashings on a regular basis while the convict served his jail time.[54] Unless the courts made greater use of corporal punishment crime would be sure to increase.[55]

White violence against Africans was, of course, integral to the establishment and perpetuation of colonialism. Across Africa, the Maxim gun cut down waves of young men in the name of the civilizing mission. Hundreds of black bodies dangled from the gallows in order to protect white lives and property. Thousands of backs were bloodied to ensure the collection of rubber, the planting of cotton, the mining of copper.[56] Settlers in Kenya understood the value of a well-placed punch or crack of the kiboko. Violence helped them control Africans, and bolstered prestige: 'For it must be remembered', the *Standard* editorialized in 1913,

> that in this country the black man is infinitely superior in number to the white and the latter's position in the black man's country is one which may well be regarded as precarious. That being so, the rule of the iron hand is still absolutely essential to the very existence of the white man in B.E.A., and the few individual beating indiscretions committed might reasonably be pardoned in view of the fact – and in consideration of the almost unendurable provocation which the white man is compelled to suffer on account of the indolence and insolence of the major portion of our native population.[57]

Whites in Kenya would not have been strangers to the business end of a paddle or switch.[58] White settlers had had their own previous experiences with corporal punishment, as victims or perpetrators. As children at home, as boarding school students, as military men, as wives: the arenas in which a white person might feel pain for disobedience, or inflict pain for insubordination, remained numerous in the later nineteenth century. British public schools carried on their tradition of flogging naughty boys, while elder students bullied juniors, who in turn tormented the next class.[59] The British military too held fast to traditions of the lash for common soldiers and sailors. It would hardly have seemed odd to settlers to resort to corporal punishment. As Elspeth Huxley remarked, flogging was a standard punishment handed out by colonial whites: 'Most of the men who imposed these sentences had themselves been beaten when young, and did not regard the whip as an insult to a man's dignity but as a valid, indeed indispensible, way to enforce order'.[60]

Whites well understood that the performance of corporal punishment was the crucial point. The officer flogs the recruit, the teacher canes the pupil, the parent spanks the child, the master whips the slave; the former has the legal or moral authority to inflict pain on the latter.[61] When one person whips another, they are acting out a ritual of power. The use of the lash thus marks the boundary between superior and inferior, powerful and powerless, he who could beat and he who could be beaten. (Thus when the inferior physically resists, he challenges his inferiority – in the language of prestige, he is insolent or cheeky: as Beryl Markham once remarked about an African her father had beaten, 'this boy was rather insulant [sic] and fought back', and so her father beat him even more.)[62] Indeed, the infliction of violence is often a very public event, to illustrate and amplify both the victim's humiliation and the perpetrator's status. Huxley was certainly wrong in suggesting that flogging did nothing to harm the victim's dignity. If so, flogging would have had little purpose at all. Hence settlers' firm belief in the rod: it was a cheap, easy and effective means of asserting superiority over Africans.

If white adults spanked their own children, and if whites acted *in loco parentis* to Africans – the conclusion was obvious. 'H.' argued that education without discipline was worthless, even dangerous – witness the 'sympathetic and spineless master' who is 'despised and taken advantage of by his class'. Government, like the schoolteacher, must not 'spare the rod'.[63] The editor of the *Leader* admitted that extra-judicial corporal punishment might not be strictly legal, but it fell in the category of acts of violence most Europeans accepted: 'In principle, violence is forbidden by the law. In fact, such violence as whipping a child, birching a recalcitrant pupil, firing into a mob of strikers, or knocking down a "cheeky" savage, are not universally accepted as crimes.'[64]

Marking Africans as infantile excused corporal punishment, while corporal punishment helped infantilize Africans. Violence was certainly not unknown in most Kenyan African communities. Children were spanked or slapped or pinched. Many women suffered domestic violence at the hands of their husbands.[65] In each of these cases, the perpetrator claimed the right to inflict violence on the basis of age and sex. Thus when whites beat African men they at once infantilized and emasculated their victims. Violence perhaps did more to turn men into boys than did language.

Settlers believed violence to be integral to labour relations.[66] Africans who made demands – fewer hours, more pay – or simply declined to work might face the lash. Noel Smith flogged his workers for demanding a shorter working day.[67] Michael Blundell, later the foremost settler politician, began his Kenya career as a labour supervisor on Captain Hill's farm. Violence there was mundane. 'Langori refused to work', Blundell told his diary on 15 February 1926, 'so I kicked him and he sobered down'.[68] Elspeth Huxley wrote of some workers who refused to weed, angering her father (whom she called Robin in her writings). Their Afrikaner neighbour, her father knew, would have 'Put them down and give[n] them twenty-five'. 'This was a sovereign remedy in those days', Huxley recalled, 'but Robin did not like it, and he dodged the necessity whenever he could'.[69] Despite his sensitive soul, Robin was first and foremost a white settler in Kenya; like it or not, beating African workers was a 'necessity'. Smith, Blundell, Robin, the Afrikaner neighbour: all joined together in training Africans to accept a particular labour – and racial – hierarchy.

Violence answered many an unintentional failure on the part of Africans. Lady Cranworth told prospective settler women that learning household management might be helpful prior to emigrating, but much had to be learned on the ground: 'One could not, for instance, learn by experience in England when is the right time to have a servant beaten for rubbing a silver plate on the gravel path to clean it, and that after several previous warnings.'[70] For 'boys' who lied, her husband advised that 'the "kiboko" has a somewhat salutary effect'.[71] A typical day for 'An Up Country Manegeress': her kitchen 'toto' deserts because of her excessive beating; she slaps another 'boy' for bringing cold rather than hot water; she smashes a rotten egg in the face of her cook; she disperses a boisterous crowd with her 'little Kiboko'.[72] Whites beat not only their own servants but those from neighbouring farms, or complete strangers.[73]

Sometimes violence had little purpose other than to release settlers' rage. Beatings could be prompted by what might appear to any unbiased observer as an utterly trivial error, or indeed for no error at all. Roger Noel Money threw a book at his cook's head ('and if it had been a bomb I still would have thrown it') because the cook had failed to make a loaf of bread; Money was sick, lonely, 'feeling abso----lutely fed up ... infernally bad tempered too', and hungry for toast.[74] Dropping a master's package in a river brought a kick to the buttocks; breaking a plate resulted in a cuffing; imitating a kitten's 'plaintive cry' was silenced by the kiboko; borrowing a razor without permission ended in 'a good flogging'; a boot helped wake a porter to stir up the campfire.[75] Simply having a bad day could lead a white to 'go about kicking every black boy who happens to get into your way'.[76]

As individual acts – a rotten egg here, a caning there, a few strokes with the kiboko again – settler violence may appear unworthy of note. Disturbing, to be sure, but a relic of a thankfully bygone era. Yet as one adds up the daily beatings and slaps and kicks, in Nairobi homes, and upcountry farms, and coastal plantations, one begins to see that more was at stake. Settlers and Africans did not speak the same language, literally and figuratively. They did not understand what each expected of the other. Settlers could not make Africans understand, or could not convince them to accept, white demands. Settlers could not, or would not, break Africans' wills through money, logic, or pretensions to civilization. They instead turned to the language of violence. This, Africans could comprehend. Violence was the lingua franca of colonial Kenya.[77]

African women, by and large, escaped the whippings and kicks their menfolk suffered. Courts did not allow the flogging of women. Settlers also had less interaction with African women than with men. The Africans with whom whites had daily contact – their domestic servants, farm labourers, syces – were men. Those nearest to hand, those who were given the most orders to obey, were the most likely to feel a sting across the cheek. If violence was meant to cow Africans and protect whites, then there was less reason to flog an African woman. Beating African women would also have complicated the civilized gender ideology settlers wished to inculcate in African men. This is not to say they did not suffer from white violence. But violence against women could never be a central part of settler rule in the same way violence against African men was.

Limits on white violence

Given that most settlers swore to the benefits of corporal punishment, few were those who spoke out against the use of the lash.[78] Only a few settlers ventured the truly radical idea that violence toward Africans was unwarranted. 'D.F.' argued against the common formulation that 'the native being child-minded, must be treated as a child'. To flog an adult African was as degrading as was flogging an adult European.[79] Within Kenya, D. F. was in a distinct minority. Virtually all whites agreed that one could hardly compare an adult African with an adult

European. In any event, was not degradation one of the most beneficial results of flogging?[80]

Rarely, whites found themselves charged with violence against Africans. Magistrates heard a sprinkling of cases and tended to assess relatively small fines for assaults. In Uasin Gishu district in 1911–12, C. E. Foster paid 5 rupees for causing hurt to Kipson Arap Gumurogor. In contrast, in the same court one Juma received twelve lashes for stealing a pipe from Mr Woodhall, Maina served two years' hard labour and received fifteen lashes for theft of clothing from Mr Tweedie, and Kipcha took fifteen stripes for deserting his employer – and was sent back to finish out his contract.[81]

More commonly, whites criticized their fellows only when they had exceeded 'acceptable' levels of corporal punishment or beaten Africans for 'illegitimate' reasons. The rise of bourgeois manners in Europe extended to controlling one's anger. In proper circles, violence was less acceptable, especially as a result of having lost one's temper. It was instead the lower classes who were thought to be violent and who lacked self-control.[82] Even in Kenya, violence had to be measured and for good cause.[83]

Thus corporal punishment was critical to race relations, but within limits. An employer constantly '"whacking" his "niggers"' was a poor one.[84] Losing one's temper did no one any good, and could injure prestige. The employer 'who is unable to control his temper', wrote 'A Resident', 'is another member of the community that the country has no need of, for it is important that a European should preserve his dignity if he wishes to preserve the respect of his labourers'.[85] 'A Colonist' instructed that corporal punishment was a crucial tool in running workers, but it had to be imposed properly. The employer should first gather the other workers, and 'when you have thoroughly laid bare [the offender's] wickedness – go for him. It is when an European employer hits a boy – makes a practice of it – in fits of passion that the damage is done. The native is then regarded as a victim by his fellows and the master is anathema.'[86]

Class thus figured into critiques of excessive white violence. When hearing a 1906 case of three white men who had assaulted a Frenchman, our beleaguered town magistrate E. W. Logan 'considered their conduct towards this Frenchman was un-English'. Not only un-English, it appeared, for the magistrate took pains to note their class standing as well: 'There appeared to be an element in Nairobi at the present time of men who came here without any visible means of existence. They loafed from one bar to another and were a menace to the peace of the town.'[87] Sixteen years later, Harold G. Robertson, editor of the *Critic*, wondered about

> The name of the low down ruffian who, while being helped into the rickshaw when 'under the influence' kicked the native servant brutally in the face as he grunted 'B..... nigger'.
>
> ...
>
> And is it not likely that the native was the better man of the two.
>
> ...
>
> Also is it not fortunate that there are few Whites of his type in Kenya.[88]

This white was 'low down' and a lesser man than his victim not because he had used violence but because he had used it inappropriately. The 'ruffian' had been publicly drunk, he had assaulted someone who had come to assist him, and had inflicted a 'brutal' kick to the face rather than a slap or some stripes with a kiboko. Too much violence, like penury or sexual immorality, could lower white prestige.

Afrikaners – almost by definition among the poor white class – were thought to be the settlers quickest to anger, and the likeliest to resort to the lash for the most inconsequential of matters. MacGregor Ross later charged that early settlers were of a 'degenerate type [who] indulged in severe punishments' and quoted two:

> 'Five minutes after I start working with these Kikuyus, I'm raving like a Dutchman', explained one employer. 'I sjambocked the nigger till my arm ached', said another, explaining how he dealt with one of the troubles.[89]

'Sjambock' is the Afrikaner version of the kiboko – the second employer was suggesting an actual or metaphorical relationship to Afrikaner violence. When Elspeth Huxley noted that her African-flogging neighbour was a 'Boer', she was pointing out more than just his national background.

Violence and the law

Only low-class ruffians used excessive violence, and 'severe floggings' were beyond the pale. Again, these distinction were clearer in theory than in practice. Lord Delamere had a violent temper.[90] Galbraith Cole's farm manager recalled that Cole acted 'like a vicious highbred horse or some fucking aristocratic snake' in his violence toward Africans.[91] But no settler would have counted himself a ruffian. They used violence only when necessary – or so each settler would have claimed. Robertson of the *Critic* did not recommend legal action to protect innocent Africans. Public opinion should be the only real limit on settlers' use of violence. Corporal punishment was too important for the law to interfere with.

As much as administrators might agree that Africans deserved a good caning now and again, they could not allow settlers to cruelly beat, torture, and kill the white man's trustees. In a series of spectacular cases, the state dragged settlers to court. But in April 1906, the Colonial Office had finally bowed to white settlers' demands for the right to trial by a jury of their peers – their only peers being other white men.[92] The state might lay a charge, but settlers determined guilt or innocence. The highmindedness of British fair play and justice would be weighed against the brutal demands of a racial hierarchy. Hence the warning of a defence attorney during J. C. van Rooyen's trial for causing grievous bodily harm and hurt to an African: 'To give a verdict against my client, you stop for ever the infliction of corporal punishment.'[93] He might well have said, you stop forever the progress of white settlement in Kenya. Even more direct was the jury who heard a charge of culpable negligence in using weapons against Claude de Crespigny. His servant had apparently brought him warm beer. Mounted for a pig hunt, de Crespigny chased the African and (allegedly by accident) stabbed the man to death with his hunting spear. At the conclusion of the case, the jury did not even bother to leave their seats before ('amidst the cheers of the Court') finding de Crespigny not guilty. As they announced, they knew 'their duty to a white man'. [94]

One of the most notorious cases concerned the Honourable Galbraith Cole. Like many of the aristocratic settlers, Cole went in for large-scale herding. Like many herders, Cole suffered regular thefts of his animals. Like virtually all settlers victimized by thieves, Cole blamed government inaction and an effete judiciary. Matters came to a head in April 1911. Cole stumbled upon three men skinning one of his sheep. Two men surrendered, the third ran. Cole shot him dead. The charge was murder or culpable homicide. The jury knew its duty: this was not just a white man but a son of an earl, and his 'crime' was defending his property when the state had failed to do so. The verdict could never have been in doubt.

Cole's acquittal seemed, to many in London and some in the Kenya administration, to be the epitome of settler arrogance and racism. Home papers charged that law and order in Kenya had collapsed.[95] A settler could snuff the life from an African, be slightly inconvenienced by a trial, then return to his vast estate a free man. Despite some sympathy toward Cole on the part of Governor Girouard, the Colonial Office determined that it was 'a very horrible case ... Cole must be deported'.[96] In October, Cole was sent from the colony for 'conducting himself so as to be dangerous to peace and good order in East Africa and endeavouring to excite enmity between the people of East Africa' and the government.[97] Now it was the settlers' turn to charge that the law had been ignored. 'From the standpoint of dignity and liberty of the citizen', the *Leader* fumed, 'the community feels that the one solid plank upon which all pride themselves as resting on – administration of open British justice – has been summarily drawn from beneath their feet'.[98]

In later years, settler juries proved to have retained some sense of British justice.[99] Juries did not release men who had undeniably inflicted extreme violence on Africans. But rarely did juries convict them of serious charges. On 6 June 1920, the Njoro farmer Captain H. M. Harries dedicated a full hour to delivering a hundred strokes on his pig herd Kamauga, who, Harries alleged, had beaten and killed several swine. The white jury found Harries not guilty on the count of grievous hurt, but convicted him of simple hurt (which Harries had admitted) with the rider that he had acted 'under intense provocation'.[100] In 1923, a settler beat an African to death in what a Colonial Office official later called 'circumstances of shocking brutality', but the white jury convicted him only of grievous hurt.[101] Believers in law and justice in London condemned the decisions. For most settlers, the verdicts were not abuses of the jury system but the proper functioning of a colonial legal system.

Violence, the law, and black peril

Unsurprising: black peril brought out the worst of settlers' obsession with the kiboko and contempt for the judiciary. If settlers approved a few stripes for lazy farm workers and irritating houseboys, then certainly nothing less was appropriate for assaulting a white woman or child. In fact, a few stripes might not suffice. Grogan, of course, made flogging into a spectacle, a message for both insolent Africans and a worthless magistrate. Most commenters on black peril similarly blasted the colonial judicial machinery. In so far as black peril was an assault on settlerdom, the failure of the state to properly punish African rapists revealed – to Africans and Europeans alike – the state's lukewarm support for settlers. With each assault there echoed ever more insistent demands for ever harsher punishment. Because government officials understood the meaning of black peril, because they too cleaved to prestige and chivalry and humiliation, they could hardly dismiss settler demands. In 1926, settler prayers were answered: rape became a capital crime.

The Grogan flogging

With their assault on the three Gikuyu in Town Magistrate Logan's courtyard completed, Grogan and his fellows mounted a verbal assault on the government. An 'Emergency Committee' of the Colonists' Association met in urgent session. Resolutions called for the creation of a defence force and for the government to issue rifles and ammunition to settlers. A delegation met with the Acting Commissioner Frederick Jackson to warn of an imminent African rising.[102] Jackson soon came to appreciate the exaggeration and political manoeuvring he faced. He reported that the Africans had committed no assault, while the flogging 'was carried out in a most brutal manner'. 'I regard the whole incident', he informed the Colonial Office, 'as deliberately engineered and planned by Grogan, Burn, Fichat, Low and others with a view to bringing the Administration, and more particularly the Judicial and Police Departments, into contempt'. Jackson requested permission to increase the white police force, not to put down a supposed African rising but to control 'this gang of European lawbreakers'.[103] And lawbreakers they were: the three floggers, as well as others in the crowd, were to be hauled to court on charges of illegal assembly.

It was not so much the violence that the government deplored. Beatings with a kiboko were unexceptional. It was, rather, the location of the assault that provoked government reaction. Jackson certainly viewed the whole episode as political theatre. Indeed, one is hard pressed to believe Grogan's protestation he had not intended to use the magistrate's courtyard as the stage for his bloody performance.

5.1 'Officers and committee of the Colonists' Association of British East Africa'

Grogan enjoyed a spectacle, particularly when he was at the centre of it. How better to deliver his message about the effeminacy of the courts than a chivalrous, manly beating on the very steps of a courthouse?

In the meantime, settlers rallied to the accused men's defence. In a spirited editorial, the *Standard* laid out the justification for the flogging. To forestall black peril demanded white unity and black deaths. 'Official and Civilian must join for the common protection of their women folk', the *Standard* called. 'The native must be taught insolence to a white woman is a crime and that white women are as a thing sacred; to touch whom obscenely means death.' If the death penalty for the rape of white women was not passed into law, 'Mob Law' could not be prevented 'when stern necessity arises for vengeance'.[104] A later article similarly absolved Grogan of any blame for acting chivalrously. 'Captain Grogan was undoubtedly justified in using physical force', the editorial went, 'as the provocation was of a kind which no man will brook, and it does not matter whether the assault was committed on a native or European. We have never heard of any man who has appealed to the law to punish his wife's insulter.'[105] Africans and the government stood accused.

Grogan and his fellows felt no guilt.[106] Sidney Fichat had run through the streets collecting white men to witness the beating. According to the *Standard*'s trial reporting, Fichat told that court: 'I can hardly call it a creditable thing to do to publicly flog niggers but I agreed with [Grogan] that it was the proper thing under the circumstances to do.' Grogan too freely admitted his actions. His reasoning could have been echoed by very many white settlers. Notions of chivalry and prestige, the inadequacy of the courts, the need to use corporal punishment on Africans – all these, Grogan lived and breathed.

> My object in flogging natives in public was because I have noticed my own natives becoming unruly owing to the impossibility (in the great majority of cases) of getting a conviction against them in a Court, or to the inadequacy of punishment if convicted. I look upon the safety of one's women-folk as a matter of such paramount importance that I do not consider I am justified as a family man in leaving such a matter to the mercy of the vagaries of the law and the application thereof. I wished natives to understand, and it should be generally understood, that any action of that nature involves a far greater risk than a dose of horse-tooth mealies [particularly tasty maize supposedly provided to jailed Africans] or a mild suggestion not to do it again.

In answer to questions (not recorded) by the Crown Counsel, Grogan showed why a proper judicial hearing was unnecessary:

> I did not ask these boys for any explanation before I flogged them. I told them simply why I was going to beat them, I did not ask them if they had anything to say.
>
> I would not anyhow take the word of a native against that of a white lady...
>
> At that time I had made up my mind to flog them publicly; nothing they could have said would have altered my mind, for I don't admit of any explanation for a native's being impertinent to a lady.

The white men in the Colonial Office, in Government House, and on the bench knew full well the danger of 'a native's being impertinent to a lady'. Black peril might crush settlerdom, and it did precious little good for the future of white colonial rule. Administrators had wives, judges had children. Yet settlers' frothing could be nearly as dangerous. In their positions as representatives of the king, as promoters and beneficiaries of serikali's prestige, government officials had to ensure law and order. Even black peril should be subject to the law.[107]

On 6 April 1907, the court handed down its judgement. Ernest Low of the *Star of East Africa* admitted having been present, but not being 'learned in the law' professed that he had not considered 'whether or not it was lawful to flog a nigger in the main street of the town'. Despite his ignorance of the law, he was given seven days in prison. Fichat, who had led the effort to gather a crowd, was sentenced to fourteen days. Russell Bowker and Captain Gray were each sentenced to fourteen days and 250 rupee fines for drawing blood. For Grogan, the magistrate reserved special words of condemnation.

> I cannot find the slightest foundation in fact, for his statement that the offence which he alleges these natives to have committed constituted a matter of such paramount importance that, having at heart the safety of his women folk, he dare not trust this matter to be dealt with by what he describes as the vagaries of the law and the application thereof.
>
> On his own showing the safety of his women folk was never involved – at most these natives had only been guilty of impertinence – and on his own admission he has no recollection of any case ever being brought before the Courts of this Protectorate in which natives have been charged with indecent conduct to white women.

Rather than an unfortunate but understandable reaction to a sexual crime, Grogan's actions were beyond the pale. Grogan put the law into disrepute. This was a most dangerous lesson to Africans. Whites must teach Africans to obey and admire the law, not defy it upon a whim. He sentenced Grogan to one month in prison and a 500 rupee fine.

The *Times of East Africa* acknowledged that the men had insulted the majesty of the law, and were due punishment – but only a fine.[108]

Imprisonment of white men for any cause deeply injured white prestige. How much more so when the white men had been trying to protect white women. 'Not a single native', the *Times* railed, 'but will conclude inevitably that five Europeans have been sent to gaol because they lifted their hands to punish an offence by natives against white women. Not a single black but will decide that he can do no wrong which will entail punishment at the hands of the law whether it be mere insult to our women or worse.' Carping humanitarians in London and those who condemned the righteous anger of whites would soon witness the results of their misguided coddling of Africans. 'An ineradicable impression has been made on the native mind, an impression that cannot fail to bear fruit'. Black peril was in the offing. All whites in Kenya were now 'absolutely at the mercy of teeming numbers of brutal savages'. The article was titled 'Beginning of the End'. (As it turns out, all the convictions were overturned on 'technicalities'.)

Black peril and the law

If the convictions of Grogan, Bowker and Fichat bore any fruit, it was a pitiful harvest. A very few African men ever dared to touch white skin, and but a tiny fraction of them ever did so in lust or rage. When they did, settlers bared their teeth and bayed for blood. Kerslake Thomas, whose little girl was ill-treated by their African worker, threatened vigilantism should the state not fulfil its duty to whites. The *Leader* and, in a further letter, Thomas both demanded that rape immediately be elevated to a capital crime.[109] In fact, Governor Girouard had already been in contact with the Colonial Office. Perhaps with a finger on the pulse of settler opinion, he feared the worst. He had telegrammed London altering them to what he called 'a very *serious case of assault*'. A change in the penal code was required allowing for harsher punishments. A strong opinion, but one that he immediately suggested he was forced to take: 'Government undoubtedly will be pressed to introduction [*sic*] of South African law', that is, the death penalty.[110] With supreme understatement, a member of the Colonial Office staff minuted that 'This is an unhappy Protectorate'.[111]

The conviction of the girl's attacker seems to have quelled – if temporarily – settlers' rage.[112] As the Colonial Office noted a few months later, Girouard had not been in further contact, suggesting that he had 'had no further trouble' from the settlers.[113] But with the next peril, in 1920, came more demands for either personal or state-sponsored vengeance. In April, the *Daily Leader* reported an 'outrage' of a European girl by two Africans, and warned that as Africans came into more and regular contact with Europeans such attacks were bound to increase: 'familiarity brings less awe into the native's mind'. What was needed was to impose capital punishment for the rape of a white woman or child by an African. In fact, the paper claimed, death was the common punishment for rape within African communities. Could white men, the paper challenged, value their womenfolk less than African men did theirs? If rape were not elevated to a capital crime, lynch law might result.[114] Editorials and letters to the editor filled the columns of the *Daily Leader* and the *East African Standard*, calling for more liberal use of the lash, threatening vigilantism, or demanding capital punishment for rapists.[115]

The collision of black peril and settler justice culminated in 1926. For several months settlers' tempers ran high with rumours of hushed-up assaults on white children Then a conviction on 11 May for an attempted rape on a white widow. Then 17 May. At 8:45 that night, sixty-nine-year-old Julia Hepzibah Ulyate retired to her bedroom. Her husband had died some years before, and she lived alone in their home in Kijabe, a small highlands town. A noise awoke her around ten o'clock. Thinking it a rat or cat, she reached for the matchbox on her nightstand. She then felt a hand on her throat at which point, she later recalled, 'I realized it was a man I had to deal with'. They fell to the floor, where the man continued to hit her on the back of the head and shoulders, and raped her. He stabbed her several times with a knife, tried to smash her head on to the floor, and pulled her ear so violently that it partially tore off. Ulyate's foot banged a dresser drawer, and the noise startled her attacker. She rattled the drawer again. He jumped up, hit her one last time, and fled out the back door.[116]

The attack was, settlers argued, the logical result of all that was going wrong in Kenya. The *East African Standard* dubbed the attack the 'Kijabe Outrage'. Headlines in enormous bold fonts filled the front page: 'Elderly European Lady Attacked by Native; Desperate Night Struggle; Dragged by the Hair and Stabbed with a knife'. In a charged editorial, the *Standard* felt sure that all whites would agree that 'the strongest possible measures are now required ... to deal with a situation which contains all the elements of grave danger to the relationship between the races'. The courts might well not be able to eliminate that danger: 'The doctrine of "an eye for an eye" is not fully satisfied by the application of the law through the Courts of Justice even in a civilised country, and it is less likely to be so in a Colony where the conditions of life demand the strictest preservation of the sanctity of European women.' The legal system might have to be set aside and justice allowed to be 'made manifest in all its stark and crude force and righteousness as a duty to humanity'. Africans were only just emerging from 'barbarism' and to teach them to respect white women and children required 'drastic measures ... even outside the law'.[117]

In a 5 June telegram, Governor Grigg warned the Colonial Office that only a change in the law could 'maintain respect for the law if another offence is committed'; the Chief Justice agreed.[118] Yet when Grigg finally called a special session of the Legislative Council, settlers were in for something of a shock. Under the bill, approved by the Colonial Office, convicted rapists could be executed – this was all well and good. Yet capital punishment could be applied regardless of the race of victim or offender.[119] This had not been Grigg's original intention. He had assured the Secretary of State that any man guilty of raping a 'non-native' woman should be executed, regardless of his race. But intra-African rape was a lesser crime: the death penalty 'could not of course be imposed for rape upon a native woman because native opinion does not regard that offence as a matter of much gravity'.[120] This belief was widely shared among white observers of African societies, but the men of the Colonial Office rejected this reasoning. Secretary of State Leo Amery acquiesced to elevating rape to a capital crime, but with the proviso that it include no racial discrimination.[121]

Yet Grigg also reassured settlers that he was, in the end, of a single mind with them. It was 'idle to ignore' that the alteration in the law was due to Africans assaulting white women. Neither did he deny the 'horror of the outrage'. Grigg succeeded in having it both ways. He was apparently successful in quieting the peril. He told settlers that the state was, after all, on their side. The courts could be used to enforce 'a high standard of conduct from natives'.[122] African rapists could be hanged. The British public could be reassured that settlers were law-abiding folk, and could be trusted to have a greater voice in local affairs.

Conclusion

The boast of British colonialism was its beneficence. The rule of law, justice for all regardless of race or station – these were the things that made the Empire great. Britons also prided themselves on the peace they brought to Hobbesian worlds of Africa. This was an achievement they found especially notable compared with the obscenities King Leopold visited upon the Congo, and the bloodbath Germans let loose in Southwest Africa. True, the African territories had been won only through a series of 'little wars' (and a big one against the Boers), but such violence was necessary for the good of the conquered. Kenya administrators believed that a restricted level of violence ensured peace and prosperity, while the slow spread of civilization would allow for the proper introduction of British law.

Kenya settlers would have agreed with all this, with one crucial caveat: the functioning of the law and the employment of violence had always to be guided by settlers' interests. Failures of the court and limits on the lash both contributed to African insolence that led to black peril. Only by forcing the legal system to bow to settlers' demands, and only through a more liberal application of the kiboko, could settlerdom survive. Only the hanging of a black rapist could fully restore the settler soul.

Notes

1. And this from the earliest days of the protectorate. A. Hardinge to Ainsworth, 20 Mar. 1896, in G. H. Mungeam, *Kenya: Select Historical Documents, 1884–1923* (Nairobi: East African Publishing House, 1978), pp. 77–8.
2. KNA: PC/COAST 1/10/70, Hobley to Chief Secretary, 28 Jan. 1912.
3. Elspeth Huxley, *White Man's Country: Lord Delamere and the Making of Kenya*, Vol. I (New York: Praeger, 1967), pp. 149-50.
4. Errol Trzebinski, *The Kenya Pioneers* (New York: Norton, 1986), pp. 107–8, 148. For similar incidents in an unnamed upcountry town, likely Kitale, see Alyse Simpson, *The Land that Never Was* (Lincoln: University of Nebraska Press, 1985 [1937]), pp. 192–3.
5. Elspeth Huxley, *The Flame Trees of Thika* (New York: Morrow, 1959), p. 184. Things had improved only slightly by 1930. Margery Perham, *East African Journey: Kenya and Tanganyika, 1929–30* (London: Faber and Faber, 1976), p. 24.
6. W. Robert Foran, *A Cuckoo in Kenya: The Reminiscences of a Pioneer Police Officer in British East Africa* (London: Hutchinson, 1936), p. 320. See also Simpson, *Land that Never Was*, p. 39.
7. Foran, *Cuckoo in Kenya*, p. 320.
8. Richards in fact suggests that 'Many of the great men of Empire were essentially boy-men'. Jeffrey Richards, '"Passing the love of women": manly love and Victorian society', in J. A. Mangan and James Walvin (eds), *Manliness and Morality: Middle-Class Masculinity in Britain and America, 1800–1940* (New York: St Martin's, 1987), pp. 92–120.
9. He had earlier passed through Lodwar, in 1894. Stephen North, *Europeans in British Administered East Africa: A Provisional List, 1899–1903*, 2nd ed. (Wantage: S. J. North, 2000), p. 262.
10. 'A Sessions case', *TEA* (20 Jan. 1906), p. 4.
11. *Kenya Gazette*, 1 Feb. 1908, p. 80; http://rainbowfamily.co.uk/archives/1 (accessed 1 Feb. 2014).
12. *Kenya Gazette*, 10 June 1914, p. 666.
13. KNA: AG 51/322, A. Rainbow to C. Ogilvie, Asst. DC Narok, 8 Dec. 1919.
14. KNA: AG 51/322, A. Rainbow to Ogilvie, 12 Dec. 1919.
15. KNA: AG 51/322, Hemsted, Officer in Charge of the Masai Reserve, to Attorney General, 2 Jan. 1920.
16. KNA: AG 51/322, K. J. Muir Mackenzie, Ag Solicitor General, to Hemsted, 16 Jan. 1920.
17. 'Charge against a settler's wife', *EAS* (24 July 1923), p. 4.
18. 'Settlers charged', *EAS* (7 May 1923), p. 7.
19. In a case the next year, Miss P. Maclean charged an African with assault for having answered her slap to his face with one to her eye. During the case, an African witness suggested she had been drunk. She broke down in tears, 'sobbing bitterly and murmuring something to the effect of natives being encouraged to heap indignities on white women'. 'Alleged assault on a European lady', *EAS* (28 June 1924), p. 14.
20. 'Mrs Rainbow's case', *EAS* (31 July 1923), p. 5. Arthur Rainbow admitted that Buxton had allowed Patrice to remain seated during the proceeding, and thus 'a

courtesy was being shown to her. He repeated, however, that Maj. Buxton had spoken to his wife "as to a dog."'

21 KNA: AG 51/322, Officer in Charge, Masai Reserve to AG, 2 Jan. 1920. District Commissioner E. B. Horne later reported on a 'Masai Traders Association to which most of the Indians and a few not very respectable Europeans belong'. Arthur Rainbow served as secretary. KNA: Narok DAR, 1923.

22 KNA: Ag 51/322, T. J. A. Salmon, Ag DC, to Officer in Charge, Masai Reserve, 10 Dec. 1919.

23 The Langridge family in Machakos also enjoyed a reputation of ignoring official summons and making spurious charges against local officials. See, for example, Montgomery, letter to ed., *Leader* (7 Oct. 1911), in Nairobi supplement; correspondence in KNA: DC/MKS.10A/14/1; and NA: CO: 533/88/27210 ('Conduct of Hon K. R. Dundas and Mr. Montgomerie: Allegations of Mr. G. L. Langridge, 1911'). A photo of the Langridges can be found in *EAS* (12 Jan. 1924), p. 20.

24 KNA: AG 51/320, Patrice Rainbow to Major Buxton and Secretary and Members, Makuyu District Association, Thika. After some consideration, the state decided simply to ignore Rainbow, thinking her 'mad'.

25 Similarly, District Officer H. Seaton once found himself faced with a settler 'storming in blind fury, stamping across the court-room, shaking clenched fists as high as he could reach. "My God," he shouted at me, "you may call this law but, by heaven, it's not justice."' Henry Seaton, *Lion in the Morning* (London: Murray, 1963), p. 79.

26 KNA: Kikuyu DAR, 1911–12. Although Delamere once wrote that he favoured 'absolute justice' in intra- and inter-racial cases, it seems he never protested against the racialism of the law. Huxley, *White Man's Country*, Vol. 1, p. 190.

27 Evidence of Capt. W. F. S. Edwards, Native Labour Commission, Evidence and Report (Nairobi: Government Printer, 1913), p. 228.

28 Letter to the editor, *EAS* (19 Sept. 1918), p. 5. Whites also pointed to the use of African and Indian assessors (meant to advise judges in serious criminal cases involving members of their 'tribe' or religion) to advance the argument that English judicial traditions were lost on non-whites. White observers, including judges, often pointed out that the assessors either did not understand their role or failed to give impartial advice. See, for example, 'Nairobi and the jury system', and 'The value of Kikuyu assessors', both in *EAS* (2 May 1908), p. 8.

29 For earlier debates on English law's applicability to non-English settings, see Radhika Singha, *A Despotism of the Law: Crime and Justice in Early Colonial India* (Calcutta: Oxford University Press, 1998), pp. 27–32.

30 Evidence of T. R. Swift, Punda Milia, Native Labour Commission, p. 218; RH: MSS Afr. s. 613, Minutes of the Lumbwa Farmers Association, 13 Sept. 1926, and 10 Oct. 1927; 'Coddling the native', *EAS* (11 Mar. 1914), p. 6; KNA: Jud 1/1465, Secretary, Kikuyu District Settlers' Association, to Colonial Secretary, 29 June 1926; KNA: Jud 1/1465, R. J. Mitchell, Secretary, Trans Nzoia Farmer's Association, to Attorney General, 2 Sept. 1931.

31 'Natives and the law in Kenya', *The Times* (26 July 1926), p. 11. See also speech by Powys-Cobb at the Convention of Associations meeting, in *EAS* (27 Feb. 1926), Special Supplement, p. 7; 'Things we want to know', *Critic* (15 July 1922), p. 15. For a fictional discussion along these lines by a former settler, see Florence Riddell, *Kismet in Kenya* (Philadelphia: Lippincott, 1932), pp. 261–2.

32 'Kenya settlers and native labour', *The Times* (1 Nov. 1926), p. 13. See also 'Cause and effect', *Advertiser* (16 July 1909).

33 Evelyn Brodhurst-Hill, *So This Is Kenya!* (London: Blackie, 1936), p. 145; Lady Evelyn Cobbold, *Kenya: The Land of Illusion* (London: John Murray, 1935), p. 214; W. S. Routledge and Katherine Routledge, *With a Prehistoric People: The Akikuyu of British East Africa* (London: Frank Cass, 1968 [1910]), p. 220. For similar comments by a former colonial official, see Herbert Reginald McClure, *Land-Travel and Seafaring: A Frivolous Record of Twenty Years Wandering* (London: Hutchinson, 1925), pp. 94–5, 101. What most settlers and administrators thus

favoured was 'substantial justice'. 'Occasional Notes', *EAS* (19 Sept. 1908), p. 9. See also 'Commonsense law', *EAS* (19 Aug. 1910), p. 2. On judicial reactions to such thinking, see Brett Shadle, 'White settlers and the law in early colonial Kenya', *Journal of Eastern African Studies* 4 (2010): 509–23, esp. p. 515.

34 'Another injustice', *Advertiser* (19 Feb. 1909). See also, for examples, G. S. Sneyd, Secretary of Rongai and Lower Molo Farmer's Association, 'Settler and native', *EAS* (30 Oct. 1920), p. 9; 'A comparison', *Nairobi News* (8 Feb. 1905), p. 2.
35 Brodhurst-Hill, *So This Is Kenya!*, p. 145.
36 'Coddling the native', *EAS* (8 March 1913), p. 22. See also 'The government's native policy: severe criticism', *EAS* (7 Mar. 1908), p. 4; 'The increase in desertions', *EAS* (5 July 1924), p. 5. Settler complaints against Kyambu Assistant DC S. V. Cooke came around to his application of the law. Particularly incensed was Aldred Ivan Rule Harries, who 'knew something of administrative work and was under the impression that officers should work hand in hand with settlers rather than to get Natives to tell untruths [in court] in order to get white men convicted'. KNA: AG 51/329, 'The Cooke Inquiry', *Daily Observer* (28 Apr. 1923), clipping.
37 'Late labour evidence, or the ballad of the cute Kikuyu', *EAS* (16 Nov. 1912), p. 26.
38 See also, for example, 'A Lover of Fair Play', letter to ed., *Leader* (7 Oct. 1911). For a fuller examination of such complaints, see Shadle, 'White settlers and the law'. Administrators, for their part, criticized settlers who worked around the law. Too freely ignoring the law might imply to Africans that the law had no force, need not be respected. 'Every [white] man', a district commissioner complained in 1912, 'wants to be a law unto himself, fines are freely extorted, stray stock confiscated and private punishment practised without regard to the law. These proceedings which in some cases I cannot describe as less than scandalous and derogatory to the dignity of the white man to which otherwise such great claim is laid, must be stopped'. KNA: Kikuyu DAR 1911–12.
39 Shadle, 'White settlers and the law', 517–18.
40 On settler-imposed fines, see, for example, KNA: AG 25/43; 'Shooting goats', *KO* (25 Aug. 1923), p. 3; C. S. Nicholls, *Elspeth Huxley: A Biography* (New York: St Martin's, 2002), p. 80.
41 See, for example, Brodhurst-Hill, *So This Is Kenya!* 145; 'Stock-stealing by natives', *TEA* (21 July 1906), p. 4; 'A distinct menace', *Advertiser* (14 Aug. 1908), p. 3; Huxley, *Flame Trees of Thika*, p. 197. See also Nicholls, *Elspeth Huxley*, pp. 46, 289.
42 'The problem of native deserters', *EAS* (5 July 1924), p. 34; C. F. Lobo, 'Native insolence', letter to ed, *EAS* (31 May 1913), p. 25. The implications of this letter extend in other directions: the name Lobo suggests he was Goan, one of the 'in-between' communities of East Africa.
43 'Critics of East Africa: a Tanganyika settler defends Kenya', *EA* (1 Oct. 1925), p. 36. As the *Standard* explained in another case, 'Swift punishment has a moral effect'. 'Delayed justice', *EAS* (3 Oct. 1924), p. 4.
44 See, for example, KNA: AG 7/2, Ag Gov. to SS, 1 Sept., 1925.
45 Evidence of Leys, Native Labour Commission, p. 273.
46 Errol Trzebinski, *The Lives of Beryl Markham: Out of Africa's Hidden Free Spirit and Denys Finch Hatton's Last Great Love* (New York: Norton, 1993), p. 40. Official opinion on settler justice was mixed. See Shadle, 'White settlers and the law'; KNA: Kikuyu DARs 1911–12, 1921; Kyambu DAR 1915–16; Ukamba Provincial Annual Report, 1918–19; KNA: AG 25/43, correspondence between Kericho DC, Nyanza PC, Ag Chief Secretary, Ag Attorney General, and Ag Solicitor General, 1918; KNA: PC/NZA 3/17/1, correspondence between DCs and Senior Commission, Nyanza, Apr. 1925.
47 Henry Tarlton, letter to ed., *EAS* (21 June 1923), p. 5.
48 'Leniency or licence?', *EAS* (22 June 1923), p. 4.
49 In fact, the courts were quite free with the lash. See David M. Anderson, 'Master and servant in colonial Kenya, 1895–1939', *Journal of African History* 41 (2000): 459–85; Paul Ocobock, 'Spare the rod, spoil the colony: corporal punishment,

50 colonial violence, and generational authority in Kenya, 1897–1952', *International Journal of African Historical Studies* 45 (2012): 29–56.
50 C. Woolcott Roberts, letter to ed., *Leader* (7 Sept. 1912), p. 15; 'Native crime', *EAS* (15 May 1920), p. 22; 'Warning to government', *EAS* (22 May 1920), p. 18D; 'Nairobi gaol', *EAS* (2 Nov. 1924), p. 6.
51 W. M. Hudson, letter to ed., *EAS* (15 May 1920), p. 2. See also, for example, E. A. Ashe, letter to ed., *Advertiser of East Africa* (22 Nov. 1907), p. 2; 'Occasional notes', *EAS* (20 March 1909), p. 9; M. C. Monckton, letter to ed., *EAS* (17 Apr. 1920), p. 29; Eve Bache, *The Youngest Lion: Early Farming Days in Kenya* (London: Hutchinson, 1934), pp. 261, 264–6; Brodhurst-Hill, *So This Is Kenya!* 185; M. H. Hamilton, *Turn the Hour: A Tale of Life in Colonial Kenya* (Sussex: Book Guild, 1991), p. 67; Seaton, *Lion in the Morning*, 23; Nora Strange, *Kenya To-Day* (London: Stanley Paul, 1934), p. 83; Huxley, *Flame Trees of Thika*, 132.
52 Curiously, these arguments were undermined by another set of justifications settlers made for their use of the kiboko. Many settlers claimed that African servants *preferred* the lash to being taken before the magistrate. Of course, these arguments were made primarily for the consumption of their critics, for logically they made no sense. If Africans took pain lightly, then what good was the lash? If Africans preferred the settler's lash to the magistrate's jail, then would not the threat of imprisonment have had greater deterrent value?
53 'Occasional notes', *EAS* (27 Mar. 1909), p. 9; W. M. Hudson, letter to ed., *EAS* (15 May 1920), p. 2. See also LegCo debates, 17 Aug. 1928, p. 565; 'Kisumu notes', *Leader* (7 Sept. 1912), p. 11; 'Inefficient sentences', *EAS* (2 Aug. 1919), p. 18; 'East African Women's League', *KO* (1 Mar. 1923), p. 4.
54 'Crime and punishment', *EAS* (17 Apr. 1920), p. 24; 'One with Experience', letter to ed., *EAS* (19 June 1920), p. 18C. Whites argued that Africans had a different relationship to pain and to their bodies than did Europeans. When patching up their patients, whites marvelled at Africans' stoicism. The impression of Africans being better able to withstand pain, or perhaps being less sentient than whites, could contribute to arguments in favour of corporal punishment. See, for example, 'One with Experience', letter to editor, *EAS* (19 June 1920), p. 18C; 'Ex-Prison Warder', letter to ed., *EAS* (19 June 1920), p. 25; A. Hardinge to Ainsworth, 20 Mar. 1896, in Mungheam, *Kenya: Select Historical Documents*, p. 78.
55 'Occasional notes', *EAS* (22 July 1911), p. 11; 'A distinct menace', *Advertiser* (14 Aug. 1908), p. 3; 'Stock-stealing by natives', *TEA* (21 July 1906), p. 4; 'Native treatment', *Leader* (30 Dec. 1911), p. 4.
56 Brett Shadle, 'Settlers, Africans, and inter-personal violence in early colonial Kenya', *International Journal of African Historical Studies* 45 (2012): 57–80; Matt Carotenuto and Brett Shadle, 'Introduction: toward a history of violence in colonial Kenya', *International Journal of African Historical Studies* 45 (2012): 1–7.
57 'Coddling the native', *EAS*, 8 Mar. 1913, p. 22. See also, on the need for a standing army in Kenya, 'Convention of Associations', *EAS* (12 Aug. 1911), pp. 19-20.
58 For some of the European inheritance of corporal punishment, see Shadle, 'Settlers, Africans, and inter-personal violence'.
59 Harry Hendrick, *Children, Childhood and English Society, 1880–1990* (New York: Cambridge University Press, 1997), pp. 23, 74–7; Lionel Rose, *The Erosion of Childhood: Child Oppression in Britain, 1860–1918* (London and New York: Routledge, 1991); J. R. de S. Honey, *Tom Brown's Universe: The Development of the Victorian Public School* (London: Millington, 1977). Tosh suggests that corporal punishment within the home may have been decreasing, however. John Tosh, *A Man's Place: Masculinity and the Middle-Class Home in Victorian England* (New Haven: Yale University Press, 2007), p. 151.
60 Elspeth Huxley, *The Mottled Lizard* (New York: Penguin, 1982 [1962]), p. 138. For one of her examples, see p. 159.
61 That corporal punishment in the West derives its meaning from the home helps explains why, although corporal punishment has long been challenged in schools, prisons, and the workplace, attempts to regulate physical chastisement of children

by parents is the last to be regulated; domestic abuse of wives by husbands comes a close second.

62 Trzebinski, *Lives of Beryl Markam*, p. 40. See also 'Nairobi Sessions', *EAS* (20 Jan. 1906), p. 7.
63 'H.', 'Native education', *EAS* (19 Aug. 1922), p. 3. The author suggested that some 'discipline' earlier on would have prevented the rise of Harry Thuku and the East African Association. See also in the evidence of the Native Labour Commission, evidence of D. Beaton (p. 49), T. R. Swift (p. 218), and Capt. W. F. S. Edwards, Inspector General of Police (p. 228); 'Editor's note', *Advertiser* (9 July 1909); 'Coddling the native', *EAS* (8 Mar. 1913), p. 22; 'Molly's world', *EAS* (3 June 1913), p. 15; 'Leniency or licence?' *EAS* (22 June 1923), p. 4. One settler demanded the right to 'give our boys a spanking occasionally'. 'Coast notes', *EAS* (7 July 1917), p. 8.
64 'Treatment of natives', *Leader* (2 Sept. 1911), p. 8.
65 On children, see Paul Ocobock, 'Spare the rod, spoil the colony: corporal punishment, colonial violence, and generational authority in Kenya, 1897–1952', *International Journal of African Historical Studies* 45 (2012): 29–56. On domestic violence, see Emily S. Burrill, Richard L. Roberts, and Elizabeth Thornberry (eds), *Domestic Violence and the Law in Colonial and Postcolonial Africa* (Athens: Ohio University Press, 2010). See also Matt Carotenuto, 'Repatriation in colonial Kenya: African institutions and gendered violence', *International Journal of African Historical Studies* 45 (2012): 9–28.
66 See, for example, *Native Labour Commission, Evidence and Report* (Nairobi: Government Printer, 1913), p. 236. See also evidence of Chief Ogola, Kisumu district (p. 163), W. E. D. Knight (p. 71), S. Anderson, Supdt of Inland Revenue and Conservancy, Mombasa (p. 105), Norman Leys (p. 273); for contrary opinions, see the evidence of E. C. Crewe-Read, ADC at Nakuru (p. 123); Capt. A. H. James (p. 125), Capt. Chapman (p. 188); See also *Native Punishment Commission* (Nairobi: Government Printer, 1923), copy in KNA: AG/7/2. (My thanks to Omukofu Richard Ambani and Paul Ocobock for obtaining a copy of this file for me.) Acting Governor Denham, queried on this point by the Secretary of State, admitted that 'It is generally agreed that the practice' of whites imposing corporal punishment 'does exist', but was in decline. Ag Gov. Kenya to SS, 1 Sept. 1925, KNA: AG/7/2. See also 'Full of Hope', letter to ed., *Advertiser* (1 May 1908), p. 3; Llewelyn Powys, *Black Laughter* (New York: Harcourt, Brace, 1924), pp. 107, 146; Trzebinski, *Kenya Pioneers*, 125. See also the *Leader*'s poem 'Jack Nigger', which ends: 'And with it all but one thing can / Disturb your lordly rest / And that, Jack Nig, you likewise know / Is twenty of the best'. Quoted in Anthony Clayton and Donald Savage, *Government and Labour in Kenya, 1895–1963* (London: Cass, 1975), n. 48, p. 105.
67 Quoted in Nicholls, *Red Strangers*, p. 56.
68 RH: MSS Afr. s. 746/1, Michael Blundell, 'Diary, 1925–26', entry of 15 Feb. 1926. See also entries of 23 and 24 Mar. and 20 Apr. 1926.
69 Elspeth Huxley, *Flame Trees of Thika*, pp. 65–6.
70 Lady Cranworth, 'Hints of a woman in British East Africa', ch. 9 in Bertram Francis Gurdon Cranworth, *A Colony in the Making; or, Sport and Profit in British East Africa* (London: Macmillan, 1912), p. 85.
71 Cranworth, *Colony in the Making*, p. 52.
72 'A day in the existence of an up country manageress', *Outlaw* (9 Feb. 1922), p. 15.
73 Simpson, *Land that Never Was*, pp. 157–8.
74 Money, letter to Carlo Plowden, 17 Feb. 1923, in Roger Noel Money, *Ginia: My Kenya Coffee Shamba, 1918–1939* (Perth: privately published by Daphne Carol Cross, 2000), p. 181.
75 Simpson, *Land that Never Was*, p. 231; RH: MSS Afr. s. 746/1, Blundell, 'Diary', entry of 9 Mar. 1926; RH MSS Afr. s. 1086, T. R. L. Nestor Papers, p. 46; RH MSS Afr. r. 93, Patterson Diary, entry of 26 Apr. 1898; 'Safari', 'A rude awakening', *Kenya Graphic* 1 (1922): 105.

76 'Matrimonial bliss in B.E.A. by one who knows something about it!', *EAS* (12 Apr. 1913), p. 22.
77 Officials relied on violence as well. See Shadle, 'Settlers, Africans, and interpersonal violence'.
78 See also the minority report of the Native Punishment Commission (Nairobi: Government Printer, 1923).
79 'D.F.' letter to ed., *Kenya Observer* (26 Oct. 1923), pp. 3, 6. His letter came in response to the report of the Native Punishment Commission, which on the whole he thought good 'except for the nauseating feeling aroused by the allusion to flogging'. 'D.F.' had previously condemned leniency in courts in cases of 'very blatant brutality' by whites against Africans. Letter to ed., *KO* (28 Aug. 1923), p. 8.
80 The only other published example I have recovered comes from 'The Echo'. In his regular column 'Echoes of the week', Echo rejected calls for outlying settlers to be given powers as justices of the peace. He thought it premature, given the extent of violence meted out by those settlers on their African employees. It was both uncivilized and gave settlers a bad name back in Britain. 'Echoes of the week', *KO* (23 June 1923), p. 6. For overseas critiques of settler violence, see KNA: AG/7/2, SS to Gov. Kenya, 19 Dec. 1924; NA: CO 533/371/4.
81 Uasin Gishu DAR, 1911–12.
82 Judith Rowbotham, 'Criminal savages? Or "civilizing" the legal process', in Judith Rowbotham and Kim Stevenson (eds), *Criminal Conversations: Victorian Crimes, Social Panic, and Moral Outrage* (Columbus: Ohio State University Press, 2005).
83 Dr Burkitt believed 'lack of self-control' to be one result of sun-induced degeneration. J. R. Gregory, *Under the Sun: A Memoir of Dr R. W. Burkitt of Kenya* (Nairobi: self-published, 1952), p. 17.
84 'Treatment of natives', *Leader* (2 Sept. 1911), p. 8.
85 'A Resident', 'Nairobi and Kenya colony', *Scottish Geographical Magazine* 37 (1921): 99-103, quote at p. 101. Similarly, one letter writer thought 'flogging when *in a temper*' was useless for dealing with thieving servants. 'Try It', letter to ed., *Advertiser* (16 Oct. 1908), p. 5. The editors of the *Standard* congratulated one Mr Powell for 'controlling his temper' and reporting some threatening Africans to the police, rather than hitting them. 'Occasional notes', *EAS* (20 Mar. 1909), p. 9.
86 'A Colonist', letter to ed., *Leader* (9 Dec. 1911), p. 6.
87 'The assault case', *TEA* (9 June 1906), p. 5.
88 'Things we want to know', *Critic* (1 July 1922), p. 15.
89 MacGregor-Ross, *Kenya from Within*, p. 90.
90 Huxley, *White Man's Country*, Vol. 1, pp. 159–60
91 Sara Wheeler, *Too Close to the Sun: The life and Times of Denys Finch Hatton* (London : Jonathan Cape, 2006), p. 76.
92 NA: CO 533/118/21531, R. M. Combe, Att. Gen., 'Trial by Jury in British East Africa', 28 May 1913. One month later came the inaugural jury trial. A white jury found Frank Oliver Tattersall not guilty by reason of insanity after he shot two Africans and sprayed bullets at others. Tatersall's madness had not clouded his understanding of prestige. A white witness reported that Tattersall had shot an askari for 'standing in a slovenly manner with his cap on one side and he thought this was an insult both to himself and his King'. 'The Tattersall case', *EAS* (19 May 1906), pp. 7, 9.
93 The accused was convicted of voluntary hurt, but not grievous hurt. 'News from Nakuru', *EAS* (20 Nov. 1915), p. 23.
94 RH: MSS Afr. s. 2046, Brig.-Gen. J. E. and Dorothy Gough, 'Letters and Diaries, 1907-08', letter of April 17; C. S. Nicholls, *Red Strangers: The White Tribe of Kenya* (London: Timewell, 2005), p. 69. Over the next few years, numerous other cases of often shocking brutality made their way through the courts. See 'Nakuru Sessions', *EAS* (22 May 1909), p. 13; 'Occasional notes', *EAS* (21 Jan. 1911), p. 11; 'Nakuru Magistrates Court', *EAS* (28 Jan. 1911), p. 13; 'Grievous hurt to native', *EAS* (11 Mar. 1911), p. 16; 'Nakuru Sessions', *EAS* (29 Aug. 1910), p. 2; 'Nakuru Sessions: alleged grievous hurt', *EAS* (12 Feb. 1910), p. 12; 'Occasional notes',

EAS (21 Jan. 1911), p. 11; 'Nakuru Magistrates Court', *EAS* (28 Jan.1911), p. 13; 'Grievous hurt to native', *EAS* (11 Mar. 1911), p. 16.
95 For extracts from British papers, see 'Cole's deportation', *EAS* (23 Sept. 1911), p. 1; 'The Cole case', *Leader* (14 Oct. 1911), p. 7.
96 Minute by Harcourt, quoted in Robert M. Maxon, *Struggle for Kenya: The Loss and Reassertion of Imperial Initiative, 1912–1923* (Hackensack, NJ: Fairleigh Dickinson University Press, 1993), p. 39.
97 The warrant of deportation is reproduced in *Leader* (16 Sept. 1911), p. 8. His deportation was reported in 'Nakuru, the Cole case, and cognate happenings', *Leader* (7 Oct. 1911), p. 8.
98 'The Cole case', *Leader* (16 Sept. 1911), p. 8. For many years, settlers continued to excuse Cole's actions and condemn his deportation. Lord Francis Scott, later political leader of the settlers, thought Cole 'perfectly justified in what he did'. RH: MSS Brit. Emp. s. 349, Lord Francis Scott, 'Diaries', entry of 14 Apr. 1920. See also 'Lord Cranworth defends Kenya', *EA* (22 Oct. 1925), pp. 90–1. McGregor Ross claimed that some settlers looked askance at Cole for not turning himself in immediately, and for neither seeking medical help nor 'finishing off' the dying man. *Kenya from Within*, p. 434. During the war Cole's deportation order was revoked by Harcourt in the CO 'in view of the general amnesty to Suffragettes and South African deportees'. (Quoted in Maxon, *Struggle for Kenya*, p. 80.) Cole returned to Kenya where he remained until his death in 1929.
99 However, it was only with the support of the Kenya judiciary that settlers did not lose their right to trial by jury, which was strongly contemplated by the Colonial Office. Chief Justice Barth in 1913 admitted 'that it is probable a whiteman charged with an offence against a native will in certain districts and under certain circumstances be given rather more than a fair trial and the tendency will be for the jury to give undue weight to evidence or statements which afford any traces of a likely defence'. If the alternative was abolishing jury trials altogether – anathema to judges cultivating British legal traditions in East African soils – they could overlook a few ill-considered decisions. Jury trials continued, although for at least thirty years the Colonial Office required the Kenya government to forward full transcripts of all inter-racial criminal cases heard by juries. NA: CO 533/118/21531, J. W. Barth, 'Notes on Trial by Jury in British East Africa', 19 May 1913, enclosure in Gov. Kenya to SS, 31 May 1913; on review of transcripts, see NA: CO 533/91/36361; CO 533/118/21531; CO 533/526/8.
100 KNA: AC 2/60, High Court at Nakuru, Criminal Case 58 of 1920. For more on the Harries case, see Shadle, 'Cruelty and empathy'.
101 NA: CO 822/52/1, Penal and Criminal Codes, Background Notes, 1934. For reaction in Britain, see the collection of letters and editorials collected by the Anti-Slavery Society, in RH: MSS Brit. Emp. s. 22 G/36.
102 'The climax', *EAS* (16 Mar. 1907), p. 9.
103 Ag Commissioner to SS, 16 Mar. 1907, in 'Correspondence Relating to the Flogging of Natives by Certain Europeans at Nairobi', Cmd 3562, 1907.
104 'Forewarned, etc', *EAS* (23 Mar. 1907), p. 8.
105 'The flogging incident', *EAS* (23 Mar. 1907), p. 9.
106 The following draws on 'Found guilty', *EAS* (6 April 1907), pp. 5–6, 9–10, 13; 'Correspondence Relating to the Flogging of Natives', Cmd 3562.
107 Thus crucial throughout the subsequent events was the question of the proportionality of the vigilantes' acts relative to their victims' alleged crime. It appears that officials would have been more forgiving of the flogging if the Gikuyu had committed an assault, or even made indecent remarks.
108 The following draws on 'The beginning of the end', *TEA* (6 Apr. 1907), in 'Correspondence' section.
109 'The native peril', and J. Kerslake Thomas, letter to ed., both in *Leader* (18 Nov. 1911), pp. 8, 12.
110 NA: CO 533/92/36964, Gov. of Kenya to SS, 15 Nov. 1911.
111 NA: CO 533/92/36964, H.B., note in file, 16 Nov. 1911.

112 Judge Pickering convicted Jaguna of attempted rape or indecent assault with violence on a child of five years, as well as criminal intimidation (for threatening to kill the girl if she reported the assault). Jaguna received twenty-four lashes, seven years' rigorous imprisonment, and a 500 rupee fine on the first count, and four years' rigorous imprisonment on the second. 'Prisoner convicted', *Leader* (9 Dec. 1911), p. 2.
113 NA: CO 533/92/36964, H.B., note in file, 2 Feb. 1912.
114 KNA: AM/1/1/5, 'Children's peril', *Leader* (9 Apr. 1920), clipping.
115 'Native crime', *EAS* (15 May 1920), p. 22; W. M. Hudson, 'Crime and punishment', *EAS* (15 May 1920), p. 2; 'Warning to government', *EAS* (22 May 1920), p. 18D; 'A Father', letter to ed, *EAS* (29 May 1920), p. 2; 'A Father', letter to ed, *EAS* (12 June 1920), p. 18B; and the following clippings in KNA: AM/1/1/5: 'A stitch in time', *Leader* (n.d., but May 1920); 'A white man', letter to ed, *Leader* (24 May 1920); 'Horrified', letter to ed, *Leader* (n.d., but early June 1920); 'To make the punishment fit the crime', *Leader* (n.d., but early June 1920); 'The unpardonable crime', *Leader* (11 June 1920); 'Maramuki Kidogo', letter to ed, *Leader* (11 June 1920); 'A Father', letter to ed., *Leader* (22 June 1920). The resulting Special Committee on Sexual Assaults of Natives upon Europeans quieted, if temporarily, the hysteria. Blackall, Crown Counsel and chair of the committee, noted later that 'excitement died down as quickly as it had arisen, as soon as the Report was published'. RH MSS Brit. Emp. S.447, Blackall Papers, p. 124. But see also NA: CO 533/162, Gov. Kenya to SS, 13 July 1926; 'Portia', letter to the ed., *Leader* (7 Aug. 1920).
116 'Elderly European Lady Attacked by Native', *EAS* (22 May 1926), p. 4.
117 Editorial, *EAS* (22 May 1926), p. 15. For further reactions, see 'Eldoret Chamber and the Kijabe outrage', *EAS* (29 May 1926), p. 14; RH: MSS Afr. s. 1506, Njoro Settlers' Association, Minutes, 13 June 1926; RH, Ulu Settlers Association Papers, 5 June 1926; 'To Correspondents', *EAS* (29 May 1926), p. 33; Arthur Barnley, letter to ed., *EAS* (22 May 1926), p. 42.
118 NA: CO 533/612, Gov. Kenya to SS, 5 June 1926, and Gov. Kenya to SS, 12 June 1926.
119 LegCo debates, 30 June 1926.
120 NA: CO 533/612, Gov. Kenya to SS, 5 June 1926.
121 NA: CO 533/612, SS to Gov. Kenya, 14 June 1926.
122 LegCo debates, 30 June 1926.

CHAPTER SIX

Conclusion

The settler soul described in these pages might be unrecognizable to the settlers themselves. The early settlers had many things on their minds – rinderpest, farming equipment, race days, hunting, locusts, currency fluctuations, and malaria. The reminiscences and anecdotes repeated these days are not about violence and fear and condescension. They are stories of adventurous, intrepid men and women who, with little more than pluck, planted themselves in Kenyan soil. They are stories with a rich cast of characters, each with eccentricities unwelcome in London but celebrated in East Africa. Stories of hard work, camaraderie, and laughter, in a land of unparalleled beauty. All of this is undeniably part of the history of white settlers.

But when Michael Blundell could not show his real fear at a thunderstorm, he revealed something else about white settlers. So too Blixen, when she composed rapturous letters about her noble savage Farah. And Lord Delamere, manning the ramparts against Russian Jews. And Eve Bach, who loved her African servants despite their ingratitude. John Rennie, punching an askari who refused to give way on the path. Harold Robertson, defending white prestige by condemning settlers who kept African prostitutes busy. A. B. Mortimer, complaining that the judiciary held 'a nigger's word' more trustworthy than a white man's. Russell Bowker, whose 'first principle [was] to flog a nigger on sight who insults a white woman'. These, too, are part of the history of white settlers.

The settler soul across the decades

The year 1928 was a kind of turning point in settler history. It is not one that scholars have noted before. It is not immediately recognizable as a historical watershed, a point where the *before* and the *after* differ starkly – the Depression, or Independence. Even in their own reminiscences, settlers did not make much of 1928. But in that year there was a rape, and there was a hanging, and the settler soul was at peace.

Dusk on 27 March, 1928 found Winifred Maud Price, a twenty-four-year-old woman only a few months in Nairobi, walking home. As she cut across a field near Lenana Road in Nairobi, she was approached from behind by an African who greeted her with 'Jambo, Memsahib' (Hello, Madam).[1] Price replied with a brusque 'Jambo, kwenda' (Hello, go). The man threw her to the ground, hit her several times in the face, and put his hands around her throat to silence her screams. He tore off her dress and undergarments. Having realized physical resistance was futile, she appealed to the logic of racial superiority: 'Don't do this to me I am English'.[2] Yet he appears to have been motivated rather than deterred by her race: Price recollected that he uttered 'me black you white'. She threatened him with arrest, promised him money, all to no avail. Ninety minutes later he sent her off, 'Kwenda nyumbani yako' (go home).[3] With Price's description of her assailant, police quickly picked up one Nyaduongo, son of Awori.

The inquest and trial left little doubt of his fate. Nyaduongo was a stranger to Price, and he had treated her brutally.[4] Nyaduongo admitted to having been present that evening, but claimed another man had assaulted Price. His story convinced no one. The other man had an alibi. Two other men testified having heard Nyaduongo say that 'he had had a very bad affair with a European woman and had laid her down'.[5] Judge Barth wondered if it was 'likely that the accused would sit there and look at another native doing that sort of thing if he had any decent feeling at all?'[6] Price had identified him in a lineup of some twenty-two men 'of the same build'.[7] Three African assessors, who sat in on the trial and offered their conclusions to the judge, all thought Nyaduongo guilty. The judge could not imagine a 'more full and proper case' for the imposition of the death penalty. (H. E. Schwartze – member of the Legislative Council, supporter of the 1926 law that allowed the death penalty for rape, and Nyaduongo's lawyer – had earlier stated that 'He had seldom seen a case of more disgusting details'. Nyaduongo may have been dissatisfied with his legal representation.)[8]

In an editorial reflecting on the death sentence for Nyaduongo, the *Standard* repeated the by-now familiar warnings: 'In a colony, such as Kenya, where races of high civilization are perforce in contact with others in descending order to the lowest, stern measures are imperative if worse is not to befall'. Nothing was worse than the rape of a white woman – 'no crimes ... so profoundly stir the feelings of all right thinking races'. The hanging of Nyaduongo would prevent 'greater evils'.[9] His death would be just desserts for his crime, and the only way to re-establish white dominance.

CONCLUSION

On 27 July 1928, the hangman slipped the noose over the head of Nyaduongo son of Awori and released the trapdoor. One wonders how many settlers denied themselves a self-congratulatory whisky with the crack of Nyaduongo's neck.

The execution of Nyanduongo marked a high point for settlerdom, a moment when black peril had been answered. For that one moment, settlers could imagine themselves protected by paternalism and prestige, and, finally, the state. Here was signal proof that settlers owned the state. Not literally, of course. More bitter struggles between state and settler lay in the future. The judiciary never really lived up to what settlers expected of it. Government officials always seemed more interested in hindering than helping settlers. But the cleaving of Nyaduongo's soul from his body announced that the government would defend all that settlers held dear. Black peril meant the death of white settlement, and black peril had been answered by the death of an African man. The souls of white folk had been adjudged more valuable than an African's very life.

Other scholars – Chloe Campbell, Will Jackson, and Janet McIntosh – have recently undertaken re-examinations of whites in Kenya from the 1930s on up to today. The stories they tell are different from mine, but in their own ways reveal that the settler soul traced here continued for some decades. Thus, for example, settlers reacted predictably to the 'female circumcision crisis', when thousands of Gikuyu deserted missionary churches rather than sign a pledge against the practice. A 1930 settler's letter to the Colonial Office brought to bear black peril, threats of vigilantism, insolence, and condemnation of the educated African:

> We are living in troublesome times, and a Kikuyu rising is imminent. Settlers are beginning to hold meetings, and a Vigilance Committee has been formed. A settler from Nyero has warned us that if any of us have any young children, that we are not to let them out of our sight for a moment. Women all over Kiambu have been warned by friendly natives never to be alone for a moment ... For the last six months all the young Kikuyus have been uppish, and cheeky, and have refused to turn out for work. It appears that the more educated they are, the more they seem to be in it ... There has been another episode recently near Nairobi concerning two white women being dragged off their horses.[10]

Eugenics too could be put to the service of prestige. Nellie Grant (Elspeth Huxley's mother) promoted eugenics to breed out or develop poor whites. It was poor whites, after all, who did not properly know how to act as whites, 'and of course these sort of people always will get raped etc'.[11]

Extra-judicial violence against Africans and complaints against colonial law and order continued. Raymond Letcher in 1936 found two Africans on an access road near his property. Thieves, he felt sure. He called on them to stop. One man, Odongo son of Bodo, fled, with Letcher in pursuit in his car. It was rough ground, Odongo fell. Letcher ran him over, shattering his back, leaving him permanently disabled. Part of Letcher's defence: he had been victim of previous thefts, and it did no good to report thefts to police. 'I found sir', Letcher explained in court, 'that unless you had definite grounds for reporting these matters it was a waste of time to bring a case to the Court where there was no evidence of the boy having stolen'. (The prosecutor commented that he preferred living in a land where conviction required evidence.)[12] Letcher served one year in prison; Father Michal Patrick Grogan was luckier. In 1943, he fired his revolver to protest against a loud celebration near his home, and the bullet entered a dwelling and killed an African woman. The jury acquitted Father Grogan of murder. The Attorney General commented that he could 'offer no intelligent reason for this perverse verdict'.[13] The settler jury considered the preservation of a white man an intelligent enough reason.

And Mau Mau. Two images of Kenya's colonial period have always fascinated – or repelled – outsiders: the settlers and Mau Mau. During the 1950s, Europeans in Kenya did a masterful job of demonizing those who took up arms against the colonial government. More recently, the British public has been made to confront the horrors of 'counter-insurgency', the torture and extra-judicial executions, the suspension of anything vaguely resembling the much-vaunted British justice.[14] While British regiments took over much of the fighting in the forests, administrators and settlers handled the everyday torture and killing of civilians and detainees. We know increasingly more, and more gory, details about what they did, their utter brutality, their consuming rage. All this can be better understood in the context of the settler soul.

Part of the reason Mau Mau so terrified settlers was the way in which it confounded paternalism and prestige. Prestige was meant to protect all whites, armed or unarmed, on their farms or on a path or walking dark Nairobi streets. Certainly there had been cases in which prestige had failed to protect white lives, but their numbers were few. With Mau Mau, however, prestige would seem to have evaporated. Mau Mau killed anyone they wished, with no regard to race. White skin offered no protection. Indeed, white skin made one a target. That a grand total of thirty-two settlers were killed over eight years gave cold comfort.

Perhaps worse: it was not just unknown Africans who slaughtered helpless whites. The possibility that one's gardener, or cook, or house 'boy' could be a Mau Mau – a savage in one's very home, ready to kill

CONCLUSION

without mercy – was deeply unnerving. More than just a physical threat, the Mau Mau within was an ideological threat. No longer the loyal retainer, no longer the trusted servant, but an ingrate, serving up murder in return for settlers' paternalistic care. Settlers had long favoured the personal infliction of punishment on their workers, holding the kiboko themselves, perhaps chastising the recalcitrant worker to his face. The Mau Mau killings on settlers' farms were generally committed with pangas. Close combat, perhaps one last glance in the eye of the Mau Mau before death.[15] This was revenge, it seemed, in spades. The more reassuring explanation, one that kept Africans in their place: Mau Mau was atavism, it was the mindless lashing out of savages who could not mentally adjust to civilization. Rather than heralding independence, Mau Mau reaffirmed the need for white rule.

If the hanging of Nyaduongo marked a high point of settler inviolability and mastery of the state, the hanging of Peter Harold Poole in 1960 marked the nadir. Poole was an English-born engineer, twenty-eight years old, a husband and father of two. On 12 October 1959, his 'houseboy' Kamawe Musunge was riding his bicycle. Confronted by Poole's dogs, Musunge threw some stones. Poole ordered him to stop, and pulled out his pistol. A bullet tore into Musunge. He died within minutes.

On 10 December, Poole was convicted of murder by an all-white jury. His appeal, which went all the way to the Privy Council, failed. Poole's fellow settlers would not let him go quietly. A petition for clemency, with some twenty-five thousand names, was handed to the governor. He refused to intervene, as did the Queen. It was a sad day for settlers, 18 August 1960, when Poole took his last breath. He was the first white man to be executed in Kenya colony for the killing of an African.

Pioneer settlers must have slumped in their chairs, their whiskies tasting foul. The eldest would have recalled the white jury that in 1908, knowing 'their duty to a white man', acquitted Count de Crespigny of murder. They may have remembered that the Honourable Galbraith Cole had been only temporarily barred from Kenya after he slaughtered an alleged poacher. Alas, Poole lived a few decades too late. Some jurors no longer knew their duty to a white man. The governor no longer felt compelled to bow to settlers' demands. A world in which a Kenya settler could defend his canines at the price of an African's life – this world was no more. The snapping of Poole's neck must have told many a settler that the game was up.[16]

Souls of white folk across the globe

White folks in early colonial Kenya came from many lands, and they would have found kindred spirits in many lands. Beginning in the midnineteenth century, and continuing for over one hundred years, British settlers around the globe shared the ideologies and emotions described here. This greater white soul was composed of particular white souls spread across South Africa, Rhodesia, Kenya, India, Fiji, Australia, New Zealand, and Papua-New Guinea, as well as the US South. In white homes across these lands, we find the emphasis on prestige and paternalism, the conflation of race and civilization, the reliance on humiliation and corporal punishment as tools of control, and an obsession with black peril. Thus the 'creed' of Southern US whites, as outlined by the educator Thomas Bailey in 1913, would have been applauded by many whites across the British colonized world:

1. 'Blood will tell.'
2. The white race must dominate.
3. The Teutonic peoples stand for race purity.
4. The negro is inferior and will remain so.
5. 'This is a white man's country.'
6. No social equality.
7. No political equality.
8. In matters of civil rights and legal adjustments give the white man, as opposed to the colored man, the benefit of the doubt; and under no circumstances interfere with the prestige of the white man.
9. In educational policy let the negro have the crumbs that fall from the white man's table.
10. Let there be such industrial education of the negro as will best fit him to serve the white man.
11. Only [white] Southerners understand the negro question.
12. Let the [white] South settle the negro question.
13. The status of peasantry is all the negro may hope for, if the races are to live together in peace.
14. Let the lowest white man count for more than the highest negro.
15. The above statements indicate the leadings of Providence.[17]

Not all Anglos would have aligned themselves with 'Teutonic peoples', and some may have tried to soften Bailey's language. But many whites would have felt comfortable endorsing the list – the essence of the white soul is there.

Several trends gave birth to this white soul. The rise of social Darwinism and the dawning of a second wave of European imperial expansion both played their parts. New ideas of whiteness and of race – of an Anglo-Saxon race – were critical. People of British descent, wherever they might be found in the world, gloried in their Anglo-Saxon blood and civilization. The Englishman Charles Wentworth Dilke travelled across the globe in the mid-1860s, in 1869 publishing a book that boasted of the 'grandeur of our race, already girdling the earth, which it is destined, perhaps, eventually to overspread'.[18] Britons of the current and former settler colonies were united by blood, culture, and sentiment.[19] Hearts of schoolchildren in Surrey and Salisbury alike beat harder as they gazed at maps coloured red for their Empire. Toss in the Americans and the superiority of the Anglo-Saxon race could hardly be denied.

But the white soul in the settler colonies differed from that in the metropole. English speakers in the colonies imagined themselves as a particular class of Anglo-Saxons.[20] They could not while away whole days readings histories of their racial forbearers. Theirs was a world both enchanting and perilous. They were epoch-making flag-bearers for the spread of Anglo-Saxon civilization, and they would be the first to perish should the rising tide of coloured races subsume the dykes. They celebrated their own daring, the fresh civilizations they created. Yet they constantly felt themselves threatened – by the indigenous, by local state officials, by the metropolitan government and interest groups.[21] In some areas, well-entrenched white rule faced the dire threat of political power being divorced from whiteness: Reconstruction and the 'New Negro' in the US South, the 'Mutiny' and the Ilbert Bill in India. Elsewhere, as in Rhodesia, Natal, Kenya, and the Antipodes, white settlement was quite new. Whites remained unsure of their ability to shape indigenous peoples to their own needs, or to simply prevent the indigenous people from wiping out a minuscule white population. To defend themselves: paternalism, prestige, violence, and racialized laws.

The exchange of ideas and individuals through the colonies furthered a common worldview. The question of Japanese, Chinese, and Indian immigration exercised whites in Kenya, Natal, Australia, the US, and Canada. They studied each other's laws, met to map out strategy, and spoke of their shared need to defend their 'white men's countries'.[22] Officials from South Africa examined US laws on mixed marriages, while the Carnegie Corporation financed a study of the 'poor white' problem in South Africa.[23] Lothrop Stoddard's 1921 *The Rising Tide of Color against White World Supremacy* warned that white civilization would soon be crushed under the weight of other races' increasing population and power. His work was read and discussed in the colonies, where the threat was most real. Careful students of racial issues in the US South, whites settlers in still-independent Fiji started their own Ku Klux Klan.[24] Individuals too circulated throughout the English-speaking world – soldiers, administrators, hunters, traders, and settlers, as well as various fortune-hunters, criminals, prostitutes, and ne'er-do-wells, all of whom flowed in and out of Indian Ocean and Pacific port cities.[25] Anglo settlers, and whites in the US South, were by choice and by circumstance one people, of one soul.

As the white soul developed, so too did its antithesis, black peril. For the century between the 1850s and the 1950s, black peril became a primary means by which whites in colonized lands spoke about their control over non-whites. Such fears were not, of course, entirely new. In North America and the Caribbean, masters found it entirely plausible that a slave uprising would be accompanied by mass rapes of white women.[26] But prior to the US Civil War, masters often defended their slaves against rape claims by white women.[27] As Jenny Sharpe notes, the trope of white women raped by colonized men only really became common after the 1857 'Mutiny' in India.[28] From that point, the fear was constant, the warnings dire and regular, the outbreak of black peril hysteria all too common.

Fundamental challenges to the white soul came after the Second World War. The championing of white people as a civilizing force for evolutionarily retarded black and brown savages seemed less palatable in a post-Holocaust world.[29] Notions of slow civilizing under white paternalism were jettisoned in favour of rapid modernization under neo-colonialism. The colonized threw off their shackles, they rejected humiliation and infantilization, they proclaimed racial equality. They also claimed political power. British officials felt slighted, unwanted in the newly independent lands (ingrates!), an embarrassment at home. Whites in India, first, much later in Zimbabwe, later still in South Africa, reluctantly released their claim over government, judiciary, and public haughtiness.

This is not to say that the bogey of the black rapist disappeared, or that suspicions of African inferiority were shunted aside. There are strong remnants of the settler soul in places where whites still dominate. Yet gone was most of the boastfulness. Books about the black savage and white prestige would now garner more condemnation than serious discussion. Articles praising the value of a good beating for a 'houseboy' no longer had a place in leading papers. The particular configuration of the settler soul could not long survive in a post-Holocaust, post-colonial, world.

The souls of white folk, the souls of black folk

Settlers tried their best to make Kenya theirs. They failed. They never really stood a chance. Settlers knew that they must maintain racial unity, but race could not paper over divisions of nationality, class, and

CONCLUSION

morality. Settlers constantly measured themselves through African eyes, and too often found themselves – or, more likely, other settlers – lacking. Nor could they convince government officials – not in London, not in Nairobi, not in the Reserves – that racial unity must supersede all other concerns.

Most of all, it was Africans' stubborn refusal to accept their subservience that kept settlers constantly on guard. Settlers thought they saw African insolence in every momentary pause after a command, a challenge in every queer look, a mocking laugh in every subdued voice. They were not always wrong. Africans did steal from their employers, they did shirk their duties, they did mutter angrily behind whites' backs. Africans did gossip about memsahib's stained sheets when her husband was away on safari, about bwana's visits to houses of ill repute on the African side of town. Africans saw settlers as they were, not how settlers wished to be seen. If all Africans had truly considered whites to be godlike, if servants had truly loved their white 'parents'? Settler letters, newspapers, and memoirs would have had much less to say about defending prestige. The kiboko would have grown stiff from disuse.

The settlers' influence on the souls of black folk is less easy to measure, but it was certainly far-reaching. Land alienation, racialized economic policies, and dictatorial white rule all altered the course of Kenyan history. But it was settlers' – and, in fact, all whites' – belief in prestige, their equation of race and civilization, that had a deeper psychological impact. Whites' constant demands for deference, and their indiscriminate use of humiliation, marked many an African soul. We know that Tebajanga, the 'boy' with the fine hat, felt stung by the words and deeds of the white men in the Nairobi street. He was but one of a vast number.

For very many Africans, humiliating incidents at the hands of whites unveiled the true nature of colonialism. It pushed many toward anti-colonialism. Bildad Kaggia was one. Kaggia, born in 1922 to the most pitiable figure in central Kenya, a landless man, proved himself brilliant in the classroom. By the late 1930s he had found work in the district headquarters at Fort Hall as a clerk-in-training. A day off from work, strolling through town with a friend. A car passes, the district commissioner and his wife. The car stops.

> 'When you see the D.C. you must take off your hat! You must have manners,' he shouted at me.
> I took off my hat and, very embarrassed, I apologized. Then he drove off. I did not discuss the incident with my friend, but I felt very indignant at being humiliated.

This 'opened [Kaggia's] eyes. It did not matter what position one held; what mattered was colour.'[30] He was soon set on the path toward militant anti-colonialism.

Even if Africans did not believe whites to be godlike, too many believed them to be a different sort of being. The unrelenting refrain of white racial superiority and of African savagery could be difficult to overcome. Kaggia recalled that 'Many Africans even believed that the rule of the *mzungu* was ordained by God ... The great majority of the uneducated masses looked on the *mzungu* with awe because of his scientific achievements and high standard of living.' The educated elite? Worse. Most of them, Kaggia wrote, 'had so much faith in the *mzungu's* continued dominance and in his intelligence, power and capability, that they simply abdicated from politics'.[31] Oginga Odinga, who fought for independence and democracy, argued that decolonization required more than just an African prime minister. It was 'a matter of liberating attitudes'. 'Brought up in the presence of the White master', he wrote, 'you are taught to defer to him, until this is ground into your soul ... The African runs the risk of growing up haltered with an inferiority complex.'[32]

Travelling to Britain proved to be a transformative experience. It revealed that whites in Kenya were exceptional – exceptional in their racism, their boastfulness, their claims to be superior beings. When Muthoni Likimani and others returned from Britain in the 1940s, they amazed friends with tales of 'how they saw a white woman cleaning their room, and how white people in England even served black people with food. They were surprised that white women did their own cooking. They even saw a white man digging in a shamba (farm) and feeding the cows. They watched a white man cleaning the hotel rooms and making beds – this was unbelievable!'[33] More than unbelievable: it was 'exciting'.[34] This would be a new way to see, to think about, white people. As a soldier, Kaggia spent time with a welcoming white family in Britain, during which time he 'learned to regard a *mzungu* as an equal. Daily contact with many of them made me lose any sense of inferiority, and this inferiority complex was a terrible disease with all Africans in those days.'[35] Veterans returned having seen white men afraid, bleeding, and dying. In Oginga Odinga's words, 'Here were men who had overcome their fear of the power of the White man'.[36]

Thus while the various anti-colonial movements fought for land and political freedom, they were also bound up in a struggle against the souls of white folk. They countered humiliation, they rejected the deference whites demanded of Africans. For Kaggia, political mobilization was intertwined with 'educating the masses' about racial equality and teaching them not to fear white people.[37] It required 'the liberation

CONCLUSION

of the mind'.[38] The pamphleteer Gakaara wa Wanjaū similarly tried to educate his readers in 1952, just months before the government declared the State of Emergency. Whites intentionally degraded Africans, casting 'seeds in us of self-hate and self-doubt'.[39] Wanjaū's goal would be to challenge white prestige: finding brave men and women 'who can stare the Europeans in the eyes', 'treat with contempt their claims that we are a nation of children'.[40]

Anti-colonialism was not, of course, simply a reaction to the humiliations of whites. It was much more complex, drawing on a wide variety of local ideas about morality, the relationship between the individual and the community, gender, and so on. But the attention Kaggia, Odinga, Wanjaū and others paid to the insults, the inculcation of self-doubt, tells us that whites often did inflict real damage. Some words were humiliating in English, and Gikuyu, and Luo.[41]

The afterlife of the settler soul

What becomes of a colonial settler when the colonial world is no more? What happens when 'boys' must now be addressed as 'Honourable', when the ridiculous semi-civilized Africans take the reins of government, when the police and the magistrates and the bureaucrats, on up to the president, no longer share one's skin colour? For some settlers, such a life appeared unliveable. As black majority rule loomed, many settlers sold out and stormed off. Angry at the British government for deserting them. Aghast that the 'prince of darkness' Kenyatta would bump aside the Queen's representative in Government House. Petulant at the ingratitude of the Africans whom whites had lifted from savagery. Despondent at the thought that all they had cultivated would soon, assuredly, go to seed – literally, in their rose bushes and ornamental gardens, and metaphorically, in their civilization.

But not all settlers left. Some had lived in Kenya their entire lives, children or grandchildren of immigrants. Reassured by Kenyatta that their lives and property would be safe, they soldiered on. This is not to say that there was no period of adjustment for whites, no psychological and emotional tolls to be paid.[42] Yet not all was lost. Some old attitudes carried over. In the mid-1970s, the writer Shiva Naipaul visited with Mrs Palmer, and witnessed her berating her African servant for not using tongs to bring ice. 'Simon seems to have a block about using those tongs', she explained.

> I can't understand it. I've told him so many times. Still, Simon has one great virtue. He hasn't been *spoiled*. Not as yet, anyway. I'm keeping my fingers crossed. It's amazing how quickly they do get spoiled, though.

> There used to be an old saying in this country: put a native in shoes and that's the end of him. Nowadays, of course, they've all got shoes and we aren't even allowed to call them natives.[43]

Palmer pined for the old days, when she could do as she wished with her natives. Now, she could only do partly as she wished with them.[44]

White Kenyans born since Independence, however, see themselves as a breed apart from their parents and grandparents. The old settler soul, they insist, is not theirs. The anthropologist Janet McIntosh has plumbed the souls of the contemporary white Kenyans, and it is in fact quite different from those of their ancestors.[45] Rather than trumpeting their whiteness and demanding deference from Africans, they attempt to distract attention from their skin. They are not primarily white or European, they say, but Kenyans first and foremost. Perhaps they are a 'white tribe', not unlike the other forty-odd ethnic groups in the country. They pride themselves on learning Swahili, unlike their parents who scrape by in Kisettla. They are, above all, disquieted by the excesses of the colonial period, the racism, the violence, the sordid Happy Valley lifestyle. Whites today, they insist, are just Kenyans, no more, no less.

This white soul is a refreshing corrective to the one of a century ago. And yet, work remains to be done. They love Swahili because it is more expressive, more warm and emotional and straightforward, than English – echoes of the noble savage? They renounce racism, yet hesitate to conduct public romances with Africans. They imagine themselves to be regular Kenyans, yet are – compared to the vast majority of their fellow citizens – immensely wealthy. They point out that colonialism ended a half-century ago and that they should not be blamed for the sins of their fathers. They continue to enjoy the fruits of those sinful but profitable lives.

Let the reader not think me too self-righteous. For I, too, have experienced the power of being a white man in Kenya. In a tiny restaurant out in the hills of Kisii, the waiter takes my order and begins to walk off, utterly ignoring – perhaps literally not seeing – my Kenyan companion. Walking into an Uchumi supermarket with a bag over my shoulder, while my two African American colleagues and every black Kenyan around us are stopped and told to check their belongings at the entrance. Must this not have been humiliating? A older Kenyan placing his left hand on his right forearm as we shake hands, a sign of respect that should be reserved only for one's elders or those of some social standing. The taxi stopped at a compound, the guard suspicious, until he sees my flesh and swings wide the gate. Why such deference? We wazungu have the

CONCLUSION

wealth to travel to Kenya, to stay in comfortable hotels, to be treated in the best hospitals, and to be evacuated should things turn ugly. Whether we be tourists, NGO workers, academics, volunteers, or citizens – these are the benefits that still accrue to whiteness, to being an mzungu. Are these not the inheritance of the settler soul?

What Kenya needs (if anyone were to ask for my opinion) is more public discussion of the meaning of whiteness, of the lingering effects of the white settler soul, of what it takes to truly decolonize the mind. It needs white people – citizens and tourists, expats and academics – to consider much more seriously our own racialized beings. We need to think, to reflect, to listen.[46] I hope that one day, in Phyllis Muthoni's words, my 'paleness / [will] be unremarkable'[47] I hope that when I am offered a deferential greeting, it is because I am a mwalimu (teacher) or have become an mzee (elder). I hope that we can overcome the ugly residue left by the souls of those departed white folk.

Notes

1 KNA: AG/52/392, Police Case 12/1928, Statement of Winifred Maud Price, 27 Feb. 1928.
2 KNA: AG/52/392, Police Case 12/1928, Statement of Nyaduango s/o Awori, 28 Feb. 1928.
3 KNA: AG/52/392, Police Case 12/1928, Statement of Price, 27 Feb. 1928; Statement of Nyaduango, 28 Feb. 1928.
4 KNA: AG/52/392, Police Case 12/1928, Statement of Price, 27 Feb. 1928.
5 KNA: AG/52/392, Police Case 12/1928, Statement of Toro s/o Biambo, 28 Feb. 1928.
6 'End of evidence in assault case', *EAS* (25 Apr. 1928), p. 8
7 'End of evidence in assault case', *EAS* (25 Apr. 1928), p. 8.
8 'Nairobi assault case heard in camera', *EAS* (24 Apr. 1928), p. 9.
9 'The death penalty', *EAS* (28 Apr. 1928), p. 8.
10 Quoted in Chloe Campbell, *Race and Empire: Eugenics in Colonial Kenya* (Manchester: Manchester University Press, 2007), pp. 134–5.
11 Quoted in Campbell, *Race and Empire*, p. 124. Similarly, one Mr Payne believed that the Kenya Society for the Study of Race Improvement should deal first with the improvement of the white population: 'whites should be taught hygiene and development rather than run the risk of trying to take the black races across a period of a thousand or 1,500 years at one step to the present stage of European development'. Quoted in Campbell, *Race and Empire*, p. 121.
12 NA: CO 533/481/1, Supreme Court Criminal Case 136 of 1936.
13 NA: CO 533/526/9, W. Harragin, minute, 16 June 1943, in Gov. Kenya to SS, 24 June 1943. I have been unable to determine if Father Grogan was related to Ewart Grogan. In recklessness, they were soulmates. Martin Wiener believes, mistakenly I think, that the shift away from racialized justice happened already in the 1930s. Wiener, *An Empire on Trial: Race, Murder, and Justice under British Rule, 1870–1935* (Cambridge: Cambridge University Press, 2009).
14 Following the work of David Anderson and Caroline Elkins, the lawsuit against the British government by Mau Mau veterans, and the unearthing of hidden, damning British archives pertaining to Mau Mau. David M. Anderson, *Histories of the Hanged: The Dirty War in Kenya and the End of Empire* (New York: Norton, 2005); Anderson, 'Mau Mau in the High Court and the "lost" British empire

archives: colonial conspiracy or bureaucratic bungle?', *Journal of Imperial and Commonwealth History* 39 (2011): 699–716; Caroline Elkins, *Imperial Reckoning: The Untold Story of Britain's Gulag in Kenya* (New York: Holt, 2005).

15 Anderson, *Histories of the Hanged*, p. 87. Anderson suggests 'White highlanders could only "understand" this gross breach of trust if their African staff were in some way deemed to be possessed, or in the control of other forces'. *Histories of the Hanged*, p. 88.

16 Nicholls, a child of settlers and living in Kenya at the time, writes that his execution 'profoundly shook white opinion. Many Europeans now understood fully that the days of white supremacy in Kenya were over'. C. S. Nicholls, *Red Strangers: The White Tribe of Kenya* (London: Timewell, 2005), p. 271.

17 Quoted in Leon Litwack, *Trouble in Mind: Black Southerners in the Age of Jim Crow* (New York: Knopf, 1998), p. 181.

18 Quoted in Robert J. C. Young, *The Idea of English Ethnicity* (Malden, MA: Blackwell, 2008), p. 197.

19 Young, *The Idea of English Ethnicity*; Marilyn Lake and Henry Reynolds, *Drawing the Global Colour Line: White Men's Countries and the International Challenge of Racial Equality* (Cambridge: Cambridge University Press, 2008), ch. 4; Bill Schwarz, *Memories of Empire, Vol. I: The White Man's World* (Oxford: Oxford University Press, 2011). For Anglo-Saxonism from the US perspective, see Paul A. Kramer, 'Empires, exceptions, and Anglo-Saxons: race and rule between the British and the United States empires, 1880–1910', *Journal of American History* 88 (2002): 1315–53; Duncan Bell, 'The Victorian idea of a global state', in Duncan Bell (ed.), *Victorian Visions of Global Order: Empire and International Relations in Nineteenth-Century Political Thought* (Cambridge: Cambridge University Press, 2007).

20 Leigh Boucher, 'Trans/national history and disciplinary amnesia: historicising White Australia at two *fin de siècles*', in Jane Carey and Claire McLisky (eds), *Creating White Australia* (Sydney: Sydney University Press, 2009), pp. 44–63.

21 Caroline Elkins and Susan Pedersen (eds), *Settler Colonialism in the Twentieth Century: Projects, Practices, Legacies* (New York: Routledge, 2005); James Belich, *Replenishing the Earth: The Settler Revolution and the Rise of the Anglo-World, 1783-1939* (Oxford: Oxford University Press, 2009); Lorenzo Veracini, *Settler Colonialism: A Theoretical Overview* (New York: Palgrave Macmillan, 2010).

22 Lake and Reynolds, *Drawing the Global Colour Line*.

23 Carnegie Commission of Investigation on the Poor White Question in South Africa, *The Poor White Problem in South Africa. Report of the Carnegie Commission* (Stellenbosch: Pro ecclesia-drukkery, 1932).

24 Gerald Horne, *The White Pacific: U.S. Imperialism and Black Slavery in the South Seas after the Civil War* (Honolulu: University of Hawai'i Press, 2007), ch. 5; Caroline Ralston, 'The pattern of race relations in 19th century Pacific port towns', *Journal of Pacific History* 6 (1971): 39–60.

25 Harald Fisher-Tiné, *Low and Licentious Europeans: Race, Class and 'White Subalternity' in Colonial India* (Hyderabad: Orient Blackswan, 2009).

26 Winthrop D. Jordan, *White over Black: American Attitudes Toward the Negro, 1550–1812* (New York: Norton, 1977), pp. 151–4.

27 Diane Miller Sommerville, *Rape and Race in the Nineteenth-Century South* (Chapel Hill: University of North Carolina Press, 2004). See also Martha Hodes, *White Women, Black Men: Illicit Sex in the Nineteenth-Century South* (New Haven: Yale University Press, 1997).

28 Jenny Sharpe, *Allegories of Empire: The Figure of Woman in the Colonial Text* (Minneapolis and London: University of Minnesota Press, 1993), pp. 2–3. Sharpe suggests that fears of inter-racial rape emerged only when colonialism was under threat, rather than, as I believe, only under a particular form of colonialism.

29 On changing ideas of whiteness after the war, see Bruce Baum, *The Rise and Fall of the Caucasian Race: A Political History of Racial Identity* (New York and London: New York University Press, 2006).

CONCLUSION

30 Bildad Kaggia, *Roots of Freedom, 1921–1963: The Autobiography of Bildad Kaggia* (Nairobi: East African Publishing House, 1975), p. 19.
31 Kaggia, *Roots of Freedom*, p. 64.
32 Odinga, *Not Yet Uhuru*, pp. 248–9.
33 Muthoni Likimani, *Fighting without Ceasing* (Nairobi: Noni's Publicity, 2005), p. 128.
34 Muthoni Likimani, *Passbook Number F.47927: Women and Mau Mau in Kenya* (London: Macmillan, 1985), p. 186. In 'Kariokor Location', one of the characters comments about being tried by a white magistrate: 'He was not one of those Kenya-born Europeans, those brought up by their parents to hate Kikuyus. He did not know Kikuyu or Swahili, so was not a local white. This was good, thought Kamau, maybe then he had some hope'. Likimani, *Passbook Number F.47927*, p. 84. See also Parmenas Githendu Mockerie, *An African Speaks for His People* (London: Hogarth, 1934), pp. 15–16. Jomo Kenyatta early on tried to puncture white prestige. In his published M.A. thesis, Kenyatta suggested that Europeans had early on decided that colonization 'did not require the selection of men with good social standing and better qualifications' to send overseas. He allowed a quote from Daniel Thwaite to make the implication clear: 'the colonies became a sort of clearing-house for failures and worse'. So much for prestige. Jomo Kenyatta, *Facing Mt. Kenya* (New York: Vintage, 1965 [1938]), p. 260.
35 Kaggia, *Roots of Freedom*, p. 46. He also describes his discussions with an African-American doctor, a major in the US army. Meeting him was, for Kaggia and others, 'an eye opener. We had always been told, and almost believed that Africans were not fit to be commissioned.' Kaggia, *Roots of Freedom*, p. 26
36 Odinga, *Not Yet Uhuru*, p. 110. See also Kaggia, *Roots of Freedom*, p. 66; Joseph Harris, *Recollections of James Juma Mbotela* (Nairobi: East African Publishing House, 1977), pp. 35–6. On African soldiers' and veterans' questioning of the colour bar, see Timothy H. Parsons, *The African Rank-and-File: Social Implications of Colonial Military Service in the King's African Rifles, 1902–1964* (Portsmouth, NH: Heinemann, 1999), p. 232.
37 Kaggia, *Roots of Freedom*, p. 65.
38 Kaggia, *Roots of Freedom*, p. 78.
39 Wanjaū, 'The spirit of manhood and perseverance for Africans', appendix five in Gakaara wa Wanjaū, *Mau Mau Author in Detention*, trans. Ngigĩ wa Njoroge (Nairobi: Heinemann, 1988), p. 229.
40 Wanjaū, 'The spirit of manhood and perseverance for Africans', pp. 236, 241. The settler leader Michael Blundell had, by 1963, come to understand some of this – even as he remained mired in older conceptions of the 'African character'. *So Rough a Wind* (London: Weidenfeld and Nicolson, 1963), pp. 221–4.
41 See also, for example, Donald L. Barnett and Karari Njama, *Mau Mau from Within: Autobiography and Analysis of Kenya's Peasant Revolt* (New York: Monthly Review Press, 1966), 385. Ngũgĩ wa Thiong'o has spent much of his career wondering how to escape the white soul. See his *Decolonising the Mind: The Politics of Language in African Literature* (London: James Currey, 1986), and his interpretation of Mau Mau as the rejection of prestige, as a claim to self-respect, in, for example, *Petals of Blood* (London: Heinemann, 1977), p. 137; Ngũgĩ wa Thiong'o and Wanguĩ wa Goro (trans.), *Njamba Nene's Pistol* (Nairobi: Heinemann, 1986); Ngũgĩ wa Thiong'o and Micere Mugo, *The Trial of Dedan Kimathi* (Nairobi: Heinemann, 1981).
42 Recent research on independent Zimbabwe and post-Apartheid South Africa reveals the struggles whites have had making their way in the strange new worlds of Africans in power. In Zimbabwe, whites tried to become part of the natural environment. In South Africa, many seem lost. Hundreds of white South Africans are seeking fresher fields elsewhere on the continent, such as Tanzania where their rands make them wealthy, their business connections make them valuable, and their whiteness does not seem the burden it does in Johannesburg and Cape Town. David McDermott Hughes, *Whiteness in Zimbabwe: Race, Landscape,*

and the Problem of Belonging (New York: Palgrave Macmillan, 2010); Melissa Steyn, *'Whiteness Just Isn't What It Used to Be': White Identity in a Changing South Africa* (Albany: State University of New York, 2001); Richard Schroeder, *Africa after Apartheid: South Africa, Race, and Nation in Tanzania* (Bloomington: Indiana University Press, 2012).

43 Shiva Naipaul, *North of South* (London: Penguin, 1978), p. 71. To be fair to Mrs Palmer, she may have been pandering to Naipaul, whose condescension toward 'modern' Africans positively drips off the page.

44 For further thoughts post-colonial humiliation, see Ngũgĩ, *Petals of Blood*, pp. 104, 198; Ngũgĩ wa Thiong'o, *Wizard of the Crow* (New York: Pantheon, 2006). Ngũgĩ in 1967 agreed to write a social history of white settlers. Yet he failed to complete it, for he must include a chapter on settler culture – and he determined that such a 'Draculan idle class could never produce a culture'. Later, detained in a Kenyan prison, he regretted his decision not to write the book, 'For the colonial system *did* produce a culture ... the culture of legalized brutality, a ruling-class culture of fear, the culture of an oppressing minority desperately trying to impose total silence on a restive oppressed majority'. Ngũgĩ wa Thiong'o, *Detained: A Writer's Prison Diary* (Nairobi: Heinemann, 1981), p. 44.

45 The following draws on Janet McIntosh, 'Unsettled: Denial and Belonging among White Kenyans', ms, 2014.

46 As Keguro Macharia has argued, this conversation is necessary, but difficult to initiate. He recounts confronting a white man who had publicly chastised – humiliated – a taxi driver. Keguro followed the man into a bank and confronted him. The white man defended himself by insisting that the taxi driver had broken some law, and repeated several times a seemingly incongruous phrase: 'I'm not listening'. 'The too-swift overlapping transitions from majority white colonial governance to majority white tourism to majority white multi-national and NGO administrators have consolidated into something that cannot be critiqued. Something that simply does not listen.' See http://gukira.wordpress.com/2011/12/09/im-not-listening-kenyan-whiteness/ (accessed 16 Feb. 2014). Keguro is a self-described 'recovering academic'.

47 Phyllis Muthoni, 'Otherness', in Billy Kahora (ed.), *Kwani?* 07 (Nairobi: Kwani Trust, 2012), p. 41.

SELECT BIBLIOGRAPHY

Media

Advertiser of East Africa
African Standard
Critic
East Africa
East Africa and Uganda Mail
East African Chronicle
East African Standard
Globe Trotter
Kenya Graphic
Kenya Observer
Leader of British East Africa
Nairobi News
Outlaw
Tattler
Times of East Africa
The Times (London)

Kenya National Archive

AC 2/60 Criminal Appeal 7 of 1920, Court of Appeal, Nakuru
AC 2/74 Criminal Case 96 of 1923, Supreme Court, Nakuru
AG 1/489 Mr Finnie's Complaint of Treatment Accorded him by Mr Humphrey, Collector, 1905
AG 7/2 Native Punishments Commission
AG 25/43 Resident Native Labour Ordinance. Fining of Squatters by Settlers, 1918
AG 42/4 Film Censorship Committee
AG 42/5 The Stage Plays and Cinematography Ordinance, Rules Under, 1910–28
AG 42/7 The Stage Plays and Cinematography Ordinance. Censorship of Films. General
AG 49/28 Swedish Woman, 1911
AG 51/320 Libellous Statements Against C. E. V. Buxton, D.C., by Mrs Patrice M. G. Rainbow, 1926–27
AG 51/322 Libellous Statement against Mr Ogilvie A.D.C. by Mr A. Rainbow, Narok, 1919–21
AG 51/329 ADC Cooke, Certain Charges Against, 1925–27
AG 52/297 Major Jolly. A Person of Unsound Mind, 1923

SELECT BIBLIOGRAPHY

AG 52/391 Supreme Court Criminal Case 19/28, 1928
AG 52/392 Indecent Assault on Mrs Price, 1928
AG 52/393 Rape. Supreme Court Criminal Case 60/26, 1926
AM 1/1/5 Report on Sexual Assaults
AP 1/108 Confinement of Nairobi Vagrants in Mombasa Jail, 1907
AP 1/547 Mr and Mrs Evans, Vagrants, 1909
AP 1/1105 Vagrancy Regulations (1900), 1919–37
AP 1/1465 Administration of the law, 1926–46
DC/MKS.10A/14/1 Disputed Boundaries. Langridge, 1911
DC/NYK 3/9/3 Justice of Peace, 1929–50
GH 7/24 East African Women's League, 1929–52
Jud 1/1104 Native Tribunals
PC/COAST 1/1/367 Miscellaneous paper, 1917–19
PC/COAST 1/3/85 Immigration and Immigrants. Inspection of, 1912–15
PC/COAST 1/3/174 Repatriation of Europeans, 1920–22
PC/COAST 1/10/70 Flogging of Natives, 1913
PC/COAST 1/10/117 Col. Molony and Mr Wickham. Complaints Against, 1921–23
PC/COAST 1/12/29 Prison Matters, 1905
PC/COAST 1/12/217 Political Unrest, European, Indian, African, 1923–24
PC/COAST 1/17/130 Prison. Plates, Cups, Tea bought for Vagrant, Mrs Hall, 1913
PC/COAST 2/3/3 Associations and Leagues. League of Mercy, 1920
PC/CP/6/4/3 Native Punishment Commission
PC/CP 7/1/2 Native Customs and Law – Circumcision, 1920
PC/NZA 3/17/1 Judicial, General Matters, 1927–29
PC/NZA 3/17/2 Judicial Cases, North Kavirondo, 1915–28
PC/NZA 3/17/18/2 Death Penalty for Rape, 1926
PC/NZA 3/18/5/1 Stock Thefts, Nandi District, 1925–27
PC/NZA 3/28/4/1 Native Marriage and Dowries, 1925–28
PC/NZA 3/32/2 Chiefs and Headmen, South Kavirondo, 1925–28
District Annual Reports, Kikuyu, Kyambu, Laikipia, Machakos, Narok, Uasin Gishu, Ulu
Papers of Sandy Herd, MSS 105/1
Provincial Annual Report, Ukamba

British National Archive

CO 533/37/11 Report of the Select Committee on Film Censorship, 1927
CO 533/85/4722 Prostitution by White Women, 1911
CO 533/85/19019 Prostitution by White Women, 1911
CO 533/88/27210 Conduct of Hon K. R. Dundas and Mr Montgomerie: Allegations of Mr G. L. Langridge, 1911
CO 533/91/36361 Trial of Mr G. L. Langridge for Striking a Native, 1911
CO 533/92/36964 Assault on a White Child by Native, 1911
CO 533/118/21531 Trial by Jury, 1913

SELECT BIBLIOGRAPHY

CO 533/162 Colonial Office: Kenya Original Correspondence. Offices: Miscellaneous, 1915
CO 533/235/42134 Flogging and Torture of Native, 1920
CO 533/236/54366 Alleged Flogging of Native at Ruira, 1920
CO 533/371/4 Labour in Kenya: Thrashing of Native by Employers, 1927
CO 533/371/11 Report of the Select Committee on Film Censorship, 1927
CO 533/384/9 Visit to England of the General Secretary of the Kikuyu Central Association, Johnstone Kenyatta, 1929–30
CO 533/526/8 Criminal Cases, 1941–42
CO 533/526/9 Criminal Cases, 1941–42
CO 544/26 Executive Council Minutes, 1923–28
CO 822/52/1 Penal and Criminal Codes, Background Notes, 1934
CO 850/47 Concubinage with Native Women, 1934
DO 119/861 Southern Rhodesia: records and correspondence in trials of case of rape and two cases of murder
DO 119/863 Visit by High Commissioner to Southern Rhodesia to discuss 'black peril', 1911
DO 119/864 Visit by High Commissioner to Southern Rhodesia to discuss 'black peril', 1911

Rhodes House Library, Oxford

Anti-Slavery Society, MSS Brit. Emp. s. 22 G/36
Birdsey, 'Sigh Softly,' MSS Afr. s. 1794
Blackall Papers, MSS Brit. Emp s. 447
Brig.-Gen. J. E. and Dorothy Gough, 'Letters and Diaries, 1907–08', MSS Afr. s. 2046
C. T. Todd, 'Kenya's Red Sunset,' MSS Afr. s. 917
Convention of Associations, Minutes, MSS Afr s. 594 1/7
E.A.P. Audit Office 'Funny Book', MSS Afr. r. 126
Elspeth Huxley Papers, MSS Afr. s. 782, Box 1
European Electors Union, Minutes, MSS Afr. s. 596
G. E. Griffiths, 'Diaries', MSS Brit. Emp. s. 349
George Nightingale, 'Memoirs,' MSS Afr. s. 1951
Lord Francis Scott, 'Diaries,' MSS Brit. Emp. s. 349
Lumbwa Farmers Association, MSS Afr. s. 613
M. W. Dobbs, 'Recollections of Kenya, 1906–1931', MSS Afr. s. 504
Margaret Elkington, 'Recollections of a Settler in Kenya, 1905–1970', MSS Afr. s. 1558
Margaret Gillon, 'The Wagon and the Star', MSS Afr. s. 568
Michael Blundell, 'Diary, 1925–26,' MSS Afr. s. 746/1
Minutes of the Lumbwa Farmers Association, MSS Afr. s. 613
Njoro Settlers Association, Minutes of Aug, 1924, MSS Afr. s. 1506
Patterson Diary, MSS Afr. r. 93
Rongai Valley Farmers Association, minutes, MSS Afr. s. 1618
T. R .L. Nestor Papers, MSS Afr. s. 1086

SELECT BIBLIOGRAPHY

Ulu Settlers Association Papers, General Meetings Minutes Book, 1908–22, Uncatalogued

Government publications

Correspondence Relating to the Flogging of Natives by Certain Europeans at Nairobi. Cmd. 3562, 1907
East African Protectorate Economic Commission, Final Report. Nairobi: Swift Press, 1919
Indians in Kenya. Cmd. 1922, 1923
Legislative Council Debates
Native Labour Commission, Evidence and Report. Nairobi: Government Printer, 1913
Native Punishment Commission. Nairobi: Government Printer, 1923

Published works

'A Resident.' 'Nairobi and Kenya Colony.' *Scottish Geographical Magazine* 37 (1921): 99–103.
Alderman, Geoffrey. *Modern British Jewry.* Oxford: Clarendon Press, 1992.
Altink, Henrice. '"An outrage to all decency": abolitionist reactions to flogging Jamaican slave women, 1780–1834.' *Slavery and Abolition* 23 (2002): 107–22.
Amussen, Susan Dwyer. 'Punishment, discipline, and power: the social meanings of violence in early modern England.' *The Journal of British Studies* 34 (1995): 1–34.
Anderson, A. G. *Our Newest Colony Being an Account of British East Africa and Its Possibilities as a New Land for Settlement.* Nairobi: East African Standard, 1910.
Anderson, David M. 'Master and servant in colonial Kenya, 1895–1939.' *Journal of African History* 41 (2000): 459–85.
Anderson, David M. *Histories of the Hanged: The Dirty War in Kenya and the End of Empire.* New York: Norton, 2005.
Anderson, David M. 'Sexual threat and settler society: "black perils" in Kenya, c. 1907–1930.' *Journal of Imperial and Commonwealth History* 38 (2010): 47–74.
Andrews, C. F. *Indian Question in East Africa.* Nairobi: Swift Press, 1921.
Arbuthnot, Col. A. G. 'Life and prospects in Kenya Colony.' *Journal of the Royal Artillery* 53 (1926): 137–51.
Aschan, Ulf. *The Man whom Women Lived: The Life of Bror Blixen.* New York: St Martin's, 1987.
Atieno-Odhiambo, E. S. 'The colonial government, the settlers, and the "trust" principle in Kenya.' *Transafrican Journal of History* 2 (1972): 94–113.
Bache, Eve. *The Youngest Lion: Early Farming Days in Kenya.* London: Hutchinson, 1934.
Baker, Richard St Barbe. *Men of the Trees: In the Mahogany Forests of Kenya and Nigeria.* New York: L. MacVeagh, 1931.

SELECT BIBLIOGRAPHY

Baker, Richard St Barbe. *Africa Drums*. London: Travel Book Club, 1945.

Baldwin, May. *Kenya Kiddies: A Story of Settlers' Children in East Africa*. London: Lippincott, 1926.

Baldwin, May. *Only Pat: A Nairobi School-Girl*. London: W. and R. Chambers, 1930.

Ballhatchet, Kenneth. *Race, Sex and Class under the Raj: Imperial Attitudes and Policies and Their Critics, 1793–1905*. New York: St Martin's, 1980.

Barnes, R. Gorell. *Babes in the African Wood*. London: Longmans, Green, 1911.

Bar-Yosef, Eitan, and Nadia Valman (eds). *'The Jew' in Late-Victorian and Edwardian Culture: Between the East End and East Africa*. New York: Palgrave Macmillan, 2009.

Bashkow, Ira. *The Meaning of Whitemen: Race and Modernity in the Orokaiva Cultural World*. Chicago: University of Chicago Press, 2006.

Baum, Bruce. *The Rise and Fall of the Caucasian Race: A Political History of Racial Identity*. New York and London: New York University Press, 2006.

Bell, Duncan 'The Victorian idea of a global state.' In Duncan Bell (ed.), *Victorian Visions of Global Order: Empire and International Relations in Nineteenth-Century Political Thought*. Cambridge: Cambridge University Press, 2007.

Bennett, George. 'Imperial paternalism: the representation of African interests in the Kenya Legislative Council.' In Kenneth Robinson and Frederick Madden (eds), *Essays in Imperial Government*. Oxford: Blackwell, 1963.

Berman, Bruce. *Control and Crisis in Colonial Kenya: The Dialectic of Domination*. London: James Currey, 1990.

Berman, Bruce, and John Lonsdale. *Unhappy Valley: Conflict in Kenya and Africa*. Athens: Ohio University Press, 1992.

Binks, H. K. *African Rainbow*. London: Sidgwick and Jackson, 1959.

Blaha, David. 'Pushing Marginalization: British Colonial Policy, Somali Identity, and the Gosha "Other" in Jubaland Province, 1895–1920.' History M.A. thesis, Virginia Tech, 2011.

Bland-Sutton, J. *Man and Beast in Eastern Ethiopia: From Observations Made in British East Africa, Uganda, and the Sudan*. London: Macmillan, 1911.

Blunt, Alison. 'Imperial geographies of home: British domesticity in India, 1886–1925.' *Transactions of the Institute of British Geographers* new series 24 (1999): 421–40.

Boucher, Leigh. 'Trans/national history and disciplinary amnesia: historicising White Australia at two fin de siècles.' In Jane Carey and Claire McLisky (eds), *Creating White Australia*. Sydney: Sydney University Press, 2009.

Boyarin, Daniel. *Unheroic Conduct: The Rise of Heterosexuality and the Invention of the Jewish Man*. Berkeley and Los Angeles: University of California Press, 1997.

Boyes, John. *King of the Wa-Kikuyu: A True Story of Travel and Adventure in Africa*. London: Methuen, 1911.

Boyles, Denis. *African Lives: White Lies, Tropical Truth, and Rumblings of Rumor – from Chinese Gordon to Beryl Markham, and Beyond*. New York: Weidenfeld and Nicolson, 1988.

SELECT BIBLIOGRAPHY

Brodhurst-Hill, Evelyn. *So This Is Kenya!* London: Blackie, 1936.
Bronson, Edgar Beecher. *In Closed Territory.* Chicago: McClurg, 1910.
Brundage, W. Fitzhugh. *Lynching in the New South: Georgia and Virginia, 1880–1930.* Urbana: University of Illinois Press, 1993.
Bulbeck, Chilla. *Australian Women in Papua New Guinea: Colonial Passages, 1920–1960.* Cambridge: Cambridge University Press, 1992.
Burrill, Emily S., Richard L. Roberts, and Elizabeth Thornberry (eds). *Domestic Violence and the Law in Colonial and Postcolonial Africa.* Athens: Ohio University Press, 2010.
Butcher, John. *The British in Malaya, 1880–1941: The Social History of a European Community in Colonial South-East Asia.* New York: Oxford University Press, 1979.
Buxton, M. A. *Kenya Days.* London: Edward Arnold, 1927.
Campbell, Chloe. *Race and Empire: Eugenics in Colonial Kenya.* Manchester: Manchester University Press, 2007.
Carberry, Juanita, with Nicola Tyrer, *Child of Happy Valley: A Memoir.* London: Heinemann, 1999.
Carlebach, Julius. *The Jews of Nairobi.* Nairobi: Nairobi Hebrew Congress, 1962.
Carnegie, Mrs V. M., *A Kenyan Farm Diary.* Edinburgh: William Blackwood, 1930.
Carotenuto, Matt. 'Repatriation in colonial Kenya: African institutions and gendered violence.' *International Journal of African Historical Studies* 45 (2012): 9–28.
Carotenuto, Matt, and Brett Shadle. 'Introduction: Towards a History of Violence in Colonial Kenya.' *International Journal of African Historical Studies* 45 (2012): 1–7.
Cell, John. *The Highest Stage of White Supremacy: The Origins of Segregation in South Africa and the American South.* New York: Cambridge University Press, 1982.
Churchill, Winston. *My African Journey.* London: Holland, 1908.
Clayton, Anthony, and Donald Savage. *Government and Labour in Kenya, 1895–1963.* London: Cass, 1975.
Cobbold, Lady Evelyn. *Kenya: The Land of Illusion.* London: John Murray, 1935.
Cohen, Deborah. 'Who was who? Race and Jews in turn-of-the-century Britain.' *Journal of British Studies* 41 (2002): 460–83.
Cohen, Paul. 'Remembering and forgetting national humiliation in twentieth-century China.' *Twentieth-Century China* 27 (2002): 1–39.
Cornwell, G. 'George Webb Hardy's *The Black Peril* and the social meaning of "black peril" in early twentieth-century South Africa.' *Journal of Southern African Studies* 22 (1996): 441–53.
Coryndon Robert T. 'Problems of eastern Africa.' *Journal of the Royal African Society* 21 (1922): 177–86.
Cranworth, Bertram Francis Gurdon. *A Colony in the Making; or Sport and Profit in British East Africa.* London: Macmillan, 1912.

SELECT BIBLIOGRAPHY

Crawford, E. May. *By the Equator's Snowy Peak: A Record of Medical Missionary Work and Travel in British East Africa*. London: Church Missionary Society, 1913.

Davis, A., and H. G. Robertson. *Chronicles of Kenya*. London: Cecil Palmer, 1928.

Davis, Alexander. *Microcosm of Empire (British East Africa): A Political, Racial, and Economic Study*. Nairobi: Caxton, 1917.

De Polnay, Peter. *My Road*. London: Allen, 1978.

Deslandes, Paul R. *Oxbridge Men: British Masculinity and the Undergraduate Experience, 1850–1920*. Bloomington and Indianapolis: University of Indiana Press, 2005.

Dinesen, Isak. *Out of Africa*. New York: Random House, 1985 (1938).

Dinesen, Isak, and Frans Lasson. *Letters from Africa, 1914–1931*. Chicago: University of Chicago Press, 1981.

Dobbin, Christine. 'The Ilbert Bill: a study of Anglo-Indian opinion in India.' *Historical Studies – Australia and New Zealand* 12 (1965): 87–104.

Dower, K. G. *The Spotted Lion*. Boston: Little, Brown, 1937.

Du Bois, W. E. B. *Souls of Black Folk*. Chicago: McClurg, 1903.

Du Bois, W. E. B. *Darkwater: Voices from within the Veil*. New York: Harcourt, Brace, 1920.

Du Toit, Brian. *The Boers in East Africa: Ethnicity and Identity*. Westport, CT: Bergin and Garvey, 1998.

Duder, C. J. D. 'The Soldier Settlement Scheme of 1919 in Kenya.' Ph.D. diss., Aberdeen University, 1978.

Duder, C. J. D. 'An army of one's own: the politics of the Kenya Defence Force.' *Canadian Journal of African Studies* 25 (1991): 207–25.

Duder, C. J. D. 'Love and the lions: the image of white settlement in Kenya in popular fiction, 1919–1939.' *African Affairs* 90 (1991): 427–38.

Duder, C. J. D., and Chris Youé. 'Paice's place: race and politics in Nanyuki District, Kenya, in the 1920s.' *African Affairs* 93 (1994): 253–78.

Dupper, O. C. 'The Construction of a South African Myth: The Houseboy and the Black Peril of 1912.' M.A. Thesis, Harvard Law School, 1991.

Durkheim, Emile. *Moral Education: A Study in the Theory and Application of the Sociology of Education*. New York: Free Press, 1961 (1925).

Durrani, Shiraz. *Never Be Silent: Publishing and Imperialism in Kenya, 1884–1963*. London: Vita, 2006.

Dyer, Richard. *White*. London: Routledge, 1997.

Efron, John M. *Defenders of the Race: Jewish Doctors and Race in Fin-de-Siecle Europe*. New Haven and London: Yale University Press, 1994.

Eliot, Charles. *The East Africa Protectorate*. New York: Barnes and Noble, 1905.

Eliot, Charles. 'The progress and problems of the East Africa Protectorate', *Proceedings of the Royal Colonial Institute* 37 (1905–6): 81–100.

Elkins, Caroline, and Susan Pedersen (eds). *Settler Colonialism in the Twentieth Century: Projects, Practices, Legacies*. New York: Routledge, 2005.

Ellison, Ralph. *Invisible Man*. New York: Random House, 1952.

SELECT BIBLIOGRAPHY

Etherington, Norman. 'Natal's black rape scare of the 1870s.' *Journal of Southern African Studies* 15 (1988): 36–53.

Evans, Maurice S. *Black and White in South East Africa*. London: Longmans, 1911.

Evans, Raymond, Kay Saunders, and Kathryn Cronin. *Exclusion, Exploitation, and Extermination: Race Relations in Colonial Queensland*. Sydney: Australia and New Zealand Book Company, 1975.

Fanon, Frantz. *Black Skin, White Masks*. New York: Grove Press, 2008.

Feimster, Crystal N. *Southern Horrors: Women and the Politics of Rape and Lynching*. Cambridge, MA: Harvard University Press, 2009.

Feldman, David. 'Jews and the British empire c.1900–1957.' *History Workshop Journal* 63 (2007): 70–89.

Fendall, C. P. 'Kenya problems.' *English Review* (1925): 158–62

Foran, W. Robert. *A Cuckoo in Kenya: The Reminiscences of a Pioneer Police Officer in British East Africa*. London: Hutchinson, 1936.

Foran, W. Robert. *The Kenya Police, 1887–1960*. London: Robert Hale, 1962.

Ford, Lisa. *Settler Sovereignty: Jurisdiction and Indigenous People in America and Australia, 1788–1836*. Cambridge, MA: Harvard University Press, 2010.

Forster, E. M. *A Passage to India*. London: Edward Arnold, 1924.

Frederickson, George M. *White Supremacy: A Comparative Study in American and South African History*. Oxford: Oxford University Press, 1981.

Frewe, Moreton. 'The dominion of palm and pine (notes on East Africa).' *The Monthly Review* 69 (1906): 43–73.

Garner, Steve. *Whiteness: An Introduction*. London: Routledge, 2007.

Giddings, Paula. *Ida: A Sword among Lions: Ida B. Wells and the Campaign against Lynching*. New York: Amistad, 2008.

Giliomee, Hermann. *The Afrikaaners: Biography of a People*. Charlottesville: University of Virginia Press, 2010.

Gill, Anton. *Ruling Passions: Sex, Race and Empire*. London: BBC Books, 1995.

Gilman, Sander L. *Difference and Pathology: Stereotypes of Sexuality, Race, and Madness*. Ithaca: Cornell University Press, 1985.

Gilman, Sander L., and Milton Shain (eds). *Jewries at the Frontier: Accommodation, Identity, Conflict*. Urbana: University of Illinois Press, 1999.

Githumo, Mwangi wa. 'Controversy over Jewish ante-chamber in Kenya: British settlers' reaction to the proposed Jewish settlement project in Kenya, 1902.' *Transafrican Journal of History* 22 (1993): 87–99.

Glenn, Myra C. *Campaigns against Corporal Punishment: Prisoners, Sailors, Women, and Children in Antebellum America*. Albany: SUNY Press, 1984.

Goffman, Erving. *Presentation of Self in Everyday Life*. Woodstock, NY: Overlook, 1973.

Gould, Stephen Jay, *The Mismeasure of Man*. New York: Norton, 1996.

Gregory, J. R. *Under the Sun: A Memoir of Dr. R. W. Burkitt of Kenya*. Nairobi: self-published, 1952.

Gregory, J. W. *The Great Rift Valley: Being a Narrative of a Journey to Mount Kenya and Lake Baringo*. London: Frank Cass, 1968 (1896).

SELECT BIBLIOGRAPHY

Gregory, Robert. *India and East Africa: A History of Race Relations within the British Empire, 1890–1939.* Oxford: Clarendon Press, 1971.

Grigg, Edward. 'British policy in Kenya.' *Journal of the Royal African Society* 26 (1927): 193–208.

Grigg, Edward (Lord Altrincham), *Kenya's Opportunities: Memories, Hopes, and Ideas.* London: Faber and Faber, 1955.

Guru, Gopal. 'Introduction: theorizing humiliation.' In Gopal Guru (ed.), *Humiliation: Claims and Context.* New Delhi: Oxford University Press, 2009.

H.B.H. [Hildegard B. Hinde], 'The "black peril" in British East Africa.' *The Empire Review* (1921): 193–200.

Hale, Grace Elizabeth. *Making Whiteness: The Culture of Segregation in the South, 1890–1940.* New York: Pantheon, 1998.

Hall, Jacquelyn Dowd. 'The mind that burns in each body: women, rape and racial violence.' In Ann Snitow, Christine Stansell, and Sharon Thompson (eds), *Powers of Desire: The Politics of Sexuality.* New York: Monthly Review Press, 1983.

Hamilton, M. H. *Turn the Hour: A Tale of Life in Colonial Kenya.* Sussex: Book Guild, 1991.

Hansen, Karen Tranberg. *Distant Companions: Servants and Employers in Zambia, 1900–1985.* Ithaca and London: Cornell University Press, 1989.

Harris, Carmel. 'The "terror of the law" as applied to black rapists in colonial Queensland.' *Hecate* 8 (1982): 22–4.

Hartigan, John, Jr, *Odd Tribes: Toward a Cultural Analysis of White People.* Durham, NC: Duke University Press, 2005.

Hawkins, Mike. *Social Darwinism in European and American Thought, 1860–1945: Nature as Model and Nature as Threat.* Cambridge: Cambridge University Press, 1997.

Haywood, Capt. C. *To the Mysterious Lorian Swamp: An Adventurous and Arduous Journey of Exploration through the Vast Waterless Tracts of Unknown Jubaland.* London: Seeley, 1927.

Heartfield, James. '"You are not a white woman!": Apolosi Nawai, the Fiji Produce Agency and the trial of Stella Spencer in Fiji, 1915.' *Journal of Pacific History* 38 (2003): 69–83.

Hendrick, Harry. *Children, Childhood and English Society, 1880–1990.* New York: Cambridge University Press, 1997.

Hinde, H. *Some Problems of East Africa.* London, Williams and Norgate, 1926.

Hinde, Sidney Landford, and Hildegarde Hinde, *The Last of the Masai.* London: Heinemann, 1901.

Hindlip, C. A. *British East Africa: Past, Present, and Future.* London: Unwin, 1905.

Hindlip, Lord Charles Allsopp. *Sport and Travel: Abyssinia and British East Africa.* London: Unwin, 1906.

Hobley, C. W. *Kenya from Chartered Company to Crown Colony.* London: Frank Cass, 1970 (1929).

Hodes, Martha. *White Women, Black Men: Illicit Sex in the Nineteenth-Century South.* New Haven: Yale University Press, 1997.

SELECT BIBLIOGRAPHY

Hodgson, Dorothy. *Once Intrepid Warriors: Gender, Ethnicity, and the Cultural Politics of Maasai Development*. Bloomington: Indiana University Press, 2001.

Hohenstein, M. A. 'Between Black and White: Ideology in the Southern African Black Peril Scares.' M.A. Thesis, Department of History, University of North Carolina, Chapel Hill, 2002.

Honey, J. R. de S. *Tom Brown's Universe: The Development of the Victorian Public School*. London: Millington, 1977.

Horn, Pamela. 'English elementary education and the growth of the imperial idea: 1880–1914.' In J. A. Mangan (ed.), *'Benefits Bestowed'? Education and British Imperialism*. Manchester: Manchester University Press, 1988.

Horne, Gerald. *The White Pacific: U.S. Imperialism and Black Slavery in the South Seas after the Civil War*. Honolulu: University of Hawai'i Press, 2007.

Hughes, David McDermott. *Whiteness in Zimbabwe: Race, Landscape, and the Problem of Belonging*. New York: Palgrave Macmillan, 2010.

Hunt, M. S. *Through English Eyes: Sunny Days and Ways in Kenya Colony and Assam*. Derby: Central Educational, 1932.

Huxley, Elspeth. *White Man's Country: Lord Delamere and the Making of Kenya*. New York: Praeger, 1935.

Huxley, Elspeth. *The Flame Trees of Thika*. New York: Morrow, 1959.

Huxley, Elspeth. *The Mottled Lizard*. New York: Penguin, 1962.

Huxley, Elspeth. *Nellie: Letters from Africa*. London: Weidenfeld and Nicolson, 1980.

Huxley, Elspeth. *Out in the Midday Sun*. New York: Penguin, 1988.

Huxley, Julian. *Africa View*. New York: Greenwood, 1968 (1931).

Hynd, Stacey. 'Killing the condemned: the practice and process of capital punishment in British Africa, 1900–1950s.' *Journal of African History* 49 (2008): 403–18.

Hynd, Stacey. 'Murder and mercy: capital punishment in colonial Kenya, c. 1909–56.' *International Journal of African Historical Studies* 45 (2012): 81–101.

Inglis, Amirah. *The White Women's Protection Ordinance: Sexual Anxiety and Politics in Papua*. New York: St Martin's, 1974.

Jackson, Will. 'White man's country: Kenya Colony and the making of a myth.' *Journal of Eastern African Studies* 5 (2011): 344–68.

Jackson, Will. 'Dangers to the colony: loose women and the "poor white" problem in Kenya.' *Journal of Colonialism and Colonial History* 14 (2013).

Jackson, Will. *Madness and Marginality: The Lives of Kenya's White Insane*. Manchester: Manchester University Press, 2013.

Jacobs, Margaret D. *White Mother to a Dark Race: Settler Colonialism, Maternalism, and the Removal of Indigenous Children in the American West and Australia, 1880–1940*. Lincoln: University of Nebraska Press, 2009.

Jacobson, Matthew Frye. *Whiteness of a Different Color: European Immigrants and the Alchemy of Race*. Cambridge, MA: Harvard University Press, 1999.

Jeater, Diana. *Marriage, Perversion, and Power: The Construction of Moral Discourse in Southern Rhodesia, 1894–1930*. Oxford: Clarendon, 1993.

SELECT BIBLIOGRAPHY

Johnson, James Weldon. *The Autobiography of an Ex-Coloured Man*. Boston: French, 1912.

Johnson, James Weldon. *Along this Way: The Autobiography of James Weldon Johnson*. New York: Viking, 1965 (1933).

Jones, Greta. *Social Darwinism and English Thought: The Interaction between Biological and Social Theory*. Brighton: Harvester Press, 1980.

Jordan, Winthrop D. *White Over Black: American Attitudes Toward the Negro, 1550–1812*. New York: Norton, 1977.

Kamante. *Longing for Darkness: Kamante's Tales from Out of Africa*. Collected by Peter Beard. New York: Harcourt Brace Jovanovich, 1975.

Kanogo, Tabitha. *Squatters and the Roots of Mau Mau*. Athens: University of Ohio Press, 1987.

Kennedy, Dane Keith. *Islands of White: Settler Society and Culture in Kenya and Southern Rhodesia, 1890–1939*. Durham, NC: Duke University Press, 1987.

Kenya: Its Industries, Trade, Sport and Climate. London: Kenya Empire Exhibition Council, 1924.

Knapman, Claudia. *White Women in Fiji, 1835–1930: The Ruin of Empire?* Sydney and London: Allen and Unwin, 1986.

Knipp, Thomas R. 'Kenya's literary ladies and the mythologizing of the white highlands.' *South Atlantic Review* 55 (1990): 1–16.

Kramer, Paul A. 'Empires, exceptions, and Anglo-Saxons: race and rule between the British and the United States empires, 1880–1910.' *Journal of American History* 88 (2002): 1315–53.

Krebs, Paula M. *Gender, Race, and the Writing of Empire: Public Discourse and the Boer War*. Cambridge: Cambridge University Press, 1999.

Lake, Marilyn, and Henry Reynolds. *Drawing the Global Colour Line: White Men's Countries and the International Challenge of Racial Equality*. Cambridge: Cambridge University Press, 2008.

Le Breton, F. H. *Up-Country Swahili Exercises*. Richmond, Surrey: R. W. Simpson, 1936.

Leakey, Louis. *White African: An Early Autobiography*. Cambridge, MA: Schenkman, 1966 (1937).

Lessing, Doris. *The Grass Is Singing*. London: M. Joseph, 1950.

Leys, Norman. *Kenya*. London: Cass, 1973 (1924).

Linden, Evelin. 'Humiliation and human rights: mapping a minefield.' *Human Rights Review* 2 (2000): 46–63.

Litwack, Leon. *Trouble in Mind: Black Southerners in the Age of Jim Crow*. New York: Knopf, 1998.

Lloyd-Jones, Brevet-Major W. *Havash!: Frontier Adventures in Kenya*. London: Arrowsmith, 1925.

Lonsdale, John. 'Kenya: home county and African frontier'. In Robert A. Bickers (ed.), *Settlers and Expatriates: Britons Over the Seas*. Oxford: Oxford University Press, 2010.

Lovell, Mary S. *Straight on Till Morning: The Biography of Beryl Markham*. New York: St Martins, 1987.

SELECT BIBLIOGRAPHY

Mangan, J. A. 'Social Darwinism and upper-class education in late Victorian and Edwardian England.' In J. A. Mangan and James Walvin (eds), *Manliness and Morality: Middle Class Masculinity in Britain and America, 1800–1940*. Manchester: Manchester University Press, 1987.

Margali, Avishai. *The Decent Society*. Trans. Naomi Goldblum. Cambridge, MA: Harvard University Press, 1998.

Martens, Jeremy. 'Settler homes, manhood, and "houseboys" : an analysis of Natal's rape scare of 1886.' *Journal of Southern African Studies* 28 (2002): 379–400.

Martinez, Julia, and Claire Lowrie. 'Colonial constructions of masculinity: transforming Aboriginal Australian men into "houseboys".' *Gender and History* 21 (2009): 305–23.

Maxon, Robert M. *Struggle for Kenya: The Loss and Reassertion of Imperial Initiative, 1912–1923*. Hackensack, NJ: Fairleigh Dickinson University Press, 1993.

McClure, Herbert Reginald. *Land-Travel and Seafaring: A Frivolous Record of Twenty Years Wandering*. London: Hutchinson, 1925.

McCulloch, Jock. *Black Peril, White Virtue: Sexual Crime in Southern Rhodesia, 1902–1935*. Bloomington: Indiana University Press, 2000.

McIntosh, Janet. 'Unsettled: Denial and Belonging among White Kenyans'. Ms, 2014.

Miller, William Ian. *Humiliation: And other Essays on Honor, Social Discomfort, and Violence*. Ithaca: Cornell University Press, 1993.

Mlambo, A. S. *White Immigration into Rhodesia*. Harare: University of Zimbabwe, 2002.

Mohanram, Radhika. *Imperial White: Race, Diaspora, and the British Empire*. Minneapolis: University of Minnesota Press, 2007.

Money, Roger Noel. *Ginia: My Kenya Coffee Shamba, 1918–1939*. Perth: privately published, 2000.

Morris, H. F. 'English law in East Africa: a hardy plant in an alien soil.' In H. F. Morris and James S. Read (eds), *Indirect Rule and the Search for Justice: Essays in East African Legal History*. Oxford: Clarendon Press, 1973.

Mungeam, G. H. *Kenya: Select Historical Documents, 1884–1923*. Nairobi: East African Publishing House, 1978.

Murphy, John F. 'Legitimation and paternalism: the colonial state in Kenya.' *African Studies Review* 29 (1986): 55–65.

Nelson, Hank. 'The swinging index: capital punishment and British and Australian administrations in Papua and New Guinea, 1888–1945.' *Journal of Pacific History* 13 (1978): 130–52.

Ngũgĩ wa Thiong'o. *Weep Not, Child*. London: Heinemann, 1964.

Ngũgĩ wa Thiong'o. *A Grain of Wheat*. London: Heinemann, 1967.

Ngũgĩ wa Thiong'o. *Petals of Blood*. London: Heinemann, 1977.

Ngũgĩ wa Thiong'o. *Detained: A Writer's Prison Diary*. Nairobi: Heinemann, 1981.

Ngũgĩ wa Thiong'o. *Decolonising the Mind: The Politics of Language in African Literature*. London: James Currey, 1986.

SELECT BIBLIOGRAPHY

Ngũgĩ wa Thiong'o. *Wizard of the Crow*. New York: Pantheon, 2006.
Ngũgĩ wa Thiong'o. *Dreams in a Time of War: A Childhood Memoir*. New York: Anchor Books, 2011.
Nicholls, C. S. *Elspeth Huxley: A Biography*. New York: St Martin's, 2002.
Nicholls, C. S. *Red Strangers: The White Tribe of Kenya*. London: Timewell, 2005.
Norden, Hermann. *White and Black in East Africa: A Record of Travel and Observation in Two African Crown Colonies*. Boston: Small, Maynard, 1924.
North, Stephen. *Europeans in British Administered East Africa: A Provisional List, 1899–1903*, 2nd ed. Wantage: S. J. North, 2000.
Nyaga, Daniel. *Customs and Traditions of the Meru*. Nairobi: East African Educational Publishers, 1997.
O'Brien, Patricia. 'Remaking Australia's colonial culture?: white Australia and its Papuan frontier, 1901–1940.' *Australian Historical Studies* 40 (2009): 96–112.
Ocobock, Paul. 'Spare the rod, spoil the colony: corporal punishment, colonial violence, and generational authority in Kenya, 1897–1952.' *International Journal of African Historical Studies* 45 (2012): 29–56.
Orwell, George. *Shooting an Elephant, and Other Essays*. New York: Harcourt, Brace, 1950.
Orwell, George. *Burmese Days*. New York: Harcourt, Brace, 1962.
Oswald, Felix. *Alone in the Sleeping Sickness Country*. London: Kegan Paul, 1915.
Paice, Edward. *Lost Lion of Empire: The Life of 'Cape to Cairo' Grogan*. London: HarperCollins, 2001.
Painter, Nell Irvin. *The History of White People*. New York: Norton, 2010.
Paisley, Fiona. 'Race hysteria, Darwin, 1938.' *Australian Feminist Studies* 16 (2001): 43–60.
Pape, John. 'Black and white: the "perils of sex" in colonial Zimbabwe.' *Journal of Southern African Studies* 16 (1990): 699–720.
Paton, Alan. *Too Late the Phalarope*. New York: Scribner, 1953.
Perham, Margery. *East African Journey: Kenya and Tanganyika, 1929–30*. London: Faber and Faber, 1976.
Pierce, Steven. 'Punishment and the political body: flogging and colonialism in Northern Nigeria.' In Steven Pierce and Anupama Rao (eds), *Discipline and the Other Body: Correction, Corporeality, Colonialism*. Durham, NC: Duke University Press, 2006.
Playne, Somerset (compiler), F. Holderness Gale (ed.). *East Africa (British): Its History, People, Commerce, Industries, and Resources*. London: Foreign and Colonial Compiling and Publishing, 1909.
Powys, Llewelyn. *Black Laughter*. New York: Harcourt, Brace, 1924.
Powys, Llewelyn, Louis Marlow, and Alyse Gregory. *The Letters of Llewelyn Powys*. London: John Lane, 1943.
Rainsford, W. S. *The Land of the Lion*. New York: Doubleday, Page, 1909.
Ralston, Caroline. 'The pattern of race relations in 19th century Pacific port towns.' *Journal of Pacific History* 6 (1971): 39–60.

SELECT BIBLIOGRAPHY

Rapp, D. R. 'Sex in the cinema: war, moral panic, and the British film industry, 1906–1918.' *Albion* 34 (2002): 422–45.

Redly, Michael Gordon. 'The Politics of a Predicament: The White Community in Kenya, 1918–32.' Ph.D. diss., Cambridge University, 1976.

Richards, Jeffrey. '"Passing the love of women": manly love and Victorian society.' In J. A. Mangan and James Walvin (eds), *Manliness and Morality: Middle-Class Masculinity in Britain and America, 1800–1940*. New York: St Martin's, 1987.

Riddell, Florence. *Kenya Mist*. New York: Henry Hold, 1924.

Riddell, Florence. *Kismet in Kenya*. Philadelphia: Lippincott, 1932.

Ritterhous, Jennifer. *Growing up Jim Crow: How Black and White Southern Children Learned Race*. Chapel Hill: University of North Carolina Press, 2006.

Rodner, Jane. *Datura: A Romance of Kenya*. London: Hutchinson, 1928.

Roediger, David. *Black on White: Black Writers on What It Means to Be White*. New York: Random House, 1998.

Roediger, David. *The Wages of Whiteness: Race and the Making of the American Working Class*. Revised ed. New York: Verso, 1999.

Rohrer, Judy. *Haoles in Hawai'i*. Honolulu: University of Hawai'i Press, 2010.

Rosberg, Carl, and John Nottingham. *Myth of Mau Mau*. New York: Praeger, 1966.

Rose, Lionel. *The Erosion of Childhood: Child Oppression in Britain, 1860–1918*. London and New York: Routledge, 1991.

Ross, W. McGregor. *Kenya from Within: A Short Political History*. London: Frank Cass, 1968 (1927).

Routledge, W. S. and Katherine Routledge. *With a Prehistoric People: The Akikuyu of British East Africa*. London: Frank Cass, 1968 (1910).

Rowbotham, Judith 'Criminal savages? Or "civilizing" the legal process.' In Judith Rowbotham and Kim Stevenson (eds), *Criminal Conversations: Victorian Crimes, Social Panic, and Moral Outrage*. Columbus: Ohio State University Press, 2005.

Salvadori, Cynthia, with Judy Aldrick (eds). *Two Indian Travellers: East Africa, 1902–1905*. Mombasa: Friends of Fort Jesus, 1997.

Schrader, Abby M. *Languages of the Lash: Corporal Punishment and Identity in Imperial Russia*. Dekalb: Northern Illinois University Press, 2002.

Schroeder, Richard. *Africa after Apartheid: South Africa, Race, and Nation in Tanzania*. Bloomington: Indiana University Press, 2012.

Schwarz, Bill. *Memories of Empire, Vol. I: The White Man's World*. Oxford: Oxford University Press, 2011.

Scott, James C. *Domination and the Arts of Resistance: Hidden Transcripts*. New Haven: Yale University Press, 1990.

Seaton, Henry. *Lion in the Morning*. London: Murray, 1963.

Seekings, Jeremy. '"Not a single white person should be allowed to go under": *swartgevaar* and the origins of South Africa's welfare state, 1924–1929.' *Journal of African History* 48 (2007): 375–94.

Shadle, Brett. *'Girl Cases': Marriage and Colonialism in Gusiiland, Kenya, 1890–1970*. Portsmouth, NH: Heinemann, 2006.

SELECT BIBLIOGRAPHY

Shadle, Brett. 'White settlers and the law in early colonial Kenya.' *Journal of Eastern African Studies* 4 (2010): 509–23.
Shadle, Brett. 'Cruelty and empathy, animals and race, in colonial Kenya.' *Journal of Social History* 45 (2012): 1097–116.
Shadle, Brett. 'Settlers, Africans, and inter-personal violence in early colonial Kenya.' *International Journal of African Historical Studies* 45 (2012): 57–80.
Sharpe, Jenny. *Allegories of Empire: The Figure of Woman in the Colonial Text.* Minneapolis and London: University of Minnesota Press, 1993.
Shaw, Carolyn Martin. *Colonial Inscriptions: Race, Sex, and Class in Kenya.* Minneapolis: University of Minnesota Press, 1995.
Shiralo, Priscilla. *A Failed Eldorado: Colonial Capitalism, Rural Industrialization, Africa Land Rights in Kenya, and the Kakamega Gold Rush, 1930–1952.* Lanham, MD: University Press of America, 2008.
Shutt, Allison. 'The settlers' cattle complex: the etiquette of culling cattle in colonial Zimbabwe, 1938.' *Journal of African History* 43 (2002): 263–86.
Shutt, Allison K. '"I told him I was Lennox Njokweni": honor and racial etiquette in Southern Rhodesia.' *Journal of African History* 51 (2010): 323–41.
Simpson, Alyse. *Red Dust of Kenya.* New York: Crowell, 1952.
Simpson, Alyse. *The Land that Never Was.* Lincoln: University of Nebraska Press, 1985 (1937).
Singha, Radhika. *A Despotism of the Law: Crime and Justice in Early Colonial India.* Calcutta: Oxford University Press, 1998.
Sinha, Mrinalini. *Colonial Masculinity: The 'Manly Englishman' and the 'Effeminate Bengali' in the Late Nineteenth Century.* Manchester: Manchester University Press, 1995.
Smith, Julian. *Crossing the Heart of Africa: An Odyssey of Love and Adventure.* New York: Harper, 2010.
Social Alternatives, Special Issue on Humiliation, 25 (2006).
Sommerville, Diane Miller. *Rape and Race in the Nineteenth-Century South.* Chapel Hill: University of North Carolina Press, 2004.
Sorrenson, M. P. K. *Origins of European Settlement in Kenya.* Oxford: Oxford University Press, 1968.
Spicer, Paul. *The Temptress: The Scandalous Life of Alice de Janze and the Mysterious Death of Lord Erroll.* New York: St Martin's, 2010.
Steyn, Melissa E. *'Whiteness Just Isn't What It Used to Be': White Identity in a Changing South Africa.* Albany: State University of New York, 2001.
Stigand, C. H. *The Land of Zinj: Being an Account of British East Africa, Its Ancient History and Present Inhabitants.* New York: Barnes and Noble, 1966 (1913).
Stoler, Ann Laura. 'Rethinking colonial categories: European communities and the boundaries of rule.' *Comparative Studies in Society and History* 31 (1989): 134–61.
Stoler, Ann Laura. *Carnal Knowledge and Imperial Power: Race and the Intimate in Colonial Rule.* Berkeley: University of California Press, 2010.
Strange, Nora. *Courtship in Kenya.* London: Stanley Paul, 1932.
Strange, Nora. *Kenya To-Day.* London: Stanley Paul, 1934.

SELECT BIBLIOGRAPHY

Summers, Carol. *From Civilization to Segregation: Social Ideas and Social Control in Southern Rhodesia, 1890–1934*. Athens: Ohio University Press, 1994.

Thompson, Joseph. *Through Masai Land with Joseph Thompson*. Evanston, IL: Northwestern University Press, 1962.

Thurman, Judith. *Isak Dinesen: The Life of a Storyteller*. New York: St Martin's, 1982.

Trzebinski, Errol. *Silence Will Speak: A Study of the Life of Denys Finch Hatton and His Relationship with Karen Blixen*. Chicago: University of Chicago Press, 1985.

Trzebinski, Errol. *The Kenya Pioneers*. New York: Norton, 1986.

Trzebinski, Errol. *The Lives of Beryl Markham: Out of Africa's Hidden Free Spirit and Denys Finch Hatton's Last Great Love*. New York: Norton, 1993.

Van Onselen, Charles. *Studies in the Social and Economic History of the Witwatersrand, 1886–1914*. Harlow: Longman, 1982.

Van Tol, Deanne. 'The Women of Kenya Speak: Colonial Welfare and Settler Philanthropy, c. 1930.' Ms.

Veracini, Lorenzo. *Settler Colonialism: A Theoretical Overview*. New York: Palgrave Macmillan, 2010.

Visser, Margaret. *The Gift of Thanks: The Roots and Rituals of Gratitude*. New York: Houghton Mifflin Harcourt, 2009.

Wanhalla, Angela. 'Interracial sexual violence in 1860s New Zealand.' *New Zealand Journal of History* 45 (2011): 71–84.

Watt, Rachel Stuart. *In the Heart of Savagedom: Reminiscences of Life and Adventure during a Quarter of a Century of Pioneering and Missionary Labours in the Wilds of East Equatorial Africa*. London: Pickering and Inglis, 1920.

Weisbord, Robert G. *African Zion: The Attempt to Establish a Jewish Colony in the East Africa Protectorate, 1903–1905*. Philadelphia: Jewish Publication Society of America, 1968.

Weller, Henry O. *Kenya Without Prejudice*. Nairobi: East Africa, 1931.

Wheeler, Sara. *Too Close to the Sun: The Life and Times of Denys Finch Hatton*. London: Jonathan Cape, 2006.

White, Luise *The Comforts of Home: Prostitution in Colonial Nairobi*. Chicago: University of Chicago Press, 1990.

Wiener, Martin *An Empire on Trial: Race, Murder, and Justice under British Rule, 1870–1935*. Cambridge: Cambridge University Press, 2009.

'Wife of a Settler.' 'Kenya: A Few Reflections.' *The English Review* (March 1931): 360–4.

Williamson, Joel. *The Crucible of Race: Black/White Relations in the American South since Emancipation*. New York: Oxford University Press, 1984.

Wilson, C. J. *The Story of the East African Mounted Rifles*. Nairobi: East African Standard, 1938.

Wilson, H. A. C. *A British Borderland: Service and Sport in Equatoria*. London: J. Murray, 1913.

SELECT BIBLIOGRAPHY

Wolfers, Edward P. *Race Relations and Colonial Rule in Papua New Guinea.* Sydney: Australia and New Zealand Book Company, 1975.

Wolff, Kurt H. (ed. and trans.). *The Sociology of Georg Simmel.* New York: Free Press, 1964.

Wray, Matt. *Not Quite White: White Trash and the Boundaries of Whiteness.* Durham, NC: Duke University Press, 2006.

Wright, Richard. *Native Son.* New York: Harper, 1940.

Wright, Richard. *Black Boy: A Record of Children and Youth.* New York: Harper, 1945.

Wylie, Diana. 'Norman Leys and McGregor Ross: a case study in the conscience of African empire, 1900–1939.' *Journal of Imperial and Commonwealth History* 5 (1977): 294–309.

Wylie, Diana. 'The Colonial Office and its critics, 1918–1940.' *Journal of African History* 18 (1977): 427–47.

Wymer, Norman. *The Man from the Cape.* London: Evans, 1959.

Young, Robert J. C. *The Idea of English Ethnicity.* Malden, MA: Blackwell, 2008.

Younghusband, Ethel. *Glimpses of East Africa and Zanzibar.* London: John Long, 1910.

INDEX

Achariar, Sitaram 89–90, 110 n.37
Afrikaners 14, 18, 22 n.17, 44, 53 n.59, 59, 69–72, 81 n.69, 115 n.108, 125, 128

Bache, Eve 37, 41–2, 54 n.75
black peril 4, 18, 103–8, 111 n.50, 115 n.113, 130–6, 152
  capital punishment 96, 103, 132, 134–6, 111 n.56, 146–7
  meaning 9, 92–6
  white men as responsible for 103–4, 115 n.109
  white women as responsible for 104–8, 115 n.117
Blixen, Karen (Isak Dinesen) 3, 29, 43, 44, 45–7, 55 n.87, 56 n.111, 56 n.114, 57 n.121, 57 n.126, 97, 145
Blundell, Michael 62, 97, 112 n.62, 125, 145, 159 n.40
'boy' 3, 35–6, 38, 53 n.68, 79 n.21, 104–5, 107, 155

capital punishment
  demands for 96, 103, 132, 134–6, 111 n.56
  of Nyaduongo s/o Awori 146–7
  of Peter Poole 149
censorship 99–100, 112 n.83, 113 n.84, 113 n.86
children
  Africans considered as by settlers 3, 8, 26, 36–8, 40–2, 46, 124–5, 155
  of settlers 35, 45, 93–6, 105–8, 135, 147
chivalry 85, 88–92, 95–6, 132–4
Christianity 33, 57 n.126, 85
  African converts to 2, 27, 31, 33–5, 47, 51 n.37
  and civilization 30, 120
civilization
  Afrikaners 69–71

'civilizing mission' 10, 19, 29–31, 75
clothing 32–3, 35–6, 61–2, 64, 70, 91
dividing line between races 4–5, 26–7, 86
emotions 39–40
gender 7–8, 39, 52 n.46, 86, 88
Jews 73
law, the 120–1
'noble savage' 34
perils of 27, 32–6, 47, 149
'poor whites' 64–6
social evolution 28–9, 36–7
clothing 32–3, 35–6, 61–2, 64, 70, 80 n.35, 91
Cole, Galbraith 35, 43, 46, 128, 129–30, 143 n.98
Colonists' Association 15, 30, 72, 75, 76, 82 n.78, 130–1
Convention of Associations 15, 30–1, 54 n.84, 58, 80 n.41, 83 n.100, 96, 111 n.50, 121
corporal punishment *see* violence

Delamere, Lord (Hugh Cholmondeley) 15, 16, 35, 44, 46, 55 n.101, 68, 72–3, 117
Dinesen, Isak *see* Blixen, Karen
Du Bois, W. E. B. 19–21

East African Women's League 87, 94, 97, 99–100, 104, 106
empathy 36, 39–40
European and African Trades Organization 6, 68–9
evolution 35–9, 120
  civilization 28–9

Finnie, John 75–7, 78
franchise for white women 87, 109 n.16

gender relations
  settlers' 86–92, 105–8

[178]

INDEX

settlers on Africans' 7, 39, 85, 101–2, 136
Gough, K. 89
government
  conflict with settlers 6, 30–1, 75–8, 96, 117–20, 121, 130–3
  prestige 6–7, 74–8
  support of settlers 6–7, 136
gratitude 39–43, 54 n.85, 55 n.91, 94, 96
Grogan, Ewart 1, 26–7, 70, 130–4

Hinde, Hildegarde 106–8
humiliation 32, 33, 35–6, 50 n.31, 94, 124, 153–5, 156–7
Huxley, Elspeth 38, 40, 41, 44–5, 58–9, 70, 82 n.88, 124, 125, 128

Indians 30, 51 n.38, 89–90
'insolence' 5, 12, 19, 59, 60–1, 67–8, 75, 78, 132, 147, 153
  toward white women 93–5, 111 n.50, 132
  violence 8, 44, 67–8, 117, 124

Jews 72–3, 82 n. 84

Kaggia, Bildad 153–4, 159 n.35.
Kariuki, J. M. 2–3
kindness 39–42

law 8–9, 148
  judiciary, the 120–2, 143 n.99
  juries 129–30
  prestige 119, 121–2
  prosecution of settlers 129–30, 131–4, 148
  punishment 122–3
  regarding sexual violence 134, 136
  settler critiques of operation of 96, 118–23, 131–5, 148
  settler justice 122, 139 n.38
League of Mercy 65
Leys, Norman 16, 122

Macharia, Keguro 160 n.46
McGregor Ross, William 24 n.32, 54 n.80, 64

Markham, Beryl 2, 45, 122, 124
medical care 40–3

Ngũgĩ wa Thiong'o 160 n.44
'noble savage' 34–5, 46

paternalism 4, 36–43, 44–7, 94, 104–5, 148
  Africans on 47–8
'poor whites' 64–9, 147
prestige 5, 58–61, 147, 148, 153–5, 156–7
  demeanour 5, 61–73, 97–100, 106–8, 154
  government 6–7, 74–8
  immorality 97–103, 114 n.97
  law, the 119, 121–2
  'poor whites' 64–9
  vagrancy 65–6
  violence 122–30
  white women 97–100, 106–8, 113 n.89, 154
  see also insolence
prostitution 32, 101, 102–3, 114 n.98, 115 n.107

Rainbow, Arthur and Patrice 118–19
Robertson, Harold 17–18, 33, 68, 98–9, 127–8

Schwaiger, L. J. C. and Marjorie 89
segregation 56 n.108
servants 43–4, 105–8
settlement,
  origins of in Kenya 12–15
  popular representations of 2–3
sex
  among whites 7, 97–9
  between white men and African women 7–8, 101–2, 103
  between white women and non-white men 8, 101, 102–3, 115 n.108
  see also black peril
Simpson, Alyse 40–1, 43, 44, 79 n.28

Tebajanga, L. M 35–6
Thomas, J. Kerslake 95–6, 134
trusteeship 29–31, 149

[179]

INDEX

vigilantism 90, 131–5, 147
violence
  by Africans against whites 9, 92, 137 n.19, 148–9
  Afrikaners 72, 128
  chivalry 85, 88–9, 91
  by courts 123, 127, 144 n.112
  critiques of excessive or improper use of 117, 122, 126–8
  as dominance 8, 116–17, 123–5, 126
  infantilization 46–7, 124–5
  pain 140 n.52
  paternalism 44, 48
  prestige 44, 48, 67, 75–7, 118–19
  prosecution for 129–31, 148
  in response to 'black peril' 1, 96, 130–4
  by settlers to discipline Africans 122, 124–6
  see also vigilantism

whiteness 5–6, 70–3, 113 n.89, 150–2, 156–7, 159 n.42

EU authorised representative for GPSR:
Easy Access System Europe, Mustamäe tee 50,
10621 Tallinn, Estonia
gpsr.requests@easproject.com